DATE DUE

The Peninsula Campaign

Yorktown to the Seven Days

Volume Three

Series Editor
William J. Miller

Savas Publishing Company

1475 S. Bascom Ave., Suite 204, Campbell, California 95008

(800) 848-6585

Manufactured in the United States of America

The Peninsula Campaign of 1862:
Yorktown to the Seven Days, Volume Three

edited by William J. Miller

Savas Publishing Company
1475 S. Bascom Avenue, Suite 204,
Campbell, California 95008   (800) 848-6585

Copyright © 1997 Savas Publishing Company

Includes bibliographic references and index

Printing Number
10 9 8 7 6 5 4 3 2 1
First Edition

ISBN 1-882810-14-7

This book is printed on 50-lb. Glatfelter acid-free paper

The paper in this book meets or exceeds the guidelines for permanence and durability
of the Committee on Production Guidelines for Book Longevity of the Council on Library Resources

73.6
D46
997

The Peninsula Campaign of 1862
Theater of Operations

miles
5 10 20

Chesapeake Bay

Fort Monroe

Hampton Roads

Gloucester Point

Yorktown

Lee's Mill

Warwick River

York River

West Point

Williamsburg

Mattapony River

Pamunkey River

Chickahominy

James River

White House Landing

New Kent Court House

Cumberland Landing

Forge Bridge

Charles City Court House

Surry Court House

Long Bridge

Richmond & York River Railroad

Beaver Dam Creek

Gaines' Mill

Seven Pines

White Oak Swamp

Malvern Hill

Harrison's Landing

City Point

Totopotomoy

Bethesda Church

Mechanicsville

Fair Oaks

Richmond

New Market

Bermuda Hundred

City Point Railroad

Norfolk & Petersburg Railroad

Richmond & Petersburg Railroad

Chesterfield Court House

Petersburg

Weldon

South Side RR

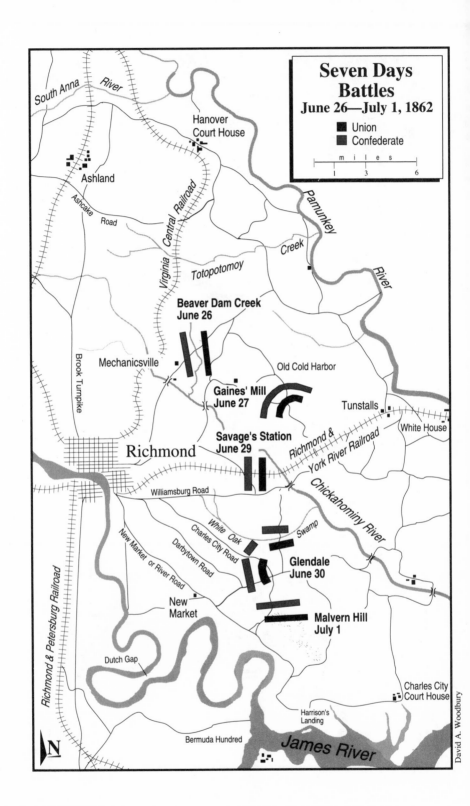

Seven Days Battles
June 26—July 1, 1862

■ Union
■ Confederate

m i l e s
1   3   6

South Anna River
Ashland
Ashcake Road
Hanover Court House
Virginia Central Railroad
Pamunkey Creek
Totopotomoy
River
Beaver Dam Creek June 26
Brook Turnpike
Mechanicsville
Old Cold Harbor
Gaines' Mill June 27
Tunstalls
White House
Richmond
Savage's Station June 29
Richmond & York River Railroad
Chickahominy River
Williamsburg Road
White Oak Swamp
Charles City Road
New Market or River Road
Darbytown Road
Glendale June 30
New Market
Malvern Hill July 1
Richmond & Petersburg Railroad
Dutch Gap
Charles City Court House
Harrison's Landing
Bermuda Hundred
James River

N

David A. Woodbury

Table of Contents

Continued . . .

Table of Contents (continued)

Illustrations

Cartography

Publisher's Preface

The third volume of *The Peninsula Campaign of 1862: Yorktown to the Seven Days*, continues the tradition of excellence and dedication to scholarship established by its preceding installments. Contents span the gamut from a full-scale examination of Federal cavalry operations, to a careful accounting of the day-to-day weather patterns and how they might have affected military operations. In between these wide-ranging monographs are a pair of essays dealing with Confederate command issues and specific battles, a regimental history of a fighting group of Pennsylvanians, and a fascinating firsthand record of the largely untold misery endured by the wounded soldiers left behind in the wake of the great armies.

As he did in the inaugural volume of this series, author Steven E. Woodworth opens this collection with a remarkable piece of work. *Dark Portents: Confederate Command at the Battle of Williamsburg*, examines what Woodworth describes as the obscure portion of the campaign, a series of events "dwarfed by the drama of the Yorktown siege and a succession of crises: the Davis-Johnston confrontations, the decision to defend Richmond, the massive but confused battle of Seven Pines and, finally, the awesome finale in the Seven Days Battles." For Woodworth, the fighting at Williamsburg revealed much about the officers who waged it. Indeed, he argues eloquently that the bitter engagement foreshadowed the failures of Seven Pines and the frustrations Robert E. Lee would eventually face later in late June.

The "California" veterans of Ball's Bluff were unprepared for the horrors that awaited them during the spring of 1862. The extended peninsular operation consisted of "almost continuous exposure to extremes in weather, severe day and night marches over impassable roads and wearisome periods of lying in drenched trenches punctuated by intervals of savage fighting." As Gary Lash notes in *"No Praise Can be too Good for the Officers and Men": The 71st Pennsylvania Infantry in the Peninsula Campaign*, the campaign "marked a rite of passage" for the collection of companies with thin ties to the far west. Originally raised as the 1st California, the regiment was later designated the 71st Pennsylvania, and it was under that moniker that it fought on the Peninsula as part of the famed "Philadelphia Brigade." Lash, a professor of Geology in New York, builds his story on a solid foundation of firsthand accounts, rendering a narrative both deeply personal and startlingly real.

Steve Newton, a professor at history at Delaware State University, broke new ground several years ago with his book on Seven Pines. He revisits that action with *"He is a Good Soldier": Johnston, Davis and Seven Pines: The Uncertainty Principle in Action*. In a unique and fascinating essay, Newton utilizes a physicist's "uncertainty principle" as a means of understanding various aspects of the intriguing relationship between President Davis and Gen. Joseph Johnston. Newton's trenchant conclusions about these men and their impact on the war differ sharply from most modern accounts, forcing readers to reconsider long-held judgments concerning Johnston's leadership abilities.

Were Northern horsemen inept? Robert O'Neill, a veteran writer on the war's mounted arm, buries that question in his series debut, *"What Men We Have Got are Good Soldiers & Brave Ones Too": Federal Cavalry Operations in the Peninsula Campaign*. O'Neill's essay is the companion piece to Ed Bearss' well-received *Jeb Stuart's Ride Around McClellan*, a detailed operational essay published in our first volume. O'Neill's keen pen treats the formative months of service experienced by the Federal horsemen, details their organizational structure and offers compelling biographical sketches of their officers. After a thorough discussion of what brought them to the Peninsula, O'Neill delves deeply into the campaign to capture Richmond, with special emphasis on the several engagements with the vaunted Southern enemy. It is his opinion that the Federal mounted arm achieved substantially more on the thin strip of swampy ground sandwiched between the York and James rivers than many have been led to believe.

William J. Miller closes out this issue with a pair of entries. The first article, *"To Alleviate Their Suffering": A Report of Medical Personnel and Activity at Savage's Station During and After the Seven Days Battles*, deals with a remarkable series of medical documents discovered by our series editor in the library at the U.S. Army Military History Institute in Carlisle, Pennsylvania. Dr. John Swinburne, a native of New York, joined the Army of the Potomac on the Peninsula, where he helped establish a hospital at White House Landing. His untiring efforts in assisting the wounded saved many lives, but it was Swinburne's detailed and illuminating report of the aftermath of Savage's Station that caught Miller's attention. As Miller writes, the report "illustrates the crucial role that civilian volunteers, like Swinburne, played in helping the wounded, and it confirms the humanity of Robert E. Lee and other Confederate military men, who cooperated with Northern medical personnel to save Northern lives."

The final section, *"Weather Still Execrable": Climatological Notes on the Peninsula Campaign, March through August 1862*, deals with the often overlooked aspects of the weather on military operations. "Drawing conclusions about the effects of the weather on the armies during the campaign has been difficult," laments the author, "because we have lacked a broad picture of what the climate was like." Tapping unofficial sources, Miller has collected a wide body of writings left by the participants themselves in order to determine "how much rain fell" and whether "that amount was extraordinary." Miller's contribution is presented in two parts: Part I is a climatological journal whose entries shed considerable light on how the weather may or may not have affected concurrent military operations; Part II, which offers comparative historical data, places the spring and summer of 1862 in context relative to "average" weather in the Tidewater.

We hope you will enjoy these essays as much as we have enjoyed bringing them to you.

Theodore P. Savas
Publisher

Steven E. Woodworth

Dark Portents

Confederate Command
at the Battle of Williamsburg

Of all the forgotten events of the much neglected Peninsula Campaign, none is more obscure than the Confederate retreat from Yorktown to the Chickahominy. As the Peninsula Campaign itself is overshadowed by the more dramatic events of the latter half of 1862, so the retreat up the Peninsula is dwarfed by the drama of the Yorktown siege and a succession of later crises: the Davis-Johnston confrontations, the decision to defend Richmond, the massive-but-confused battle of Seven Pines and, finally, the awesome finale in the Seven Days Battles. In the midst of these monumental events, the muddy miles of retreat from the Yorktown works to the banks of the flooded Chickahominy have attracted less notice than most other Civil War events of equal importance. Yet, in the course of that dismal retreat, the Confederate army fought a battle that in other circumstances would have gained considerable attention, a battle that was all the more important because of what it revealed about the shortcomings of the officers of that army. The Battle of Williamsburg foreshadowed in many ways the failures of Seven Pines and the frustrations Gen. Robert E. Lee would face during the Seven Days. Had the men responsible for the leadership been able—and willing—to assess and correct the problems revealed at Williamsburg, the course of the later battles—and the war—might have been changed.

On the evening of May 3, 1862, a heavy rain began to fall on the already none-too-dry armies, fortifications and countryside around York-town, Virginia. As the sheets of water coursed down from the blackened skies, the night was suddenly illuminated by the flash of cannon, the red glow of burning fuses tracing fiery arcs across the cloudy heavens, and the lurid bursts of the shells. In the Confederate fortifications, every gun had opened fire in what one observer called "a magnificent pyrotechnic display." The purpose of the bombardment, was to cover the withdrawal of the Confederate army of Gen. Joseph E. Johnston from the fortifica-tions it had held for over a month. Through the flash and thunder of the bombardment and the storm, Southern troops began filing out of their muddy trenches and onto the muddy roads leading back toward Rich-mond. By morning, the Yorktown defenses were silent, the guns spiked and the fortifications empty as the first Federal troops moved gingerly into the stronghold.[1]

At that moment, Johnston and his army were still only seven or eight miles away. For the Confederate commander and his men, the march had been a nightmare of rain, mud, mired horses and hopelessly bogged wagons and guns, with the thought constantly present that McClellan's Union army would no doubt take up the pursuit in the morning. The tired troops continued their struggle with elements and the wretched Virginia roads through at least part of the day on Sunday, May 4. By afternoon, Johnston's forces had reached the old colonial capital at Williamsburg. About two miles short of Williamsburg and roughly 12 from the lines around Yorktown, the two roads on which Johnston's army had been marching, the Yorktown Road on the north and the Lee's Mill Road on the south, converged into a single thoroughfare. At the intersection of the roads, stood Fort Magruder, the centerpiece of a line of fortifications built by Maj. Gen. John B. Magruder while he was commanding the Peninsula before Johnston's arrival earlier that spring.

The Peninsula narrowed at Williamsburg and this and other terrain features offered the Confederates an opportunity to make a stand there. Magruder had thus, with the approval and supervision of Confederate President Jefferson Davis' military advisor Robert E. Lee, constructed a system of works here as a possible second position should Yorktown fall. When in March of that year President Davis, after a lengthy conference with Lee, Johnston, Secretary of War George W. Randolph and generals Gustavus W. Smith and James Longstreet, had decided that the Peninsula ought to be defended, he and Lee had almost certainly expected that Johnston, while his troops delayed McClellan at Yorktown, would improve the defenses at Williamsburg and occupy them for a determined stand against the advancing Federals. This would at least give Davis and Lee more time to prepare the Richmond defenses and to gather reinforcements and recruits from the rest of the Confederacy.[2]

Yet Johnston had no intention of doing anything of the sort. His attitude from the start had been one of going through the motions of defending the Peninsula while actually planning to force the president into accepting his own strategic idea: rapid concentration of all the Confederacy's available forces for a showdown battle on the outskirts of Richmond.[3] It was not that Johnston was so very anxious to give battle—quite the contrary. He was the sort of general who could fearlessly expose his person to enemy fire but was paralyzed by fear at the thought of exposing his reputation to mishap in the ultimate test of an army commander's skill—pitched battle. For him, tomorrow was always a better day for fighting than today, and the day after was better still. Since defending the Peninsula meant immediate confrontation with the hostile army, Johnston preferred retreat, staying well clear of the enemy as long as possible and hoping in the shadow of Richmond to find more troops—or at least more nerve.

Johnston thus had neither the desire nor the intention of meeting the Federals at Williamsburg or anywhere in the vicinity. He planned to abandon the fortifications and continue his retreat. The first suggestion he got that this might not be entirely possible came when Union cavalry began skirmishing with his own mounted soldiers in front of Fort Ma-

gruder on the afternoon of the 4th. The Northern riders were successfully brushed off, but their infantry support could not be far behind. An
encounter with them would be another matter entirely, and it would take
a good deal more than Brig. Gen. Jeb Stuart's brigade of Confederate
cavalry to keep them at bay.[4] This was significant since the army's
wagon trains were making poor time on the muddy roads. By the evening of May 4, Johnston seems to have realized that he was going to
have to hold the road junction at Williamsburg for at least part of the
next day. Stationed there in support of Stuart's cavalry were two brigades of infantry under Brig. Gen. Lafayette McLaws. McLaws' brigades were part of Magruder's Division. They had helped build these
fortifications, and they knew them well. The natural course would have
been to let them man the works, reinforced, perhaps, by another brigade
or two, until the army's trains were safely out of the way. Instead,
Johnston ordered McLaws' troops to march at the head of the army's
column the next day, while other troops assumed the duties of rear
guard. The reason for this strange decision probably had something to do
with the man to which Johnston entrusted these duties. The division now
called on to provide a rear guard was that of Maj. Gen. James Longstreet.[5]

Longstreet was a man of massive physique and even larger self-con-
fidence, a fact that was all the more surprising since he had graduated
54th out of the 56 men in his West Point class of 1842 and had done
little to distinguish himself since then. Yet the sense of self-assurance he
exuded could be well nigh overpowering. In battle this made him an
encouragement to those around him, and in those and other times of
stress, it could make him a temptation to a weaker-willed superior who
might seek emotional relief by leaning on the decisions of Longstreet's
feeble intellect—delivered, as always, with the greatest of confidence.

Johnson was almost neurotic in his fear of risking his reputation by
undertaking any endeavor in which all of the arrangements were not
absolutely perfect. The story was even told that in pre-war days he had
returned empty handed from quail hunts rather than risk his reputation
for marksmanship by taking a less-than-perfect shot.[6] His heart was now

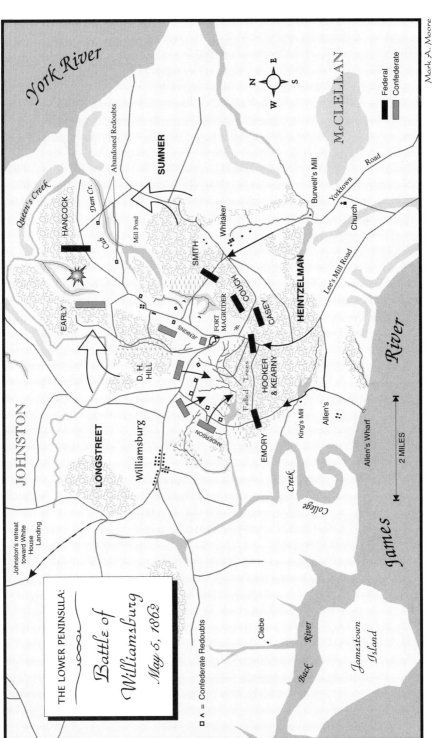

Mark A. Moore

THE LOWER PENINSULA:

Battle of
Williamsburg
May 5, 1862

□ ∧ = Confederate Redoubts

set on the perfect shot he planned to take at McClellan once he received large reinforcements near Richmond, and he desperately wished to avoid battle for the present, especially with his army tired, wet and hungry and stretched out along several miles of muddy roads. Yet, in view of the fact that he obviously could not avoid at least some sort of battle at Williamsburg on May 5, the actions he took that morning seem strange. Having turned responsibility for the rear guard over to Longstreet, he rode off with the army's leading units, abandoning the scene of likely battle and placing as many miles of muddy road as possible between himself and risk of confrontation with the enemy. In Longstreet's air of self-assurance, he had found a way to put an unpleasant circumstance out of his head for at least the time being.

Longstreet, for all his confidence, had very little idea what to do. Throughout the war he was to demonstrate himself to be skillful in the mechanics of moving his brigades around the battlefield but hopelessly incompetent in devising strategy or tactics. Handling troops skillfully was a very important asset, however, one lacked by many an officer of greater intellect and even greater strategic insight than Longstreet. His ability to get troops where they were needed, along with the steadiness he could impart to those around him and those under his command, would eventually make him a valuable lieutenant to any general who could induce him to use his skills in accordance with a wise plan of the superior's devising. Unfortunately for the Confederacy, Robert E. Lee was the only general who ever succeeded in doing that. Left to his own devices, Longstreet had pride enough to get himself into trouble and not brains enough to get himself out. Left by Johnston to cover the army's retreat, Longstreet made no effort to reconnoiter the ground he was to defend, but virtually tuned over command of the operation to Brig. Gen. Richard Anderson, with two brigades posted in and around Fort Magruder.[7]

The precipitation, which had stopped during the day on the 4th, started again during the night, and continued throughout the day of the battle and the night after that. The morning of May 5 had just dawned cold, gray and dripping under a leaden sky and a steady soaking rain when Federal skirmishers began to press forward along either side of the Lee's Mill Road, exchanging fire with the Confederates around Fort Magruder and the nearby redoubts. Union artillery came forward and joined the long-range firing. The Confederates answered in kind, but for some time the contest remained low-key.[8] These Union troops were part of Brig. Gen. Joseph Hooker's division of the Army of the Potomac's III Corps. By advancing toward Williamsburg over the Lee's Mill Road, they were approaching the right of the Confederate line. Opposite the Rebel left, the Yorktown Road angled toward the intersection in front of Fort Magruder. On that road another Federal division was approaching, Brig. Gen. W.F. Smith's of the IV Corps. McClellan and Johnston had been friends before the war, and the Northerner was a man after the Virginian's own heart. He, too, had found ways to be away from the troops that would likely fight a battle that day. Commanding in his stead on the field of battle was 65-year-old Brig. Gen. E.V. Sumner. Whatever the old general's strengths—and they may have been considerable—he did not seem to have a very clear head on this day. The result was that he allowed Hooker to go forward unsupported, while Smith, for most of the day, was kept chafing in inactivity.[9]

Meanwhile, Longstreet, still not having visited the battlefield himself, began making the other brigades of his division available to Anderson. Around 7:00 a.m., the brigade of Brig. Gen. Cadmus M. Wilcox, which had already taken up it march through town behind the rest of the retreating army, was countermarched to the vicinity of Fort Magruder to be ready if Anderson needed it.[10] About an hour later, Brig. Gen. A.P. Hill was ordered to get his brigade up and moving toward the battle-field.[11] Brig. Gen. George Pickett's regiments had started early from their camp at the College of William and Mary, and about the same time Hill got orders for the front, Pickett, too, was directed to countermarch and await further orders at William and Mary. About 10:00 a.m., the word came for this brigade to proceed to the scene of the fighting.[12] Longstreet's remaining brigade, under Brig. Gen. Raleigh Colston, was farthest from the battlefield, but was turned back toward the action by mid-morning.

Anderson, who had started the day with his own and Brig. Gen. Roger A. Pryor's brigades, was not slow to flex the extra muscle Longstreet had given him. He ordered Wilcox to cross a field to the right and enter the woods leading down to the James River to see what was in there. Seeing was no easy matter in this forest so dense a colonel could not see the whole of his regimental front at one time, but as Wilcox pushed forward a line of skirmishers, he found out soon enough what he was up against. Hooker had all three of his brigades off on this side of the road now, probing for a way around the daunting bulk of Fort Magruder. Realizing he could not cover the entire enemy front and that the Federals overlapped him badly on his right, Wilcox sent an urgent summons for aid not to Anderson but directly to A.P. Hill. Hill was not sure that his orders from Longstreet authorized this; after all, he had been directed to move up and support Anderson. The result was delay while Hill sent a courier dashing of to find Longstreet and get permission to make the move.[13]

Anderson, who was actually responsible for directing the action, was not consulted by anyone. At some point as the fighting was heating up that morning he left the fort and rode down toward the right to take command in person. Messages to him appear to have missed him during his move. Unable to exercise effective command from his advanced position, he may have returned to the vicinity of Fort Magruder. Wherever he was, he did little to coordinate the division's fighting on this day. Brave and talented, Anderson had nevertheless been dogged for many years by rumors of a bent toward drunkenness. His ineffectiveness on this day—indeed, even his whereabouts during most of the fight—remain a mystery.[14]

Cadmus Wilcox, however, needed reinforcements and quickly. He mentioned his plight to Stuart, who happened along at that time, and Stuart carried the request to Pryor, whose brigade held the redoubts near Fort Magruder. It was still only about 9:00 a.m., and the rest of the reinforcements Longstreet had ordered had not yet come up. In response to Wilcox's dilemma, Pryor marched into the woods with half of his brigade, though by whose order this occurred remains in some obscurity.

Anderson later reported having ordered the movement, while Wilcox reported that Pryor had received his request intended for Hill and acted on his responsibility. Pryor recounted that he had "received verbal orders from several sources," some of which apparently involved abandoning the redoubts altogether and taking his whole command into the woods. Feeling bound by his previous orders from Anderson to hold the redoubts "at every hazard," and believing it was actually Hill who was supposed to go to Wilcox's support, Pryor took only one under-strength regiment and three companies of another.[15]

Strangely, when Hill and Pickett came up around 10:00 a.m., Anderson still did not make use of their brigades. He may have been out of touch someplace between fort and front. Or, he may have had only the sketchiest of ideas of what was going on in the underbrush, as the other brigade commanders, particularly Wilcox, seem not to have realized they were to continue reporting to him. Both Hill and Pickett had sent aides to inform him of their arrival, and both riders had returned to their respective commanders to report that Anderson declared he needed no support. The men of the two brigades had thus been waiting as peacefully as their nerves would allow as they listened to the thump and rattle of the simmering exchange of fire between the fort and the enemy lines a few hundred yards away. Yet within half an hour Anderson seems to have changed his mind, for around 10:00 a.m. he gave orders to both Hill and Pickett to advance to the support of the comrades in the timber.[16]

Meanwhile, Wilcox, upon receiving Pryor's reinforced regiment, immediately threw the entire force at Hooker's division. The Federals had something less than three brigades with which to meet this thrust, since Hooker was using some of his troops to engage the Confederates at Fort Magruder and the nearby redoubts.[17] They still enjoyed a better than two to one advantage over Wilcox's short gray line, over-lapping him substantially on the right. The Confederate attack made little headway beyond driving in the enemy skirmishers. As the battle lines collided, this advantage told on Pryor's command and on the right regiment of Wilcox's brigade, the 9th Alabama, both of which reeled backward in confused retreat.[18] Wilcox's center regiment, the 10th Alabama, on the initiative of its colonel, swung its left flank forward to bring the regiment up to a rail fence that ran through the woods, then side-stepped along the fence to the right rear until it could confront the enemy head-on. The two sides poured fire into each other, often at very close range, deadlocked in the dense, now smoke-filled woods.[19]

How long Wilcox's men could have stood this uneven exchange is an open question. They were required to stand it perhaps half an hour, for shortly after 10:30 Hill's brigade wheeled into position on the right. Hill discovered it was by this time futile to try to link up with Pryor's right or even the right of Wilcox's brigade—the broken 9th Alabama. Instead, Hill seems to have moved into position on the flank of the 10th Alabama, helping it to break the impetus of the Federal pressure it had been resisting along the rail fence and covered the battered 9th, along with Pryor's units, as they attempted to re-group. The cheering of Hill's men as they stopped the advancing Yankees and turned them back could be heard the whole length of the Southern line.[20] Ambrose P. Hill was nothing if not aggressive and needed no one to urge him to follow up his advantage. Completing the deployment of his regiments with some difficulty in the dense woods, he now turned the left flank of the Federals who had been destroying Wilcox's right. Swinging his right-flank regiment forward on the rest of his line like a gate on a hinge, he broke the Union line and drove the bluecoats back through the woods in disorder.[21]

That Hill was able to enjoy this degree of success was probably due to the fact that one of Pickett's regiments was just then going in even farther to the right, fully occupying Federals who might have turned the tables on Hill yet again as he swung his flank across their front in the process of crushing the exposed left of the Union troops that had defeated Wilcox. Pickett had originally been ordered by Anderson to send in his other three regiments at the same place, in hopes of completely overlapping and rolling up the Federal line. Before he could comply, however, he was called back, probably by an urgent summons from Wilcox or from one or more of his regimental commanders whose situation was still dire. Pickett's other three regiments thus went into action in support of these already hard-pressed units. Wilcox, who had borrowed a regiment from Hill to bolster the shaky 9th Alabama, now directed at least one of Pickett's regiments to move up and support his left-flank regiment, the 19th Mississippi.[22]

With his own front now shored up by reinforcements from both Pickett and Hill, and with the remainder of those generals' brigades rolling forward on his right, Wilcox again ordered his line to advance. The 10th Alabama swarmed over the rail fence, the 19th Mississippi rushed forward with bayonets fixed and the various companies of the 9th Alabama, now acting independently or in small battalions, joined the advance. Still on this end of the front where no advantage could be gained by flanking, northern resistance proved to be stubborn. The 19th Mississippi got into a furious fire-fight at a range of less than 30 yards with a line of Federals behind a log barricade, losing its colonel but finally driving the Unionists from their cover. The 10th Alabama fared worse and was thrown back in disorder from its attempted assault. The impetus of Hill's thrust, however, served to carry the fragmented Confederate line forward. Anderson had sent forward the remainder of Pryor's brigade, spreading his own regiments to cover both fort and redoubts. Thus, the Confederates now had four brigades committed in the woods, while Hooker had only three Union brigades, and at least some of his forces were still confronting Fort Magruder. The Rebel advance carried their battle lines forward to the edge of a large clearing covered with felled pine trees and here the Federals dug in their heels. They would give no more ground.[23]

By this time Longstreet's division was approaching a state of almost complete disorganization. Wilcox was exercising a general sort of leadership on the left part of the line, but he no longer commanded anything like a brigade. Under his direction was a collection of regiments from Hill's and Pickett's brigades. Of his own troops, the 10th Alabama had rallied but was now fighting under Hill. The 19th Mississippi had come apart after its ordeal in front of the log barricade. Half the regiment was still fighting but now as part of Pryor's command. The other half had become entangled in the felled timber, then drifted off to the right to take possession of several abandoned Federal guns from two batteries that had been engaging Fort Magruder. Seizing the guns simultaneously with elements of at least two other Confederate regiments, the Mississippians came under the fire that the gunners in Fort Magruder had been sending at the Federal batteries. Thereafter, that half of the 19th Mississippi drifted out of the fight. Companies of the 9th Alabama were all over the battlefield. Independent of Wilcox and apparently unknown to him, Pickett, with two of his regiments and a fragment of one of Pryor's, was operating along more or less the same stretch of the Confederate line. Pryor himself had only one of his own regiments and one of Wilcox's, while Hill's command was the most nearly intact brigade left on the battlefield. At least three regiments, two of Pryor's and one of Pickett's, seem to have fought entirely independent of any brigade command. Ominously, by this time virtually everyone was getting low on ammunition. The division's supply wagons had already been started on their way to the rear, and there was no reserve supply of ammunition. Regimental and brigade commanders were reduced to ordering their men to scavenge the cartridge boxes of the killed and wounded Federals they had just overrun.[24]

It was about noon now, and listening to the sound of the fighting from a point well to the rear, Longstreet noticed a sudden change in the combination of sound reaching his ears. A new set of notes—deep, hammering, and insistent—had been added to the symphony of battle that had been swelling through the misty rain for more than five hours already. Longstreet would have recognized it as field artillery. That was nothing new—each side had employed several batteries so far in the battle. It was not the nature but rather the direction and the proximity of the source of this sound that would have been startling, for the booming of these guns was issuing from a point well to the left and rear of Fort Magruder, the adjacent redoubts or any Confederate units. It could not have been a welcome sound to Longstreet, for it could only mean one thing: the division was flanked. "From the swelling noise of battle," Longstreet blandly noted in his memoirs years later, "I concluded that it would be well to ride to the front."[25] He would have done well to have done so a good deal earlier. By this point, five of Longstreet's six brigades, all the infantry then within reach, were fully committed and largely disorganized in a vicious fight in a pine thicket. Only Stuart's cavalry was available as a reserve, yet till now Longstreet had not so much as observed the action or taken stock of the situation. Riding out on the field a little after noon, he found a situation bad enough to have shocked even a man of his own near-legendary imperturbability.

Somehow as Anderson's two brigades had relieved McLaws' men the previous evening, at least four of the redoubts on the far left of the line had simply been missed. No one in Longstreet's division seemed to be aware of their existence, and neither Longstreet nor Anderson had taken the trouble to find out. By mid-morning the Federals had found out, and they also knew that the position was readily accessible from the Yorktown Road, up which William F. Smith's as yet unengaged division was advancing. The ground around the unoccupied left redoubts, which looked down a long, open, gradually sloping farm field toward Fort Magruder, enfiladed the fort and the entire left of the Confederate position around Williamsburg. The Federals had but to walk in and take possession and Longstreet was check-mated. His entire division would likely have been cut off and captured or dispersed. The Confederates were saved by Sumner's bull-headed obtuseness. The crusty old general was letting Hooker's outnumbered division fight on unsupported while enough Northern troops to flatten Longstreet's whole division and walk straight over the thinly held Williamsburg works waited within call. Now, Sumner did the Confederates another favor by allowing Smith to send into the key position only a force too small to have a decisive effect. Brig. Gen. Winfield S. Hancock, with a reinforced brigade and two batteries of artillery, seized two of the undefended redoubts and then, unable to effect more with his small force, unlimbered his artillery and began to shell Fort Magruder and the other redoubts from the left rear. Incredibly, his 3,400 men and 10 guns, maneuvering in the open within plain view of the Fort had not been noticed by a single high-ranking Confederate officer up to this time.[26] Col. Micah Jenkins, the highly competent young officer left in command of the fort when Anderson left, was understandably preoccupied with the troops of Hooker's division engaging his position from the front. Longstreet had not yet deigned to visit the scene of his division's struggle, and where Anderson was and what he was about remains an open question. Nevertheless, Hancock had arrived, like a ghastly apparition squarely on the Confederate flank. For the time being, the Pennsylvanian held his position and continued his shelling of the Confederate fortifications.

The situation was bad enough for all that. The rear-enfilade artillery fire by itself was proving so hard to take that it appeared for some time Fort Magruder might have to be abandoned, which would have had disastrous results for the Southerners. The possibility also existed that the Federals would reinforce Hancock, which was exactly what he and his division commander were hoping Sumner would finally allow. Longstreet knew at once that he was in trouble. Ordering his remaining brigade, Colston's, to hasten its march to the field, he sent an order to Maj. Gen. D.H. Hill, whose division was next up the column from his own, to countermarch to his support.[27] Though he would not have shown it, Longstreet must have endured an uneasy couple of hours as he waited for the additional troops to come up and hoped the Federals would not press their advantage.

By 3:00 p.m. he might have breathed a little easier, as Colston's troops and the leading brigade of D.H. Hill's division marched through Williamsburg and came sloshing down the muddy road toward the battlefield. He would at last have some sort of a force available to try to avert disaster on his badly exposed left. By this time, however, trouble was brewing again on the right. While Sumner continued to hold most of the Union troops in the area in inaction, Union Brig. Gen. Phil Kearny had brought his division of the III Corps marching up the Lee's Mill Road in Hooker's wake. Kearny was the most experienced combat officer and one of the toughest fighters in the Army of the Potomac, and since he was not under Sumner's command, he wasted no time in throwing his troops into action in support of Hooker. His troops hit the tired and disorganized Confederates hard, rolling their line back into the woods. The Southern ammunition situation was becoming critical, as the troops frantically searched the knapsacks and pockets of the fallen for extra rounds. Some regiments were forced to pull out of the line for want of cartridges. A. P. Hill reported that upon the exhaustion of his ammunition he had led his troops in a successful bayonet charge. Wilcox was still senior officer on the field—Anderson still being curiously absent—and sent Longstreet an urgent appeal for reinforcements. In response, Longstreet dispatched Colston's brigade and two regiments of Brig. Gen. Jubal A. Early's over-sized brigade. With these troops Wilcox was able to mount a small-scale counterattack, and the situation was stabilized.[28]

With D. H. Hill's fresh troops had come a rider who must have been far less welcome to Longstreet. Army commander Joseph E. Johnston had left Williamsburg that morning hoping that nothing would happen there and that if something did, Longstreet would somehow deal with it. The distant thunder of battle to the rear had shattered these delusions, and Longstreet's call for help from D. H. Hill, explained as it was with the report that "the enemy was threatening to turn his left," would have removed all doubt as to the seriousness of the situation.[29] No longer able to ignore Williamsburg, Johnston turned back toward the battlefield himself, arriving about mid-afternoon. Incredibly, in view of the fact that his entire division was engaged in a hot fight with major enemy forces and that he had called on a neighboring division for aid, Longstreet had not communicated with Johnston in any way. This omission was too bizarre to have been an oversight. Clearly, Longstreet, who would spend much of the war conniving to gain independent command and who was campaigning for a corps command, had not wanted his commanding general present. He was also probably unenthusiastic about the prospect of Johnston's viewing what even Longstreet must have realized by this time was his highly questionable use of his division.

If he worried about facing Johnston's disapproval, or even having Johnston take over direction of a battle that was now threatening to involve close to half the army, Longstreet's mind was soon put at rest. Johnston was content, as he related in his report a few days later, to be "a mere spectator, for General Longstreet's clear head and brave heart left me no apology for interference."[30] The fact was that Johnston did not want to touch this mess with a 10-foot pole, and as he was to demonstrate after Seven Pines a month later, Johnston was not above falsifying the historical record to cover Longstreet's clumsy tracks, since admission of Longstreet's failures would for Johnston be a form of self-indictment, demonstrating the foolishness of granting Longstreet so much responsibility and autonomy.[31] So the army commander stood quietly by and allowed his subordinate to extricate himself as best he could from the predicament into which he gotten himself.

If Johnston was unwilling to take the unpleasant situation off of Longstreet's hands, Sumner was far more accommodating. Having steadfastly refused to send reinforcements to Hancock to allow the exploitation of his incredibly advantageous position, he now ordered the Federal brigade to pull back and rejoin the rest of Smith's division. Hancock prepared to do so, and had the Confederates simply left well enough alone—as they had left him alone to their own great discomfiture all day long—he would, without further ado, have withdrawn himself from his threatening position and alleviated Longstreet's embarrassment. At this point, however, Brig. Gen. Jubal A. Early entered the equation of Confederate command. Early's was the lead brigade of D. H. Hill's division. Even after two of his battalions had been detached to blunt Kearny's counterattack on the Confederate right, he still had four excellent regiments in his command. Thankful to have at last some sort of force to cover the nakedness of his left flank, Longstreet posted Early some distance to the left and rear of Fort Magruder.[32]

Most of the Confederate brigade commanders so far this day had proved to be remarkably aggressive. Now Early would surpass them all. He was posted, as he later described in his report, "on the crest of a ridge in a wheat field, and near a barn and some houses, with a wood some 200 or 300 yards in front, in which position we were not in view of any body of the enemy."[33] The situation seemed to offer little enough chance for Early to emulate the reputedly successful efforts of Longstreet's brigadiers in driving the Federals back on the right, and the ambitious

Virginian may well have reflected on this as Hill's other three brigades took up reserve positions behind his line. All the while he listened to the thumping of what sounded like at least a full battery of artillery firing away steadily someplace just the other side of the woods his men were facing across the empty wheat field. Clearly that sound had to be coming from a Union battery, undoubtedly the one that had been shelling Fort Magruder all afternoon from near the location of the far left redoubts now in Federal hands. Thus it was that Early conceived the idea of an attack through the woods to take the Union battery in flank and win easy laurels with the capture of these guns the Federals had so obligingly set down on his doorstep. Riding off to get permission for this attack, he found Johnston, Longstreet and D. H. Hill together, and directed his request at first directly to Johnston. The army commander deferred to Longstreet, who agreed, but who ordered Hill to accompany the assault since he did not trust Early.[34]

What Hill did not know at the time, was that Early had made absolutely no reconnaissance of the ground over which he proposed to hurl his brigade. His information was limited to the sounds he could perceive coming from the other side of the dense woods to his front. Early's mind was apparently already occupied with counting the guns he was going to capture—it sounded as if there might be a dozen of them—and thinking how good all this would look in his report. Whatever occupied his thoughts, taking a look on the other side of the woods before sending his troops there seems not to have entered his mind. By not it was about 5:00 p.m., and hurrying lest darkness close in on this already gray and gloomy day before they could launch their attack, Hill and Early got the brigade moving forward. Hill rode with the right-flank, where two regiments from his native North Carolina were in line. Early took the two Virginia regiments on the left, and a certain degree of competition seems to have started between the troops of the two states and their commanders as to which state would have the honor of capturing those guns. By the sound of things, if they pushed straight ahead, they ought to come out of the woods right on the flank of the Federal battery. The gunners might not even be able to swing their cannon around in time for a single shot. Eagerly they pushed across the wheat field and plunged into the woods.[35]

Here things began to go wrong. Visibility was virtually nil in the dense underbrush. The regiments lost sight of each other and soon lost contact. A small, swampy stream had to be crossed. Hill's North Carolinians had just dragged themselves through the thicket and waded the stream when the general stopped them to re-establish contact with Early's two regiments. He sent an aide down the line to locate him but not five minutes had passed before Hill was shocked to hear shouting and firing in front of them and just to the left, "and a voice, which I took to be General Early's above all the uproar, crying, 'Follow me.'"[36] It was indeed Early. In his eagerness to capture the guns, he had raced ahead without thought of alignment or the security of his flanks. His men had burst out of the wood full tilt and straight ahead toward a wide open field of mud—just plowed whenever last the weather had permitted such an activity. In front of them was nothing else—all the way to the woods on the far side of the Yorktown Road. To their right the sodden furrows of the plowed field stretched down in a long gentle slope to where Early could see Fort Magruder in the distance through the misty rain. On their left a more interesting scene presented itself. Early's guess about the location of the sounds he had been hearing had been a little off. There, just about 400 yards away and smack across his left flank was not one but two batteries of artillery, 10 guns in all, and supporting them was Hancock's reinforced infantry brigade with some 3,400 men.[37]

Early's reaction was characteristic. He ordered his regiments to wheel to the left and charge, and the accompanying shouting and opening shots were the sounds that had so shocked Hill down in the woods. The only thing Early had going for him was that Hancock's men were just in the process of obeying the order to retreat. Another few minutes and they would have been gone altogether. Now, they had just limbered up their guns and started for the rear when the Virginians burst into the open behind them. Early interpreted what he saw as flight and was all the more encouraged to pursue. The time needed by the Federals to get their infantry back into line and their guns back into battery, coupled with the relatively short distance he had to cover, gave him a chance. In the stiff fire-fight that followed, however, the Virginians had much the worst of it. Early was wounded in the shoulder and, weak from loss of blood, had to relinquish command and go to the rear. His troops were not far behind, retreating diagonally toward the woods to seek the cover of the underbrush as quickly as possible.

Meanwhile, Hill had hurried his troops forward to join the fray and emerged into the open field to view the near hopeless tactical situation. To make matters worse, he had only one regiment still with him, the 5th North Carolina. His other regiment, the 23rd North Carolina, had gotten lost some after they had crossed the creek and was still wandering around the woods. Hill, perhaps, wished the 5th were lost as well, and that Early's troops had never entered the open field, but it was too late now, and since something might perhaps be accomplished by joining the Virginians' attack, he reluctantly gave his consent to the eager colonel of the 5th to wheel to the left and advance across the open field, angling farther out into the field all the while, so as to get around Early's regiments, now directly between them and the enemy.[38]

The result was an unmitigated disaster. Because their position on the right of the original brigade line put them further away from the Union position, the men of the 5th had to slog their way across more than a half-mile of muddy field under the fire of Hancock's entire brigade and both batteries, now free to concentrate on the Carolinians as the Virginians fled for the cover of the woods. Hill's men got to within about 100 yards of the Federal line, where they sought shelter—such as it was—behind a rail fence. They could go no farther, and Hill, who could see as much, sent the order for them to fall back. The retreat proved to be another ordeal—a nightmarish attempt to run through the soft mud while shells and bullets continued to tear through their ranks. In all, the 5th North Carolina lost 302 men in the assault, 68 percent of those it had taken into battle that day. While this disaster was unfolding, Hill endeavored to get the other three regiments of the brigade into line and into the fight. It was no use. With the exception of the 38th Virginia, which

accidentally emerged into the open and just as quickly hustled back to
the protection of the forest, none of them so much as got out of the
woods.[39]

As the survivors of the 5th North Carolina regained the relative
safety of the thicket, Hancock's men once again took up their withdrawal. As darkness settled over the field a couple of hours later, Longstreet's division disengaged and pulled back toward Williamsburg and,
beyond it, Richmond. Fort Magruder was abandoned. The battle of Williamsburg was over. Each side was quick to claim victory. For as much
as it might be worth, the Confederates had at least accomplished what
they set out to do. Their supply trains had escaped unmolested. Johnston
himself was not a bit behind others in claiming victory and praising
those of his subordinates who had directed the fighting. Those higher up
the Confederate chain of command were not inclined to question the
matter, especially as more pressing issues were at hand. Officially, it was
a battle with which Southerners could be satisfied.

Yet future events might possibly have been different, had Joseph E.
Johnston observed more closely and pondered more deeply the events of
May 5, 1862. The troops had performed well at Williamsburg, and regimental officers had led them with dash and vigor. The higher one moves
up the Confederate chain of command, however, the more questions
arise about the quality of leadership. Confederate brigade leadership at
Williamsburg was at best uneven. Among the brigadiers engaged in the
battle were men whose names were to become well known within the
Army of Northern Virginia: A. P. Hill, Cadmus Wilcox, Jubal Early,
Richard H. Anderson and George Pickett. Some of these turned in per-
formances at Williamsburg that foreshadowed their future successes.
Wilcox had performed about as well as could be expected of a brigadier
who is ordered to conduct a battle in a dense woodland and is left in
charge of several other brigades without much help or direction from his
division commander. That he essentially lost control of the fight is less
surprising than that he was able to accomplish as much as he did. His
greatest fault—indeed, the greatest fault of all the Confederate brigadiers
on this day—was an over-aggressiveness that led him to advance with-

out adequate reconnaissance and even when he should have realized his forces were badly out numbered. A. P. Hill did even better. Having perhaps less opportunity than his brethren to display over-aggressiveness, he made no major errors and turned in the best performance of any of the brigade commanders.

Pryor, a political general pure and simple, had held that rank less than three weeks on the day of the battle. He had performed about as well as such qualifications gave cause to expect, courageously but unskillfully. Pickett, a West Pointer, had done little better. He would eventually rise to division command—not through his merits but rather through the favoritism of Longstreet. Anderson is the enigma of the battle. He did not re-enter Fort Magruder after leaving it in midmorning until at least sometime after Early's brigade came up late in the afternoon.[40] He was supposed during that time to have been directing the battle on the right, but it is clear from the reports of the officers engaged there that after sending in Hill and Pickett, he was doing nothing of the sort.[41] Where he was and how he occupied his time remains a mystery. His own report of the battle is curiously short and vague.[42] He, too, would rise to division command, he was undeniably skillful, and sometimes he could be an excellent brigade or division commander, yet throughout the war there remained questions about him. Lee would essentially relieve him of command the day before Appomattox. At Williamsburg, Anderson had shown the darker side of his generalship. Early's was by far the worst performance of the Confederate brigadiers at Williamsburg. His over-eagerness and carelessness in a business that was very intolerant of human error led to the butchery of his brigade. As a group, the brigade commanders had had their flaws—they would require good division leaders over them for the army to function smoothly—but they had shown much promise and there was good reason to believe they would grow into their jobs.

It was in the area of division leadership that the most glaring faults were displayed at Williamsburg. In D.H. Hill's defense it can at least be said that he probably thought that either Early or Longstreet had dealt with the matter of a reconnaissance of the ground over which Early's brigade would be attacking and the Federal position it was to assault. Yet he ought to have made sure. His oversight was a costly mistake for the men of the 5th North Carolina and the rest of the brigade. It was perhaps the least impressive day in the career of an otherwise highly competent combat commander.

Longstreet had displayed some tendencies that should have been alarming to his commander. He had abdicated the leadership of his division to his brigadiers. Five of his six brigades were sucked into a vicious fight in a dense tangle of thicket, disorganized and almost out of ammunition in the face of potentially crushing Union numerical superiority before he even came on the battlefield. He completely lost control of his division not because he lacked the technical skill to manipulate his brigades but simply because he had no idea what to do with them. The five brigades thus fought without coordination by a division commander. Even more glaring was Longstreet's neglect in failing to watch the Yorktown Road, to reconnoiter the approaches to his position and to see that all of the prepared defensive positions were occupied. Well might D. H. Hill have failed to imagine that any division commander—much less Johnston's favorite—could commit such a stupendous dereliction of duty. Had Longstreet effectively performed the most basic functions of a division commander, Early's debacle could never have happened.

Indeed, even at this early stage of the war, no excuse existed for the overall Confederate conduct of the Battle of Williamsburg. For a division commander to allow his brigades to advance into dense woods to meet a potentially superior enemy when he could instead have accomplished his mission by holding prepared defensive works and forcing the enemy to advance toward him across open muddy ground, through an abatis of felled trees, displayed an ignorance of the art of war worthy of a man who had been just two places removed from being the "goat" of his large West Point class and who had learned little since then. Yet Johnston, eager to make himself look good and virtually enthralled by Longstreet's glib self-assurance, had high praise for that general in his report. From that day to this, historians have generally echoed his praises, without a closer examination of what actually took place on the field of Williamsburg.[43]

From all this, Johnston might have learned, had he studied the matter closely and with an open mind, that Longstreet, while he could be very useful to a commander who knew how to take advantage of his strengths and suppress his weaknesses, could also be a dangerous subordinate. His deliberate refusal to notify Johnston of the serious situation at Williamsburg betrayed a lust for independent command that would—26 days later—lead him to demolish Johnston's clever plan for the Battle of Seven Pines by disobeying orders to get himself command of one wing of the army. Longstreet's tactical blundering should have warned Johnston that here was a division commander who would require close supervision. Lee learned this lesson early, and almost invariably kept his headquarters close to Longstreet. If Johnston ever learned it, he did so too late. At Seven Pines he gave Longstreet oral instructions only and a good deal of latitude. It was a mistake for which he was to pay in defeat at the only Civil War battle he stood a fair chance of winning at the outset.

The small action at Williamsburg, with its few hundred casualties on each side, was soon relegated to the status of "skirmish" and then all but forgotten as it passed into the shadows of the momentous events of the weeks that followed it. Yet this test of new commanders had lessons to teach, if it had found a ready learner in the man whose success depended on the wise use of these men. Had Joseph E. Johnston rightly assessed the strengths and weaknesses of his subordinates at Williamsburg, particularly Longstreet, he might have adjusted his employment of these men in such a way as to have improved his chances for victory at the only major offensive battle he would ever conduct as an army commander—Seven Pines. That he did not was a flaw in his own generalship, and thus Williamsburg, insignificant as its fighting might have been to the course of the war, might have revealed to anyone concerned enough to look a serious shortcoming in Joseph Johnston.

This faded image was taken in Camp Oregon, north of Washington D.C., after First Bull Run but before September 1861. It depicts members of the 71st Pennsylvania Infantry. Identified individuals include: Lt. Richard Penn Smith; Lt. George W. Kenney; Cpl. Burton P. Johnson; Cpl. N. L. Willard, and Pvt. George C. Moore. Note the obvious color contrast between those wearing dark blue uniforms and the men wearing gray uniforms issued in 1861 to the 1st California. *Dr. George Oldenburg, Jr., Berkeley, California*

Gary G. Lash

"No Praise Can be too Good for the Officers and Men"

The 71st Pennsylvania Infantry in the Peninsula Campaign

For the men of the Army of the Potomac, the Peninsula Campaign marked a rite of passage. It was their first extended operation, and it was, for many, their first blooding. Indeed, for some it turned out to be this and all too much more. Their time on the Virginia Peninsula was marked by almost continuous exposure to extremes in weather, severe day and night marches over impassable roads and wearisome periods of lying in drenched trenches punctuated by intervals of savage fighting. All of the trials that the men of the Army of the Potomac would face in future campaigns they faced first in their 150 days on the Peninsula.

The 71st Pennsylvania Volunteer Infantry Regiment was one of many Federal regiments that struggled on the thin strip of swampy land between the York and James Rivers. The 71st was a typical regiment, and its history in the Peninsula Campaign is the account of an ordinary regiment composed of average men who dutifully slogged through more than five months of arduous campaigning only to be withdrawn when they believed Richmond to be within their grasp. It is a story repeated by many other regiments of Maj. Gen. George B. McClellan's Army of the Potomac during the spring and summer of 1862.

Fewer than 10 days after Confederate cannon fired on Fort Sumter, 46-year-old Edward Dickinson Baker, an ardent anti-secessionist and Republican senator from Oregon, offered to recruit and organize an infantry regiment in California. To his chagrin, Baker encountered serious obstacles to raising men and money from California. Democratic Senator James A. McDougall from Washington state, however, offered to bankroll the regiment and supply arms if Baker could find enough men to fill its ranks. The senator's only stipulation was that regardless of where the men were raised, the regiment would be known as the "California Volunteers."[1]

Baker, who was by this time practicing law in Philadelphia, began recruiting men from that city and its environs for the "1st California Volunteers." Newly recruited companies moved to Fort Schuyler in New York City for training. By June, the 1st California had attained its full compliment of 10 companies. Edward Baker, now Colonel Baker, would command the regiment.[2]

On June 20, 1861, Colonel Baker returned to Fort Schuyler from Fort Monroe on the tip of the Virginia Peninsula with two important orders. One was to increase the size of his regiment to 1,500 men. This meant the addition of five companies, L, M, N, P and R, to the 10 companies already in camp. The other order, much anticipated by the rank-and-file, was to make ready to depart for the war front.[3]

Colonel Baker's regiment reached Fort Monroe on the morning of July 6. The "Californians" spent much of the month fighting the tedium of camp life and becoming more knowledgeable in the basics of military drill. Near the end of the month, however, about 300 of Baker's eager troops participated in a bloodless amphibious operation against a Confederate battery several miles from Hampton at Black River.[4]

The 1st California's sojourn at Fort Monroe was cut short by the Federal defeat at the Battle of First Bull Run on July 21, 1861. Colonel Baker's command rushed to Washington and bivouacked south of the Potomac River. The men settled into a monotonous routine of fatigue duty in the fortifications around Washington.[5] During this time, the five additional companies authorized in June, one of which had been recruited in the District of Columbia, arrived in camp.[6]

Early in October 1861, the 1st California marched into Maryland and joined the Third Brigade of Brig. Gen. Charles P. Stone's Corps of Observation of the Department of the Potomac. The brigade also included the 69th, 72nd and 106th Pennsylvania regiments, each of which had been raised in and around Philadelphia. Colonel Baker became commander of the brigade, which became known as the "Philadelphia Brigade," and Lt. Col. Isaac Wistar ascended to command of the 1st California.[7]

The 1st California received its baptism of fire by the Potomac on October 21. At about 8:30 a.m. that day, Lt. Col. Wistar, with as many of his men as he could cram into the small number of boats available, began crossing the river at a place called Harrison's Landing. The men clambered out of the boats and ascended the bluffs on the Virginia shore to the staccato of skirmish fire. Colonel Baker arrived and ordered his men into line of battle.[8] The "Californians" struggled to the top of the bluff and deployed on the left of the Union line. Two companies were thrown forward as skirmishers. These men had advanced only a short distance when they were hit by a volley delivered by troops of Col. Nathan "Shanks" Evans' Confederate brigade hidden in some woods. The skirmishers stood their ground until mounting casualties compelled them to fall back to the edge of the bluff.[9]

At about this time, Colonel Baker, who had been strolling back and forth in an open part of the field urging his troops to remain steady, was mortally wounded. The situation became critical at this time and the Northerners were ordered to fall back. Triumphant Confederates followed in hot pursuit, and what had started out as an orderly retreat deteriorated into a rout of the Unionists down the bluffs and into the Potomac. The first action involving the 1st California had ended in utter disaster.[10]

After the Battle of Ball's Bluff, the men of the 1st California spent several relatively quiet months drilling and picketing along the Potomac.

It was during this time that the Commonwealth of Pennsylvania claimed the regiment as one of its own and designated it the 71st Pennsylvania Infantry.[11]

Brigadier General William Wallace Burns assumed command of the Philadelphia Brigade shortly after Colonel Baker's death. The 36-year old brigadier, a native of Coshocton, Ohio, had been graduated from West Point in 1847. After serving as a recruiting officer during the Mexican War, Burns saw duty at a number of posts in the west and southwest. Burns was promoted to brigadier general at the end of September 1861, and served as General McClellan's chief commissary officer during the future army commander's campaign in western Virginia. Sergeant Benjamin Franklin Hibbs of Company I, 71st Pennsylvania, considered Burns "a perfect soldier. He understands his business, and those under him must understand theirs."[12]

Early 1862 witnessed command changes in the eastern Federal army. On February 19, Brig. Gen. John Sedgwick assumed command of General Stone's division. General Burns' brigade now was officially the

Third Brigade of Sedgwick's division. Five days later, the Philadelphia Brigade, with one other brigade of Sedgwick's division, was ordered to support Maj. Gen. Nathaniel P. Banks' operations in the Shenandoah Val-

Brig. Gen.
William Wallace Burns

Generals in Blue

ley.[13] General Burns marched his men to within several miles of Winchester before he was ordered to take his command back to Harpers Ferry. The Southerners had withdrawn from Winchester and army command concluded that Brig. Gen. James Shields' force could occupy and hold the village. This turn of events frustrated some of the 71st who longed "to avenge our Baker's untimely end." Colonel Wistar's men were back in camp near Harpers Ferry by March 15, "much to the disgust of every member of the regiment."[14]

The Army of the Potomac underwent a major organizational transfiguration at the end of the first week of March. President Lincoln directed that the army be reorganized into four army corps. General Sedgwick's division now would be known as the Second Division of Brig. Gen. Edwin V. Sumner's II Corps. Brig. Gens. Israel B. Richardson and Louis Blenker were assigned to command of the First and Third Divisions, respectively.[15]

General McClellan's original design for his spring campaign was to transport the Federal army down the Chesapeake Bay and up the Rappahannock River to Urbanna, Virginia. He would then march on Richmond thereby forcing the Confederates to abandon their lines near Manassas and Centreville. The preemptive evacuation of these works by the Southerners during the end of February and early part of March changed all that and, as McClellan wrote, "the Urbana [sic] movement lost much of its promise." McClellan received Lincoln's approval to transfer the Army of the Potomac by water to the tip of the Virginia Peninsula where, according to the army commander, it would make "Fort Monroe and its vicinity the base of operations." On March 17, elements of the III Corps, lying in wait at Alexandria, boarded steamers bound for Fort Monroe; the Peninsula Campaign was underway.[16]

The 71st Pennsylvania, with its sister regiments, departed Bolivar Heights on March 23. Five days later, Col. Wistar's men, carrying only their rubber blankets as shelter, crowded aboard the steamer Louisiana bound for Fort Monroe. On the morning of March 30, after surviving a drunk steamer captain, heavy snow and wind storms, the Louisiana reached the waters just off Fort Monroe. The transport anchored near the

U.S.S. Monitor, which one member of the 71st Pennsylvania described as a "raft sharpened at both ends with a cheese box on it." The Philadelphians were roused early the next morning, formed column and marched the short distance to Hampton, where they encamped.[17]

General Burns' brigade began marching to Richmond at 6 a.m. on April 4. The men had traveled only six miles when the column was halted, and General McClellan and his staff rode by. Private John Burns of Company G, 71st Pennsylvania, recalled that "instantly every man was on his feet, and cheer after cheer greeted him [McClellan] seeing him for the first time." That rainy evening, the 71st camped near Big Bethel, the small town that hosted one of the early battles of the war. The wet troops were on the road the next day at 5 a.m. in a heavy rain that would continue almost uninterrupted for the next week. The marching was difficult, and the men covered only five miles in four hours.[18] The historian of the 5th New Hampshire of General Richardson's II Corps division provided a particularly descriptive narrative of the trying march to Yorktown:

> It had rained for many hours. Thousands of men, hundreds of wagons and scores of cannon had passed over the roads during the last two days. It rained a cold, chilling rain, literally soaking the men to the skin. The roads were awful, being obstructed with brush, tree-tops, logs, holes filled with water, sloughs, and pit-falls....Officers and men blundered along. Nothing could be more uncomfortable, wearisome, distressing and demoralizing.[19]

The wet and tired troops plodded along, all the while listening to an artillery duel in the distance, until early evening when they pulled up in front of Confederate Maj. Gen. John B. Magruder's entrenchments that screened Yorktown.[20]

General McClellan quickly determined that there was no point along the Confederate entrenchments "where an assault promised any chance of success," and on April 5 decided to lay siege to Yorktown. The army commander ordered the siege guns to the front, an undertaking which would require the construction of numerous corduroy roads through the dense woods and across the low-lying, marshy land before Yorktown.[21]

The fatiguing work on these roads was made all that more difficult by an almost continuous artillery and sniper fire.[22] As if this were not enough, it rained continuously. One member of the 71st Pennsylvania recalled that "everybody felt wet and miserable in their rubber tents."[23]

General Sedgwick's entire division was assigned to Battery Number Eight on the left flank of the Federal line and due east of the Confederate works at Wynn's Mill in April. Confederate assaults on the battery were common at any time of the day and though they were always repulsed by Union pickets, the Northerners began to feel the effects of this new type of combat, trench warfare. The soldiers slept little, lying in a constant state of readiness. The general lack of prolonged rest would continue for much of the 71st's time on the Peninsula.[24]

Though the 71st Pennsylvania suffered few casualties from artillery or small arms fire In April 1862, the number of men laid low by the unhealthy conditions in the trenches in front of Yorktown grew. Colonel Wistar wrote:

> No other campaign was attended with more privation, sickness and death than prevailed in the muddy trenches of Yorktown. . . .The result of hard work, constant exposure by night as well as by day, with inadequate food was wholesale sickness. . .kept the actual strength and mobility of the army reduced to a low figure.[25]

Men fell victim to malaria, diarrhea and typhoid fever in alarming numbers. Colonel Wistar showed symptoms of malaria near the end of the month and was soon carried "in an unconscious condition" to a hospital transport on the York. Major Charles Smith assumed command of the 71st.[26]

Good news traveled through the 71st Pennsylvania's camp on the morning of May 4. The Confederates had evacuated Yorktown and Federal troops were entering the colonial town.[27] The Philadelphians marched into Yorktown in a heavy rainstorm the next day, as the Battle of Williamsburg was being fought about 10 miles to the northwest. The Southern defenses and town displayed all the signs of a hasty retreat. Tents still stood and a bounty of ammunition had been left behind. One member of the 71st counted almost 100 abandoned heavy artillery pieces, most of which had been spiked. Dummy or "Quaker" guns fashioned from logs lay scattered about, some of which were guarded by "soldiers" fashioned from clothing stuffed with straw.[28]

May 6 dawned clear and warm. The men of the Philadelphia Brigade took advantage of the pleasant weather to continue their tour of the Yorktown defenses. Federal troops had serious concerns in spite of the absence of their enemy. The Southerners had seeded the roads with torpedoes—primitive land mines—as they had withdrawn from the town. Some of the explosive devices had been planted "near object[s] of interest that would likely attract a crowd."[29] A mine killed a member of the 69th Pennsylvania, and the Northerners were outraged over what they deemed underhanded tactics. Sergeant Schurtz of Company P, 71st Pennsylvania, compared this type of warfare with "cutting the throats and bayoneting the wounded men that fell in the marshes," a reference to atrocities allegedly perpetrated by Confederate soldiers during the recent siege of Yorktown.[30]

Early the next morning General Burns led his brigade to Brick House Landing on the York. The 71st and 106th Pennsylvania crowded aboard the steamer State of Maine and set off on a roughly 25-mile trip up the river to West Point at the confluence of the Pamunkey and Mattaponi Rivers. General McClellan ordered this movement "to force the evacuation of the [Confederate] lines at Williamsburg, and, if possible, [to] cut off a portion of the enemy's force and trains." By the time they arrived at their destination late that afternoon, Brig. Gen. William Franklin's I Corps division and Brig. Gen. N. J. T. Dana's brigade of Sedgwick's command had already fought with Brig. Gen. William H.C. Whiting's Confederate division.[31]

The men of the 71st, disappointed by their late arrival, disembarked and helped Lt. Edmund Kirby, commander of Battery I, 1st United States Artillery, maneuver his Napoleons off the wharf. The infantry made camp along the banks of the York and contemplated the future. "Richmond is only 30 miles distant," wrote Sergeant Schurtz, "and I hope that my next [letter] will be written in that well remembered city of rebels and tobacco warehouses."[32]

On the afternoon of May 9, the 71st Pennsylvania moved three miles to Eltham on the Pamunkey River where they bivouacked. After six days of much needed rest, the Philadelphians tramped about 10 miles toward New Kent Court House in a heavy downpour, which turned the road into a quagmire.[33]

On May 18, General McClellan reorganized the command structure of the Army of the Potomac. With the blessings of President Lincoln, McClellan formed two new corps; the V and VI Provisional Corps to be commanded by Brig. Gen. Fitz John Porter and General William Franklin, respectively. Porter's corps included his own III Corps division, to be commanded by George W. Morell, and Brig. Gen. George Sykes' Regular Army brigade. The VI Provisional Corps would be composed of Brig. Gen. William F. Smith's IV Corps division and Franklin's I Corps division under charge of Brigadier General Henry Slocum.[34]

May 21 was an oppressively hot day. At about 5 a.m., General Sedgwick's division set off on a particularly difficult march of what one soldier recalled was "about thirteen miles to accomplish a distance of eight or nine." Potable water was almost impossible to obtain along the route of march. Private Burns of the 71st fell out of the struggling column to get a drink of water and ended up standing one hour of guard duty for his transgression. That night, Burns and his comrades camped on the plantation of ex-President John Tyler near Bottom's Bridge over the Chickahominy River.[35]

One member of the 5th New Hampshire painted a particularly grim picture of the miry Chickahominy lowlands close to where the Philadelphians bivouacked:

> This land is covered with a rank, dense, tangled growth of trees, reeds, grasses and water plants. Vines climb and mosses festoon the trees; the soil is productive, but its stagnant water is poisonous; moccasins and malaria abound; flies and mosquitoes swarm; turtles and lizards bask; cranes and herons wade; buzzards and polecats stink; bitterns boom, owls hoot, foxes yelp, wild cats snarl and all nature seems in a glamour or a gloom.[36]

The weather was becoming a major factor in the campaign. Powerful thunder and hailstorms did little to alleviate the unseasonably warm temperatures. On May 22, a particularly heavy storm flooded many of the camps including that of the 71st Pennsylvania. The hot and humid weather, poor drainage and prolonged exposure of the men continued to cause many cases of fever and diarrhea. One member of the Philadelphia Brigade, partly with tongue in cheek, wrote that the number of sick men in the army at this time was almost as large as the army itself.[37]

On May 23, the 71st and its sister regiments struggled six miles through a steady downpour before they bivouacked in a field near the crossroads known as Cold Harbor.[38] Five days later, General Sedgwick's entire division hurried off to the support of Fitz John Porter's corps. The booming of cannon fire was heard throughout the day, portending serious work in the near future. The next day, however, "Uncle John's" men marched back to their original position near the Tyler plantation in a terrific electrical storm.[39]

The storm was vivid in the memory of many of the troops. A member of General Richardson's division wrote that:

> The lightning was blinding and incessant, the thunder one continual roar, and the rain fell in torrents, turning the gentle incline on which we were encamped into one complete sheet of water, which ran like a river. The storm lasted far into the night, turning every brook, rivulet and river into a raging torrent far above its natural level, and the Chickahominy was one wide sea of swift-rushing, muddy waters.[40]

The quiet of the 71st Pennsylvania's camp was shattered late in the morning of May 31 by the swelling sound of artillery fire coming from south of the Chickahominy. The barrage served as the prelude to Maj. Gen. Daniel H. Hill's assault of Federal lines near the village of Seven Pines. At about 1 p.m., Hill's men moved east along the Williamsburg Road and engaged Brig. Gen. Silas Casey's division of Brig. Gen. Erasmus Keyes IV Corps west of the village. Faced with the prospect of being flanked on their left, Casey's men fell back through Brig. Gen. Darius N. Couch's division deployed in line of battle at Seven Pines.[41]

General Sumner, who was becoming increasingly impatient at the sounds of the distant battle, rode his horse back and forth in expectation of leading the II Corps across the Chickahominy. Major Smith anticipated a sudden movement and ordered his men to fall in. The troops were issued rations which they stuffed in pockets and haversacks. Tents and knapsacks would have to be left behind.[42]

The restless Sumner finally reached the limits of his patience, and at about 2 p.m. he directed his corps forward to the Grapevine Bridge. Thirty minutes after this, General McClellan ordered Sumner to push his troops across the bridge. This would be no easy task for General Sedgwick's brigades in the van of the corps. The heavy rains had flooded the lands adjacent to the bridge. Segments of the corduroy road leading to the bridge were actually floating. Nonetheless, Brig. Gen. Willis A. Gorman's brigade led Sedgwick's command onto the bridge. Gorman's men were followed by General Burns' brigade, General Dana's brigade and the remainder of the division's artillery.[43]

Lt. Edmund Kirby's Battery I, 1st U.S. Artillery had a particularly difficult time crossing the shaky bridge and some of the pieces broke through the planks. General Burns understood the importance of artillery and determined to do whatever was required to get the Napoleons to the south side of the river. Men unhitched battery horses and Burns' men, working feverishly with the artillerymen, actually carried the guns to solid ground. Meanwhile, the impatient General Sumner dispatched three messages urging Burns to get his men across the bridge.[44]

When the Philadelphians finally reached the south bank of the Chickahominy, Sumner ordered them forward at the double-quick. Major Smith's troops trotted off to the west and up a ridge, where they encountered a stream of wounded men and stragglers fleeing from the fighting a short distance to the west. These men were probably some of General Couch's IV Corps troops who had retreated north toward Fair Oaks Station from the action at Seven Pines. Smith's undaunted Northerners charged down the slope and crossed a small stream.[45]

At about 4:30 p.m., Gorman's brigade pulled up in an open field near the Adam's house where they found Brig. Gen. J. J. Abercrombie's brigade of Couch's division under severe attack. The IV Corps troops were valiantly standing their ground southwest of the Courtney house, a short distance west of the Adam's house, against a Southern brigade commanded by Col. W. Dorsey Pender. Gorman placed his regiments in line of battle, with the 1st Minnesota deployed on both sides of the Courtney house and the remainder of the brigade on General Abercrombie's left flank.[46]

The Philadelphia Brigade reached the field just as Gorman's regiments moved into line of battle. A member of the 71st Pennsylvania recalled that there were "woods to the left and right and open fields to the front" of his regiment's position. As General Burns prepared to push his men forward the Confederates rushed to turn Gorman's right flank. Sedgwick ordered Burns to send two regiments to the threatened flank. The brigadier chose the 69th and 72nd Pennsylvania which moved roughly "300 yards through a tangled swamp" to a position on the right of the 1st Minnesota. Sedgwick then lead the 71st and 106th Pennsylvania forward to the support of Kirby's threatened cannons. Throughout all of this, the lieutenant's battery ripped holes in the Hampton Legion and 16th North Carolina, of Brig. Gen. Wade Hampton's brigade, and the 6th North Carolina of Dorsey's brigade.[47]

Major Smith's men advanced a short distance and quickly went to ground. Soon they were ordered up and a bit farther to the right. The Philadelphians found themselves behind the 65th New York (1st U.S. Chasseurs) of Abercrombie's brigade, and the 1st Minnesota. Sergeant Hibbs recalled, "Our regiment did not fire a shot [from this position], but a great many stray bullets came among us, being fired at the men in our front." Private Burns claimed that the fire on their front was "terrible." The Confederates made several attempts to take Kirby's battery; each time they were turned back with awful loss by galling artillery and small arms fire.[48]

The action north of Fair Oaks Station lasted for roughly one and one-half hours and was over by about 7:30 p.m. Both sides held their lines at the end of the fighting. Lieutenant George Kenney of Co. N, 71st Pennsylvania, penned the following letter to a Philadelphia newspaper as he lay in support of Kirby's battery. It conveys his spontaneous feelings of anticipation and exhilaration as he realized that the tide had turned in the Federals' favor, and that the right flank had been saved:

> As I now write, a terrible battle is raging at our right, and has been doing so all afternoon. The enemy are trying to turn our flank. Now our brave boys are cheering, now we can hear the Rebels yelling. We have just three days rations on hand, ready to join the fight; just now the command is given to fall in without arms. Some good news I am sure, I must go. [He returns.] Yes, it is good news! good news! General McClellan wishes to announce to the men that we have met the enemy in large force on our right and defeated him, and oh, such cheering along our lines! It is worth a hundred dollars to hear it; I cannot tell you how wild I am to participate in it. Thanks be to God for his goodness to us! Listen! Listen! The whole heavens resound with the noise. There! our bands are playing the Star Spangled Banner! we are filled with great joy.[49]

Near midnight, General Burns was directed to move the 71st about one mile to the rear. Before they vacated the line, the Philadelphians handed over all of their extra cartridges to the men of the 34th New York, who were low on ammunition. The 71st, with 19th Massachusetts, 42nd New York and 63rd New York, were instructed to protect the line of communication to the north side of the Chickahominy, as well as to provide cover for artillery crossing the Grapevine Bridge.[50]

The fighting resumed early the next morning, June 1, on the right flank of the II Corps southeast of Fair Oaks Station and north of Seven Pines. The men of the 71st moved toward the sounds of the fighting shortly after awaking, and Major Smith's troops double-quicked to a large field southeast of the railroad station. There they engaged Confederate skirmishers. Soon, the Southerners withdrew, and by noon the Battle of Fair Oaks was over. Later that day, the 71st marched to a new position near Golding's farm, approximately two miles north-northeast of Fair Oaks Station and one-half mile south of the Chickahominy. Pickets from the regiment guarded the Federal right flank just south of the river.[51]

The 71st Pennsylvania had come through its action at the Battle of Fair Oaks with few casualties: Two men had been killed and two officers and 11 men wounded. Of the wounded, it appears that three were mortal.[52] Major Smith had been struck by two minie balls during the fighting but remained on the field. The fierce combat of the past two days revealed to the Philadelphians, and most others of the Army of the Potomac, that the road to Richmond would be fraught with difficulty. "Everything indicates stern resistance to our entering Richmond," observed Sergeant Schurtz, "but we are full of hope and possess the greatest confidence in our gallant young leader."[53]

Nothing had prepared the veterans of Ball's Bluff for the hideous sights in the woods and fields around Fair Oaks Station. It was, exclaimed Private Burns, "last field after battle I wish to witness." Another member of the regiment noted that the dead Confederates, who had not yet been gathered in piles or laid in rows by Union burial details, could be found lying, "in every conceivable position. They had been literally mowed down, and the intense heat had already produced a putrefication [sic] that rendered them all most disgusting to look upon." This Philadelphian noted that some compassionate Northerners had covered the faces of their dead enemies "from the gazes of the curious." One of Major Smith's men stumbled upon the body of Colonel Champion Davis, commander of the 16th North Carolina of Hampton's brigade. The Northerner remembered the Confederate officer as "a fine looking man."[54]

On the evening of June 2, the 71st and 106th Pennsylvania trotted off toward the left flank of the army to the support of Brig. Gen. Joseph Hooker's III Corps division. An anticipated attack never occurred, and the next morning the two regiments retraced their route back to their brigade near Golding's farm. The Pennsylvanians trudged across the recent battlefield as they made their way back to the farm. A member of the 106th recorded his impression of the field four days after the fighting in that area:

> The dead, in large numbers, still lying unburied or only partially buried, now terribly disfigured and rapidly decomposing. . .the sickening odor

making it almost unbearable, clinging to our wet clothes and even tainting the food in our haversack.[55]

The proximity of the Philadelphia Brigade to the swampy Chickahominy lowlands and to decaying men and horses, created what one member of General Burns' command charitably referred to as an "unwholesome atmosphere." Men continued to fall sick daily and problems obtaining proper medical and sanitary supplies exacerbated an already deadly situation. To some, it seemed that the wounded from the recent fighting were better off than those men who had contracted fevers and other maladies.[56]

On June 7, two companies each of the 71st and 106th Pennsylvania and one of the 69th Pennsylvania were ordered to the advanced picket line. The Confederates attacked this tempting target and almost flanked the Federal line. Lieutenant Maurine C. Moore of Company H, 71st Pennsylvania, and two privates of Company C were killed, and a number of men were wounded in this brief action. Small arms fire along the picket line continued throughout the day and was accompanied by Confederate artillery fire that afternoon. The men sensed a certain meanness to this sniping. Sergeant Schurtz of the 71st concluded that "The custom long adhered to by us of no shooting pickets, the rebels have entirely disregarded, and necessarily compelled us to do likewise."[57]

During June, the men of the 71st deviated little from their standard routine of picket duty, digging trenches or chopping down trees to open fields of fire.[58] "There was scarcely a day we had no fight," declared Sergeant Hibbs. A member of the 106th Pennsylvania recalled that the men were under constant threat of attack and typically slept on their arms, "as no day or night passed that we were not hastily summoned into line by an attack on our pickets." This man claimed that there was virtually no time when the rank-and-file were afforded "five consecutive hours of undisturbed repose. We might lie down, thinking to have a good sleep, but soon one, two, three guns would be fired, and then it was 'fall in,' 'stand in line,' 'sleep on arms.'"[59]

So it went for almost four weeks. The effects of seemingly endless picket duty and the attendant exposure took its toll on the 71st. "Sickness to an alarming rate prevailed" in the brigade, wrote the historian of the 106th Pennsylvania.[60] Poor sanitary conditions and grinding "labor and anxiety" continued to sap the strength of the Army of the Potomac.[61]

On June 19, General Franklin's VI Corps crossed to the south side of the Chickahominy, thereby isolating from the rest of the army Porter's V Corps, which remained north of the river. William Smith's division of Franklin's corps deployed near the Golding house displacing the II Corps, which shifted to the area west of Fair Oaks Station. Brigadier General Samuel P. Heintzelman's III Corps stood on the left of Sumner with General Hooker's division deployed across the Williamsburg Road in front of Seven Pines and Brig. Gen. Philip Kearny's division south of the road. General Keyes' crippled IV Corps was held in reserve.[62]

General McClellan had decided to move on Richmond when "the conditions of the ground and the completion of the bridges and entrenchments" were to his satisfaction. by late June, it seems, that time had finally arrived, and McClellan instructed General Franklin to have his corps on the road to the village of Old Tavern roughly one and one-half miles to the west of his lines early on June 25. General Heintzelman was ordered to push the III Corps east along the Williamsburg Road in support of Franklin's command. The operation would be supported by General Richardson's II Corps division. Heintzelman's men engaged the enemy at about 8 a.m. and pressed eastward until they were stopped by Maj. Gen. Benjamin Huger's division at about 11 a.m. Early in the afternoon, McClellan ordered the III Corps forward and, with the help of reinforcements culled from the IV Corps, Heintzelman's troops reached the area around Old Tavern by about 5 p.m.[63]

The Philadelphia Brigade was not involved in this action known to history as the engagement or Battle of Oak Grove. Nonetheless, Private Burns and his comrades on picket duty did skirmish with their Confederate counterparts throughout the day. The Seven Days Battles had begun.[64]

General Lee launched his operation against General Porter's isolated corps north of the Chickahominy the next day, June 26. The impetuous Major General A.P. Hill drove his troops against Porter's men deployed along Beaver Dam Creek at about 3 p.m. The battle ended after a fierce fight along the banks of the sluggish creek. Porter's line stood intact.[65]

Sergeant Hibbs and others of the 71st heard the "tremendous cannonading" of the Battle of Mechanicsville, but saw no action. Later that evening, General Burns' men were ordered into line without arms. An officer read an announcement proclaiming that Generals George A. McCall and George W. Morell had gained a victory north of the Chickahominy. Hibbs recalled that the assembled troops "gave three hearty cheers" which were quickly answered by the rebel yell delivered by Southerners just across the picket line. Indeed, some members of the 71st reported a great deal of cheering in the Confederate camps suggesting that, for some reason, they were at least as elated as the Northerners. Optimism was soon transformed to discouragement. "The truth was," one of the 71st affirmed, "the rebels had by their overwhelming numbers gained advantageous positions."[66]

That night General McClellan was informed that Maj. Gen. Thomas J. "Stonewall" Jackson's command was approaching dangerously close to the right flank and rear of the V Corps along Beaver Dam Creek. The Federal army commander promptly issued orders for a change of base from White House to Harrison's Landing on the James River. Fitz John Porter began withdrawing from his Beaver Dam Creek entrenchments before daylight on June 27. General Lee soon got wind of this and set his men in pursuit of Porter's corps. The Northerners retired southeastward along the north bank of the Chickahominy to a new defensive position on the lip of a plateau overlooking Boatswain's Swamp. George Morell's division formed the left flank of the new line and George Sykes placed his men on right.[67]

General A.P. Hill launched an uncoordinated attack against the center and right of Morell's command and the left of Sykes' division that afternoon. The Southerners were forced to retire after about two hours of hard fighting.[68] Around 4 p.m., General Lee ordered Maj. Gen. James Longstreet to initiate a diversionary move on A.P. Hill's right flank. Before this occurred, Maj. Gen. R.S. Ewell's division of Jackson's corps moved into a gap between A.P. Hill's and D.H. Hill's divisions. Then, as

Longstreet prepared his command for the diversion against Porter's left flank, Ewell launched an unsuccessful assault of Sykes' line. The seasoned Longstreet concluded that a full-scale attack would be more effective than a diversionary movement. Meanwhile, A.P. Hill's battered division was pulled out of line and replaced by General Whiting's division. At about 7 p.m. Longstreet's, Whiting's and Jackson's commands attacked the Federal line. Morrell's men, supported by George McCall's Pennsylvanians, broke under the overwhelming pressure of the grand assault. Sykes' troops, however, were able to fall back in good order, fighting all the way to the Grapevine Bridge.[69]

Lieutenant Colonel William G. Jones, recently installed as commander of the 71st Pennsylvania, and his men spent much of June 27 near Fair Oaks watching the Confederates on their front. While Fitz John Porter's men fell back to the high ground overlooking Boatswain's Swamp that morning, elements of William Smith's VI Corps division ventured west from Golding's farm. These men met Confederate artillery near the Garnett farm buildings.[70]

The men of the 71st Pennsylvania on picket duty south of Smith's line found their counterparts in a particularly "quarrelsome" mood. The tenuous situation could not have been helped by hearing, but not understanding, the vicious fighting involving Smith's men a short distance to the north.[71]

At some point during the day, General McClellan road his lines south of the Chickahominy and the men greeted their commanding officer "with loud cheers." The boisterous displays of affection for McClellan may have convinced the high-strung Confederates opposite the Federal trenches that an attack was imminent. The Southerners unleashed an artillery barrage followed by a fierce, but unsuccessful assault of the Northern picket line.[72]

During the night, General Porter transferred essentially all of his command to the south side of the Chickahominy. McClellan met with his corps commanders at Dr. Trent's mansion which was served as army headquarters, and issued marching orders for the following day. The army commander decided to array elements of his command in a defensive line behind which he would move the trains and artillery to the south. The II, III and VI Corps were to remain in position near Golding's farm, Fair Oaks Station and Seven Pines, respectively, during June 28 to protect the withdrawing column. However, the three corps were to fall back eastward approximately one mile and cover Savage's Station on the Richmond & York River Railroad.[73]

John Magruder's artillery began shelling General Smith's troops near the Golding farm early on June 28. Two Georgia regiments followed the cannonade with an assault on the Federal line, which was "repulsed with great carnage."[74] Later that morning General Burns issued orders to his regimental commanders to prepare to move. "Wagons began to hurry here and there," Sergeant Hibbs wrote, "bacon was burned, crackers were emptied into the roads and ditches, extra guns were hammered to pieces and cartridges were scattered everywhere." Though most of the wounded and sick men were sent to Savage's Station, some were simply ordered to return to their regiments or, as one of Hibbs' comrades recalled, "make the best of their way to the James River."[75]

The men of the 71st Pennsylvania struck tents on the evening of June 28. They packed their knapsacks and haversacks, stacked arms and anticipated marching orders. Of the arrangements to move south, Private Burns disdainfully scribbled in his diary: "preparing to Skedaddle from Fair Oaks."[76]

Late that night, the three corps facing Richmond finally began withdrawing from the Golding's farm-Fair Oaks Station-Seven Pines line. The VI Corps occupied the van of the retrograde movement and would be followed by Sumner's II Corps and Heintzelman's III Corps. Confederate troops across the fields and woods stands from the Philadelphia Brigade's line appear to have been alerted by Federal preparations to move and unsuccessfully attacked what they believed was the rear of the retreating column. The Philadelphians were forced to sleep, or try to sleep, on their arms that night as they listened to the artillery begin to withdraw from the lines.[77]

General Burns finally received orders to begin moving east along the Richmond & York River Railroad at about 4 a.m. on June 29. His men awakened and soon found themselves marching under cover of a morning fog and drizzle.[78] A member of the 106th Pennsylvania recalled that shortly after daylight on June 29, he and his comrades were instructed to pitch their tents in order to mask the rearward movement. As they went about this task, Burns reigned up and ordered the men back into line and ready to move out.[79]

As they marched east, the Federal troops observed the destruction of the great amount of military stores that had accrued at Fair Oaks Station and could not be transported away with the departing army. The expressive historian of the 5th New Hampshire provided a particularly graphic image of the spectacle around the railroad station:

> Just now the scene about Fair Oaks was one to illustrate the desolation and destruction of war. The abandoned camp, woods and fields were covered with the waste of war. Thousands of broken muskets; tons of ammunition burning and exploding; barrels of beef, pork, molasses, sugar, vinegar; boxes of hard-bread, soap and candles in great piles were being destroyed. The ground was strewn in all directions with immense quantities of food, clothing, books, papers and sutler's goods.

This man added a figurative exclamation point to the Army of the Potomac's withdrawal from the lines they had held for the past month by declaring that "This was the ending of the siege of Richmond."[80]

Lieutenant Colonel Jones' men marched a short distance east along the railroad to Orchard Station where they helped destroy more supplies. This task completed, the troops set off for Allen's farm, approximately one and one-quarter miles east of Fair Oaks Station.[81] Sumner's command reached the farm after a rapid march and deployed in line of battle with General Richardson's division on the right and General Sedgwick's brigades on the left. The men of the 71st Pennsylvania stacked arms and fell out next to the railroad.[82]

General Burns received orders to "reoccupy our former lines as advanced pickets." He ordered Jones to carry out this assignment. The lieutenant colonel led his men west along the railroad and soon arrived at their recent campsite near Fair Oaks Station. They were surprised to find three Confederates in an abandoned tent. One of the men ran and although fired at by several Federals, made a clean escape. The remaining Southerners wisely surrendered. When more Confederate troops, probably the advance of General Magruder's division, appeared from the east, Jones ordered his command into line of battle and attacked. Soon, however, the 71st came under threat from another Confederate line on their front and, more menacingly, a column moving along the railroad on their left flank.[83] Jones concluded that his small command would be engulfed and passed orders to retreat. The Philadelphians withdrew along the railroad, fighting all the way, to a "favorable position" on the left of some woods behind the Allen house.[84]

Magruder's advancing division was poised to strike the right and center of Sumner's line by about 9 a.m. The Allen house, which the 71st Pennsylvania had deployed behind, just happened to be close to the focus of the Confederate attack. Magruder's column fell upon the right of Sedgwick's division and the left of Richardson's line.[85] The 71st was forced back through the woods to the edge of a field. Sergeant Hibbs deemed this position as less than satisfactory: "We fought at a disadvantage, they being in the woods behind trees, and we in a clear field, where the bullets were more certain." Hibbs estimated that the regiment lost 30 men killed and wounded at this location.[86] Lieutenant Colonel Jones finally received relief from the 53rd Pennsylvania, which had occupied the Allen house and out buildings a short time earlier, the 63rd New York and the 15th and 20th Massachusetts. The 5th New Hampshire also came to Jones' assistance.[87]

Soon Confederate reinforcements compelled the 71st to fall back "under a severe fire," to a safer position. Though this "brisk fight," otherwise known as the Battle of Peach Orchard or Allen's Farm was over for Jones' men, the fighting continued. Later in the morning, Capts. Rufus D. Pettit's and George W. Hazzard's batteries went into action against the advancing Confederates, and, by about 11 a.m., Magruder's men had been repulsed.[88]

Lieutenant Colonel Jones' stalwart men had fought a stubborn rear guard action from near Fair Oaks Station to the Allen farm, a distance of more than a mile. One man estimated the regiment's casualties in this fighting to be 96 men and officers. A more realistic estimate of losses is probably no more than 68 killed, wounded and missing.[89] The worn out survivors would have little time to rest on their well-earned laurels.

At about noon, General Sumner learned "that the enemy was crossing the Chickahominy and advancing in large force upon" William Smith's VI Corps division near Savage's Station. As senior officer on the field, Sumner ordered that his corps, the III Corps and elements of the VI Corps concentrate at Savage's Station.[90]

The men of the 71st Pennsylvania had rested only a short time when some men of the regiment were detailed to the picket line to watch Magruder's men. General Burns put his brigade on the Williamsburg Road to Savage's Station. The day was quite warm, and at times the Federals moved on the nearly two-mile march at the double-quick. Men succumbed to heat and fell by the wayside; some of these unfortunates became prisoners. The Philadelphians lightened their loads along the route. A member of the 106th Pennsylvania recalled that "the road was strewn with knapsacks, blankets, tents, overcoats, etc." John Burns of the 71st had a particularly rough time as he struggled to Savage's Station. "On this march," the private wrote at the end of this long day, "I had to throw away my knapsack, I took my blanket and India rubber out and left the rest of the things for the rebels, I was so exhausted that I nearly dropped with the heat and excitement."[91]

General Burns' men toiled along the Williamsburg Road throughout the early part of the afternoon. They reached Savage's Station between 3 and 3:30 p.m. after passing through some of Heintzelman's III Corps troops who had been instructed to guard the road.[92] The jaded men of the 71st fell out and stacked arms in a stand of trees close to a field hospital from where they observed the destruction of military stores at the station.[93]

General Sumner quickly prepared his command for an imminent attack. Richardson's division stood in reserve in an open field north and east of the railroad station. Sedgwick's division held the center of the Federal line in a field south of the station between the railroad and the

Williamsburg Road. The division commander deployed the Philadelphia Brigade approximately 700 yards to the west of the station with its right flank close to the railroad and its left extending toward the Williamsburg Road. To the rear and left of Burns' regiments lay Gorman's (now commanded by Col. Alfred Sully of the 1st Minnesota) and Dana's brigades. Captain Pettit's Battery B, 1st New York Light Artillery, Capt. Thomas W. Osborn's Battery D, 1st New York Light Artillery and Capt. Hazzard's Batteries A and C, 4th United States Artillery supported the infantry. Brigadier General W. T. H. Brook's brigade of Smith's VI Corps division formed in a stand of woods south of Savage's Station and to the rear of Sedgwick's division.[94]

General Magruder's command advanced cautiously toward the railroad station while Sumner deployed his command. The Confederate division commander formed his troops in line of battle when they reached a position roughly one-quarter of a mile in front of General Burns' advanced line. Brigadier General Howell Cobb's brigade deployed just north of the railroad, Brig. Gen. Joseph Kershaw's brigade of Maj. Gen. Lafayette McLaws' division formed on Cobb's right immediately south of the railroad and Brig. Gen. Paul J. Semmes' brigade of the same division fell in on the right of Kershaw's line and spanned the Williamsburg Road.[95]

Soon Southern artillery rumbled up and began firing at Federal troops deployed about the railroad station. A number of rounds fell among the prone men of the 71st Pennsylvania. A noncommissioned officer recalled that "a shell came screaming over our heads, cutting off a large limb of a tree, which fell among us." Some of these Confederate shells may have been delivered by an artillery piece mounted on a railroad flat car.[96]

General Sumner was resting at his headquarters on the Williamsburg Road just south of Savage's Station when the Confederates began their attack. Awake and fully informed of the developing situation, Sumner ordered General Burns to dispatch two regiments into a wood on the brigade's front and south of the railroad. Burns selected the 72nd and 106th Pennsylvania. At the same time, the 1st Minnesota of Gorman's brigade advanced to the left of Burns' line and deployed with its left wing extended across the Williamsburg Road. Sumner sent the remainder of Gorman's brigade as well as Dana's full brigade to the aid Burns' advanced line.[97]

General Burns directed the 72nd Pennsylvania farther to the right to cover the railroad along which the mounted artillery piece was moving. This, plus the movement of the 1st Minnesota to the left across the Williamsburg Road, weakened the center of Burns' line; General Kershaw's South Carolinians were quick to move toward the gap and, according to General Burns, "attacked most furiously." The air was dense with minie balls. Burns was wounded in the face during this action, but he regular army officer remained on the field and in command of his brigade.[98]

The brigadier faced an immediate threat on his center and left flank near the Williamsburg Road. Indeed, General Sumner pondered why Semmes' men were able to move so easily along the road. The II Corps commander later learned, to his "utter amazement," that Heintzelman had withdrawn his corps from the left of the II Corps thereby uncovering the road.[99] The 69th Pennsylvania rushed to the aid of the 1st Minnesota. Sumner hurried the 88th New York and the 5th New Hampshire, both of Richardson's division, up the Williamsburg Road. John Burns wrote that it "was a splendid sight to see them [the 88th] with the American, Irish and state flags at the head" of the charging column. This attack, made in the face of fire delivered by Southern batteries on the road, forced Semmes' men to fall back.[100]

Shortly after the 88th New York make their gallant counterattack along the Williamsburg Road, orders came for John Burns and his comrades to move forward. Lieutenant Colonel Jones' regiment, with the 7th Michigan of Dana's brigade, was ordered to the threatened center of General Burns' line. The Philadelphians advanced out of the woods into an open field where, as Private Burns noted, "the bullets were flying very thick." They moved across the field and into the woods that the 72nd had charged into a short time earlier. The "firing was terrible," and

Jones' men and their comrades from Michigan quickly went to ground. They remained here for the duration of the fighting.[101]

The Battle of Savage's Station ended between 7 p.m. and 8 p.m., with the Federal line intact. Scattered fire continued throughout the night and the 71st was ordered to remain in its forward position. The nearness of the Southern and Federal positions precluded efforts to help any of the wounded men trapped between the lines. John Burns was shaken by "the cries and groans of the wounded begging for water and praying for help;" there was nothing he could do about it.[102]

General Sumner's men held their positions in the fields and woods around Savage's Station until about 10 p.m., when they began withdrawing.[103] The Confederates learned of the retrograde movement by the fires and many explosions set off by the destruction of Federal stores at the station. Perhaps the greatest losers in this stage of the "change of base" were the many wounded and sick men left on the field and in hospitals to, as the historian of the Philadelphia Brigade put it, "the tender care of the rebels."[104] The plight of these men was allayed somewhat by surgeons and other medical attendants who volunteered to remain behind.[105]

While the fighting raged in the fields and woods west of Savage's Station during the late afternoon and evening of June 29, portions of the Army of the Potomac joined elements that had already crossed to the south bank of White Oak Swamp. General Keyes' IV Corps had marched across White Oak Bridge by noon on June 28. That night and the early part of the next day saw the battered V Corps divisions of Morell and Sykes cross the swamp. General McCall's division crossed at noon and Henry Slocum's division of the VI Corps reached the south bank of the swamp at about 2 p.m.[106]

General Smith's VI Corps division led the withdrawal from Savage's Station, followed by Sedgwick's men. The hard march south took the men through dark, dank forests and swamps. A rain storm did not alleviate the great thirst that General Burns' men suffered from. Many soldiers were happy to guzzle stagnant, fetid water from puddles in the road that had been trodden by the army's trains and artillery.[107] The difficulties of this march were perhaps best described by a member of the 71st Pennsylvania in a letter to his hometown newspaper:

> It commenced to rain and we, weary and exhausted, plodded on through the mud and water, we scarcely knew where. The horrors of that night's march no one can imagine. Men declared that they could go no further, and I saw them take their guns from their shoulders, break the stocks off, and sit down by the roadside, to be taken prisoners in a few hours. Wagons, artillery, cavalry and infantry blocked the road, and the wounded were endeavoring to get on with the moving mass. How much further to go? Some said one or two, some four or five miles. It was impossible for regiments to keep together—we would become separated before we knew it, but all tried to follow the same road.[108]

One of Lieutenant Colonel Jones' Philadelphians claimed that the regiment finally arrived at the White Oak Bridge "soon after midnight," though this estimate may be several hours too early.[109] The exhausted men were guided to the bridge by lights set along the road. Some of the soldiers were so parched from the march that they jumped into the swamp. Others hurried across the bridge to the south bank for fear of being captured by Confederate cavalry close of the Army of the Potomac's heels. Several of the 71st, including Private Burns, gained the relative safety of the south side of the swamp and promptly fell asleep.[110]

The last Federal troops to cross White Oak Swamp were those of General Richardson's II Corps division, who reached the bridge just before daybreak. These men helped herd stragglers across the bridge. Richardson wrote in his post-battle report that "By the greatest exertions of myself and staff I succeeded in getting this mass over by sunrise." By 10 a.m. on June 30, the White Oak Bridge had been burned.[111] The division commander then formed his troops on the west side of the road south of the bridge in a defensive line facing northward, whence the Confederates were expected to appear.[112]

General Sedgwick's brigades slogged two miles southwestward of the burning bridge to an open field on Nelson's farm along the Quaker or Willis Church Road where the tired troops stacked arms and tried to get some rest. The relative calm of the afternoon was broken by an artillery fusillade echoing from the direction of White Oak Swamp. Sergeant Hibbs recalled that the cannonade caused some of his comrades in the 71st "to speculate as to the next move in the change of base."[113]

The commotion heard by the men of the Philadelphia Brigade issued from "Stonewall" Jackson's artillery deployed along the north side of the swamp. Jackson's command had crossed the Grapevine Bridge that morning, marched through Savage's Station and appeared on the north bank of White Oak Swamp at about noon. The Confederate artillery opened fire on the Northerners deployed along the south bank. The Federals requested reinforcements, and General Sumner, in command of the field with headquarters at Glendale, ordered Dana's and Gorman's brigades, both under Dana's command, of Sedgwick's division back to the swamp to support Richardson's men.[114]

Burns' brigade, now all that remained of Sedgwick's division near Nelson's farm, rested in reserve to the right rear of General Hooker's III Corps division which held the left of the Federal line. Hooker's line lay somewhat to the west of, and parallel with the Quaker Road, its right flank approximately a quarter of a mile west of the Nelson house. General McCall's V Corps division, stood in front of Sedgwick's command athwart the Long Bridge Road. Phil Kearny's III Corps division stood on McCall's right between the Long Bridge Road and the Charles City Road.[115]

Pickets of General Longstreet's division, commanded at this time by Maj. Gen. R.H. Anderson, advanced northeastward along the Long Bridge Road and engaged and drove McCall's pickets. Longstreet, in command of the 20,000 Confederate troops on the Long Bridge Road, ordered his column forward in a grand assault.[116]

The initial brunt of the Confederate attack fell on McCall's Pennsylvania Reserves causing the left flank of that line to crumble. Some of the routed troops retreated through the Philadelphia Brigade. General Sumner took command of the brigade and formed a battle line with the 72nd Pennsylvania on the right flank, the 69th Pennsylvania in the center and the 106th Pennsylvania on the left. The 71st Pennsylvania was placed in support of Lieutenant Kirby's battery, which had just reached the field.[117]

As more refugees emerged from the woods, followed by Confederates, General Sumner directed the 69th Pennsylvania to support Brig. Gen. Cuvier Grover's brigade on Hooker's right flank. General Burns was ordered to personally lead the 72nd Pennsylvania into the woods through which McCall's left flank troops had fallen back. Three of General Dana's four regiments, which had just returned from White Oak Swamp, moved into a gap that had opened between the 69th and 72nd.[118]

Burns' regiments helped stabilize the situation for a short time until the Confederates struck the center of McCall's line. The 71st was still in support of Lieutenant Kirby's battery, which one infantryman recalled was "firing shells vigorously and with effect." The batterymen "worked so fast at their guns," John Burns proclaimed, "that we could not see the sun for the smoke." The 69th Pennsylvania moved forward to shore up the crumbling part of the Reserve's line. Colonel "Paddy" Owen's "Sons of Erin" pitched into the Southerners and regained some of McCall's lost ground, and the 72nd and 106th Pennsylvania regiments supported the 69th. General Sedgwick directed the 71st Pennsylvania, with the 19th Massachusetts of Dana's brigade which had been held in reserve, to the support of the front line. "We threw off our knapsacks," Sergeant Hibbs recalled, "crossed the field and entered the woods." Confederates among the trees fired with great accuracy at Lieutenant Colonel Jones' troops racing across the field, hitting several men, including stragglers whom the regiment had "adopted" earlier by order of General Sedgwick.[119]

The Southerners renewed their offensive against the left center of the Federal line as the Philadelphians and Bay Staters rushed to the broken part of McCall's line. The fervent Confederates broke through Dana's 42nd New York and 7th Michigan. General Burns redirected the 71st and 19th into this gap, and, as he noted later, "nobly did they redeem the faults of their comrades." The two regiments quickly formed a battle line and unleashed several volleys that compelled the Confederates to "fall back a short distance." Private Burns described this action in most understated terms: "We made a charge here, had quite a right smart fight." Burns bragged that "for nearly one hour [the 71st Pennsylvania and 19th Massachusetts] poured into them [the Confederates] such a tremendous volley that no further attack was had at that vital point."[120]

Among the fallen of the 71st Pennsylvania that afternoon was Lieutenant George Kenney, the officer who had written with such exuberance from near the Fair Oaks just four weeks ago. The young lieutenant was hit by a minie ball below the waist on the left side of his body as he lead his company toward the breach in Dana's line shouting "Let us forward boys and give it to them." Major Parrish claimed to have heard Kenney cry out, "My Savior, My Savior," before he sank to the ground.[121]

The Battle of Glendale ended at about dark. General McClellan's men had held their positions, keeping the road to the James River open. Nonetheless, Sergeant Hibbs recalled that firing along the line on the left of the 71st continued "with unabated fury until long after dark." The wounded caught between the lines suffered through the night. Hibbs remembered that wounded Confederates begged for help by crying out the name of their regiment. He claimed that the most common regimental number called out was the 17th Virginia of Kemper's brigade.[122]

Generals Franklin and Heintzelman decided to withdraw from their lines near Glendale and move southward shortly after the fighting ended. Sumner learned of this at 9 p.m. and, although not pleased with the prospect of again leaving the field to a defeated enemy, began pulling his troops out of their lines.[123] Shortly thereafter, the Philadelphians found themselves in column of march with the rest of Sedgwick's division. They left many of their wounded comrades behind, including Lieutenant Kenney, whose desperate condition precluded his transportation south.[124]

Elements of the Federal IV and V Corps began gathering on Malvern Hill as the Battle of Glendale was being fought three miles to the north.[125] The remainder of the Army of the Potomac filed into position on the hill throughout the morning of July 1. General Heintzelman's III Corps was placed on the right of General Couch's IV Corps division, and Franklin's VI Corps held the extreme right flank of the army. Sumner's II Corps was the last to arrive and was placed in reserve near the center of the Federal line. The 71st Pennsylvania occupied a small hollow from where they could be sent to the support of nearby batteries.[126] Sergeant Hibbs was able to view the James River and the smoke stacks of the U.S.S. Galena from his regiment's position. The sight of the ironclad was comforting to the sergeant who averred that "The rebels now could not assail us from that [the south] side."[127]

The Army of Northern Virginia pursued McClellan's army. At about 9 a.m., massed Federal artillery on Malvern Hill began shelling Confederate troops and batteries deploying along the northern base of hill. Southern artillery responded to this fire and lobbed shells into John Sedgwick's position.[128] Confederate batterymen focused some of their fire on an artillery battery close to where the 71st Pennsylvania lay. Several of the Southern rounds overshot the battery and landed among the Philadelphians. The 71st—and Sedgwick's division in general—was forced to move several times during the late morning and early afternoon to avoid the Confederate bombardment.[129]

The artillery duel waned at about 1 p.m. An assault planned by Southern commanders to begin at 1:30 p.m. was delayed because of the ineffectiveness of the Confederate batteries, but the attack did come and it came with fury.[130] The 71st was fortunate in that it remained in reserve during the Battle of Malvern Hill. The men of the Philadelphia Brigade observed some of the action that was unfolding on their front. Years after the war, a brigade staff officer wrote:

> we could overlook most of the operations going on at the left, and as we heard the loud cheers of our troops engaged, and saw each repulse of the enemy, the unpleasant remembrance of the struggles and marches of the last few days was almost lost in the thoughts of victory.[131]

The fighting at Malvern Hill ended at about 9 p.m. in a decisive defeat for General Lee's Army of Northern Virginia. Nevertheless, Federal artillery kept the heat on Lee's men well into the night. The 71st Pennsylvania was sent out on the picket line from where Sergeant Hibbs and his comrades witnessed "streams of fire from the cannon" illuminate the hillside. The Philadelphians were so close to the Confederate lines that they could hear Southern officers issuing orders.[132]

Sedgwick's division vacated its position on Malvern Hill around midnight and marched toward Richmond. Burns' men, flush with their recent victories, anticipated a glorious march into Richmond. Their glee was quickly transformed to dejection when the column halted, turned away from the Confederate capital and trudged toward Harrison's Landing on the James River. Staff Officer Charles Banes probably spoke for most of the men of the 71st Pennsylvania when he offered a succinct overview of the Philadelphia Brigade's experience on the Peninsula and the most recent "change of base":

> After the three-months' campaign on the Peninsula, with all its privations, the perils of battle, and the wearisome fatigue of the march, to make a retreat when victory seemed within the grasp required all the fortitude of men to exhibit the obedience of soldiers.[133]

Sedgwick's command arrived at Harrison's Landing at about 10 a.m. on July 2 after a short, but difficult march through a severe rainstorm. Private Burns recalled the miserable journey, noting that he and the other members of the 71st Pennsylvania reached their destination "in a state of demoralization[,] all very wet."[134]

General Burns' regiments slogged into a wheat field, which had been transformed into a large "mud hole" by the recent rain. Later, rations of hardtack, coffee and sugar were distributed. "Somewhat rested with the sleep that many had secured," a member of the 106th Pennsylvania wrote, "the inner man was then attended to, and all hands felt much better and in better spirits." John Burns scribbled in his journal that despite of the wet and cold conditions, he and his companions were "very thankful for being spared" in the recent fighting.[135]

July 4, Independence Day, dawned bright and beautiful. At about noon Federal batteries unleashed a national salute accompanied by the playing of patriotic airs by numerous regimental bands. The men were reviewed by President Lincoln and General McClellan. After this, the army commander read a statement to his gathered audience congratulating the troops for their "valor and endurance" demonstrated during the recent fighting against "superior forces, and without the hope of reinforcements."[136]

For the next two weeks, the men of the 71st Pennsylvania remained in camp and devoted much of their time to fatigue duty, digging rifle pits and felling trees for fields of fire. An almost constant rainfall during much of this time made the boredom of camp life that much more tedious. On July 23 General McClellan issued Special Orders 212 which read in part: "The fifteen companies of the 71st Penn. Vols. will be consolidated under the direction of the Division Commander so as to reduce the regiment to 10 companies subject to the approval of the War Dept." In response to this directive, Companies L, M, N, P and R were disbanded and the men transferred to the remaining ten companies.[137]

The Army of the Potomac suffered in the unhealthy environment around Harrison's Landing. A member of the medical staff of the 5th New Hampshire, who was not with his regiment at Harrison's Landing, nonetheless provided a graphic, and no doubt accurate, portrait of the miserable conditions in the miry lowlands along the James River:

> The weather was intensely hot, and much sickness prevailed on account of the heat, bad location and miserable water. The hospitals were filled with men sick with fever, diarrhoea [sic], malaria, nervous exhaustion-all resulting from exposure, over-work, malarious air, badly prepared food, and last, but not least, mental depression, homesickness and a general weariness of heart and soul. Many died.[138]

Sergeant Hibbs of the 71st Pennsylvania judged the regiment's location at Harrison's Landing to be "the most unhealthy place our army was ever in." He went on to accuse army surgeons of keeping sick and wounded soldiers in this pernicious area until they were nearly dead. Hibbs blamed the poor handling of the maimed and infirm on the "cowardly officers and men" who themselves had gained entry on "sanitary steamers" to be taken to their homes in the north.[139] Private George Beidelman of Company C, had just returned to the regiment after recuperating from typhoid fever and was struck by the conditions at Harrison's Landing:

> The flies exist here in swarms, and they are very troublesome, but strange to say, there is almost an entire absence of mosquitos [sic]. The water is poor, and is the chief complaint. Diarrhea is prevalent. A good many have died since the great battles.

The continuous marching and fighting at the end of June and the disagreeable conditions at Harrison's Landing may have combined to induce at least 17 men of the 71st to desert in July.[140]

Toward the middle of August rumors were afloat that the army was about to move. On August 10, John Burns recorded, the men were issued 40 rounds of ammunition and two-days' rations, and ordered to be ready to march. The anticipated move was not to be, and for five days the men lay "around in the dirt like old shoes," as one Philadelphian put it. Finally, and no doubt thankfully, marching came early on August 16, and the 71st, with the rest of the II Corps, trudged off in the rear of the army.[141]

The march from Harrison's Landing was not without its problems. Stifling dust plagued the soldiers. Private Beidelman claimed that "in most places [it is] like wading through the snow in winter. We eat dust, drink dust, breathe dust, and are thoroughly filled and covered with it from head to foot."[142]

The hot and tired men of the 71st Pennsylvania collapsed out of column a short distance west of Yorktown early on the morning of August 20. The next day's tramp covered 16 miles and was remembered by some as the most difficult part of the march since leaving Harrison's Landing. "Besides being awful dusty," George Beidelman declared, "it was also hotter than usual." Water was scarce and several men of Sedgwick's division died from sunstroke and fatigue.[143]

Elements of the Army of the Potomac sailed back toward Washington at the end of August. George Beidelman realized that he would soon leave the Peninsula and lamented the losses and lack of success during the recent campaign:

What a great pity that after a campaign of nearly five months, this large and splendid army must be transported from the chosen position back to its original one, and that without having accomplished anything save the sacrifice of half a hundred thousand lives, and the expenditure of hundreds of millions in money![144]

Early on August 25, the men of the 71st Pennsylvania were issued two-days' rations and marched to a nearby landing on the James River, where they boarded the steamer Knickerbocker. The Knickerbocker weighed anchor at sunrise the next morning and made for the mouth of the James River. After 149 days, the 71st Pennsylvania was off the Peninsula.[145]

The men of the 71st Pennsylvania, like most other regiments of the Army of the Potomac, had spent their roughly five and one-half months on the Virginia Peninsula, slogging along muddy roads, living in flooded trenches, eating poorly cooked rations, rushing to arms at all times of the day and night and fighting off a variety of little understood maladies common to the sultry lowlands between the York and James Rivers. The seemingly endless tedium of trench warfare and camp life was periodically shattered by several running battles in which the Philadelphians fought well enough to win the praise of their brigade and division commanders.

For all of their difficulties, the men of the 71st Pennsylvania Infantry probably suffered neither more nor less than most Northern regiments on the Peninsula. The 106 men lost to the regiment from the Battle of Fair Oaks through the Seven Days Battles—no doubt a minimum figure that does not take into account those who deserted or were lost because of illness—is less than the loss of some regiments and more than others.[146]

Perhaps the most important result of the failed spring 1862 campaign for these veterans of Ball's Bluff was the great amount of experience gained on the Peninsula. General McClellan, much criticized for his handling of the campaign but loved by his men, realized that the army had fought well and was better prepared for coming campaigns. The former army commander provided an assessment of his command that could certainly apply to the 71st Pennsylvania:

No praise can be too great for the officers and men who passed through these seven days of battle, enduring fatigue without a murmur, successfully meeting and repelling every attack made upon them, always in the right place at the right time, and emerging from the fiery ordeal a compact army of veterans, equal to any task that brave and disciplined men can be called upon to undertake.[147]

In a sense, the war was just beginning for the men of the 71st Pennsylvania. The regiment departed the peninsula only to be rushed to Centreville, where it would help cover the rear of Maj. Gen. John Pope's Army of Virginia retreating after the Battle of Second Bull Run. In less than three weeks, the Philadelphians would face General Lee's battle-tested troops again in a stand of woods just west of Antietam Creek. Three months later, the 71st, with the rest of the II Corps, would participate in the senseless and bloody assaults of the high ground west of Fredericksburg. Almost two months to the day after the Federal disaster at Chancellorsville, these men would help repulse a Confederate wave rolling up a gentle ridge just south of the village of Gettysburg, Pennsylvania. The stolid men of the 71st Pennsylvania would also take part in Lt. Gen. Ulysses S. Grant's brutal spring 1864 Overland Campaign just before they were finally mustered out of service.[148]

But that was all in the future. In the meantime, the soldiers of the 71st Pennsylvania had left a solid legacy of their first real experiences of the horrors of the Civil War in their record on the Virginia Peninsula.

Gen. Joseph E. Johnston

Valentine Museum, Richmond, Virginia

Steven H. Newton

"He is a Good Soldier"

Johnson, Davis and Seven Pines:
The Uncertainty Principle in Action

During the Congressional inspection of the curriculum at West Point in 1860, Professor William H. C. Bartlett described his course in "Natural Philosophy" as discussing "all the laws of equilibrium and motion of connected systems," which included "the composition and resolution of forces, work, center of gravity, center of inertia, vertical motion of heavy bodies, projectiles, planetary motions, system of the world, perturbations, universal gravitation, impact, simple, compound, gun, and ballistic pendulums."[1] It is hardly surprising that a college of civil engineering would produce graduates who employed analogies from classical Newtonian physics to explain the outcomes of battles and campaigns. For example, when writing to Gen. Braxton Bragg on November 16, 1862, Gen. P. G. T. Beauregard advised his successor in command of the Army of Mississippi that "in *tactics* as in *statics*, the force is equal to the mass multiplied by the square of the velocity, as Professor Bartlett used to teach us at West Point. We must profit by his lessons to put to rout these abolition hordes."[2]

Allusions to classical physics have enjoyed tremendous popularity in the memoirs of generals and the narratives of historians, especially when it comes to the descriptions of battles and campaigns. Columns of regiments attacking an exposed flank can be explained metaphorically in terms of mass and velocity, the shattering impact of a cavalry charge described not as the impact of flesh against steel, but as the action of predictable—even inexorable—physical forces. This calculus of combat is often employed for predictive rather than descriptive purposes. Historians have endlessly quantified troops, armaments, supply, terrain factors and even the effect of specific leaders in attempts to generate theses on combat efficiency, the cultural precursors of tactics or the effect that a live "Stonewall" Jackson might have had on the battle of Gettysburg.[3]

At the bottom of all this, one might suspect, is not only the Newtonian assumption that the world is an orderly place (the same forces dependably producing the same result time after time) but the very human attempt to categorize the efforts of soldiers expending their lives as something other than senseless, random and chaotic. Unfortunately, as quantum physicists and researchers in the new science of chaos have shown, the universe is an inherently disorderly place, where the same cause does not always consistently lead to the same effect. While this ideological shift has discomfited weather forecasters and physics teachers, it also creates interpretive opportunities for the historian.

For example, eminent physicist Dr. Werner Heisenberg argued with his famous "uncertainty principle" that every particle can be described in terms of location and velocity. Unfortunately, the more precisely the observer defines the location of that particle, the less will be known about the particle's velocity, and vice versa. If the particle can be placed without doubt at a specific point, then it cannot be moving. On the other hand, if the speed and direction of movement can be calibrated, then the particle can no longer be located at a specific point. The uncertainty principle is a reflection of the fact that there exists an inherent limitation of the accuracy with which physical phenomena can be measured; it also implies that the very act of observation changes the subject under consideration.[4]

So, too, for human relationships, such as the tortured relationship of Gen. Joseph E. Johnston and Confederate president Jefferson Davis, which, as historian Richard McMurry observed, "contributed to the ruin of a nation for which each of them would willingly have laid down his life."[5] From the earliest estrangement over the general's rank in 1861 to the summer day in 1864 when Davis relieved Johnston of command, historians and biographers have graphed the progressive deterioration of the pair's ability to cooperate. Not a single item of evidence has escaped scrutiny, from detailed examinations of the salutations and closings in the official correspondence between the two men to the gossip surrounding their wives. There seems to be an implicit Newtonian assumption operating here that, if we can just collect enough evidence, it will be possible to discover both the precise velocity at which the Johnston-Davis relationship declined, as well as the exact measure of animosity that the feud contained on any given day. This precision, however, may be much more the construct of historians than an accurate description of reality.

Consider as a case in point the five-and-one-half-month interlude between Johnston's wounding on the battlefield at Seven Pines and Davis' appointment of the Virginian in November 1862 to command the sprawling Department No. 2, incorporating major Confederate armies in Mississippi and Tennessee. These armies were commanded by two men in which Davis had nearly unlimited personal trust—Lt. Gen. John C. Pemberton and Gen. Braxton Bragg—and their divisions guarded the path into the industrial and agricultural heartland of the Confederacy. By the late autumn of 1862, Maj. Gen. Ulysses Grant was contemplating his first advance on Vicksburg, and Maj. Gen. William Rosecrans had forced Bragg's retreat from Kentucky into middle Tennessee. The Federal preponderance in numbers threatened to overwhelm the Confederates if some coordination was not introduced into the area. There was no theater of war more critical to the Confederacy in the fall of 1862 than Department No. 2.

Unlike the lengthy and acrimonious cabinet debate that preceded Johnston's succession to command of the Army of Tennessee in 1864,

Davis alone made the decision to give the important 1862 post to Johnston, and he did so with alacrity and every appearance of enthusiasm. The appointment came the same day that Johnston reported himself fit for duty, though Davis well knew that the general had not completely recovered from his injuries. The president also knew that Johnston had spent his convalescence working against Davis's policies, lending his support to nearly every opposition politician who happened to pass through Richmond. Nonetheless, Davis felt Johnston merited the command on the basis of his military skill, having written privately on June 23, 1862, "Genl. J. E. Johnston is steadily and rapidly improving, I wish he was able to take the field. Despite the critics who know military affairs by instinct, he is a good Soldier, knows the troops, never brags even of what he did do and could at this time render valuable service."[6]

Yet, by all the indicators most commonly cited, Davis' respect for Johnston should already have been nearly non-existent. Johnston's retreat from Yorktown to the vicinity of Richmond during May had certainly strained an already mistrustful relationship. Johnston is usually painted as balky, uncommunicative, and unwilling to commit his army in a stand-up fight without massive reinforcements. Both the president's most recent biographer, William C. Davis, and western theater historian Steven Woodworth, have even accepted the old canard that Davis believed Johnston was about to

President
Jefferson Davis

National Archives

abandon Richmond. They present Davis as repeatedly prodding Johnston to stand and fight. Woodworth asserts that it was only "under this threat to his proud position [that] Johnston finally summoned up the nerve to fight."[7]

Nor should Johnston's conduct of the Battle of Seven Pines, in the eyes of the historians, have done anything to raise Davis's esteem for the balky army commander. The general, first of all, had not informed the president that a battle was imminent, and when Davis appeared on the field, Johnston galloped off in another direction, pretending not to see him. The president soon found himself forced to participate in rallying disorganized troops at the rear of the battlefield; "Davis saw with alarm that his generals knew little of the enemy's positions, showing poor reconnaissance by Johnston," writes William C. Davis.[8] After Johnston had been knocked out of the battle by a stray shell fragment, the president discovered that even the army's second-in-command, Maj. Gen. Gustavus W. Smith, had not been privy to the plan of attack.[9]

So the question should loom large: Why would Jefferson Davis be willing to entrust most of the trans-Allegheny west to an officer who had proved to be uncommunicative, incapable of cooperating with his civil superiors, obsessed with a strategy contrary to his government's policy and tactically maladroit? Davis himself claimed in a February 1865 memorandum that by the time Johnston was appointed to command Department No. 2 he already had good reason to suspect the Virginian's competence.

Many historians have tended to accept the premise that the president retained a substantial respect for Johnston despite his conduct on the Peninsula and his mishandling of the Battle of Seven Pines. Woodworth, for example, argues that "Davis's confidence in Johnston had been shaken somewhat by that general's apparent willingness to retreat up to and right through Richmond without a fight, but he still thought Johnston was skillful and needed only to be put in a position where he could overcome his skittishness in order to be effective." In the Mississippi Valley and Tennessee, Woodworth continues, "Davis may have reasoned, Johnston could use his skill as a strategist without needing the nerve to commit an individual army to battle."[10] Historian Craig Symonds suggests that "Johnston's battlefield wound probably saved him from having to face a more rigorous public investigation of his own conduct of the battle," and suggests that in November 1862 Johnston represented Hobson's Choice to the president, because Braxton Bragg recommended him, and because he "hated Beauregard more than he hated Johnston."[11]

Richard McMurry and Joseph Glathaar, on the other hand, both champion the idea that Davis in 1865 substantially overstated his suspicions about the general's abilities two-and-one-half years earlier. "Despite these differences," McMurry believes, "Davis sincerely regretted Johnston's May 1862 wound and retained an appreciation of and a respect for the general's ability." According to Glathaar, "some of Johnston's lustre as a great military man had rubbed off before Davis's eyes. But in Davis's opinion he remained a good commander and an asset to the Confederacy."[12] Not a few historians simply fail to discuss the question at all.

What these interpretations have in common is the underlying assumption that the velocity of the deterioration of the Davis-Johnston relationship can, in one manner or another, be employed to describe their relationship at any given point in time. The logic would seem unassailable: between Manassas and Seven Pines hostility increased between the two men, moderated with only limited success by Robert E. Lee. At Seven Pines, Davis witnessed a terribly mismanaged battle. Within weeks of establishing Johnston in his new command the following November, the two men were at odds over strategy. Certainly it seems to follow that the Battle of Seven Pines must have represented another item in the president's lengthening indictment of Johnston—an element he had to intentionally overcome, put aside or rationalize to reemploy the general.

An historical application of the uncertainty principle, however, argues against such a chain of deterministic logic. Understanding where Seven Pines lies in the chronology of the Davis-Johnston feud is not the same as understanding how it affected the speed with which the quarrel deepened. What historians know of the details of Seven Pines is in fact much more than Davis did in the summer of 1862, and what we know of Davis's contemporary reactions to the battle contradicts the idea that he viewed Johnston's conduct in a negative light. Viewed only from the perspective of November 1862, President Davis had actually come to consider the battle as a positive indicator of Johnston's skill. Furthermore, the president likely retained a much higher overall opinion of Johnston's abilities than historians have allowed.

Admittedly, this was not the case on the afternoon of May 31, when Davis rode down the Nine Mile Road to observe the unfolding battle. This was the third time in little more than a week that the president had visited the front lines of the army defending Richmond. On both previous trips, Davis had witnessed what he interpreted as such complete disorganization that he had admonished Johnston on May 22 that "My conclusion was that if, as reported to be probable, General Franklin, with a division, was in that vicinity, he might easily have advanced over the turnpike toward if not to Richmond."[13] On May 29, Davis had thought to witness an announced attack by Johnston's army, only to find a trio of disgusted generals—presided over by Maj. Gen. James Longstreet—none of whom seemed to know what was going on. The attack, he discovered quickly, had been cancelled. Johnston's attempts to elude the president by riding off toward Fair Oaks, as well as the considerable disorganization in Brig. Gen. W. H. C. Whiting's Division could not have increased his confidence in the general, nor would Davis's temper have been improved by Lee's subdued admission that Johnston had left him in the dark all day or by Gustavus Smith's failure to produce a plan of battle after Johnston fell. It would be doing less than justice to Davis as a keen observer and a trained military man to suggest that all these negative impressions were somehow wiped out by his emotional concern for the wounded general.

But in the days and weeks that followed, Davis's opinion of Johnston's conduct of the Battle of Seven Pines underwent a dramatic if gradual change. This process may well have begun as soon as the afternoon of June 1, when the president realized that, for all the faults attending Johnston's disjointed attack the previous day, Gustavus Smith had in fact accomplished even less on the second morning, leaving Lee, now commander of the army, little choice but to withdraw from the ground gained and move closer yet to Richmond. As June passed, and the Army of the Potomac remained inactive outside the Confederate capital, quite a few observers began to draw the conclusion that Johnston had in fact wounded the Federals more severely than it had first appeared; Davis's letter of June 23 suggests that he was among them.

Lee's offensive campaign, the Seven Days Battles, which was designed as nothing less than an ambitious attempt to destroy McClellan's army, ironically provided further vindication for Johnston's conduct at Seven Pines. At the battle of Mechanicsville, Lee attempted a complex plan of battle aimed at overwhelming the exposed Federal V Corps, north of the Chickahominy River. In a maneuver reminiscent of Johnston's original intention a month earlier, Lee's battle was to open when Maj. Gen. Thomas J. Jackson's divisions swarmed down on the Union right flank. Maj. Gen. A.P. Hill was to launch his own attack when he heard Jackson engage the enemy. Hill's attack would signal Longstreet to join the battle.

But, like Johnston four weeks earlier, Lee failed to account for the possibility of having his orders misconstrued—either willfully or unintentionally—by a key lieutenant. When Jackson's attack failed to materialize, Lee reacted as had his fellow Virginian almost a month earlier. He vacillated and missed the opportunity to call off the whole operation before an impetuous subordinate, in this case A. P. Hill, committed the army to a bloody repulse. So primitive were Lee's staff arrangements that for critical minutes he did not realize that Hill had attacked without the essential prerequisite of Jackson's advance.

As he had been present at Johnston's discomfiture, so, too, was Davis there to observe Lee's tactical shortcomings. While the president was infinitely more favorably disposed toward Lee, he could not have helped but reflect that Lee had repeated, as if by rote, every one of Johnston's mistakes, with even worse results. Johnston's attack had nearly shattered one Federal corps and pushed another back nearly three miles; Lee had accomplished nothing of the sort.

The difference came in the succeeding days. Not having been knocked out of the battle, Lee attacked again and again. Gaines' Mill was not a textbook battle, but it represented a vast improvement in tactical coordination over Mechanicsville, and it ended with the retreat of the Federal V Corps. This precipitated the Army of the Potomac's ignominious "change of base" from the York to the James River, a maneuver which looked suspiciously like a retreat to everyone but George McClellan. Over the next week, the tired troops of the Army of Northern Virginia battered the Federals repeatedly, with far more bravery than skill as the butcher's bill mounted, but it was possible for Davis to discern growth and improvement in his army commander's conduct of operations. Even in the wake of the disastrous frontal assault at Malvern Hill, the president was more than satisfied with Lee's overall performance.

Lee's perseverance and improvement changed the light in which the president would have then read Johnston's official report on Seven Pines. Johnston finished the document on June 24, two days before Mechanicsville, which makes minuscule the possibility that Davis saw it prior to observing Lee's first battle. In his report, Johnston omitted all mention of the confusion caused by Maj. Gen. James Longstreet's unauthorized modification of his battle plan, and attributed the failure of the army to crush two Union corps entirely to the dilatory movements of Maj. Gen. Benjamin Huger on the far right flank. "Had Major General Huger's division been in position and ready for action when those of Smith, Longstreet, and Hill moved, I am satisfied that Keyes' corps would have been destroyed instead of merely being defeated," Johnston wrote. "Had it gone into action even at 4 o'clock the victory would have been much more complete."[14]

Johnson's report enjoyed a great deal more credibility with Davis than it did with his contemporaries or historians thereafter. There were a number of important reasons for this. First among them was the example of Mechanicsville, which had transpired before the president's eyes, in which he witnessed just how easily the intentions of a commander could unravel due to the failure of a subordinate—in this case "Stonewall" Jackson. Johnson's report had the ring of truth to it in late June 1862 because it seemed to describe accurately both Seven Pines and Mechanicsville.

Equally important was the supporting documentation Johnston provided in the form of the reports of Longstreet and Smith. Longstreet had his own motivation for passing the blame to Huger, which was, of course, to avoid close scrutiny of his own disobedience. During the initial planning for the attack at Seven Pines, Johnston had instructed Longstreet to lead the attack on the Nine Mile Road with his six brigades, while those of D. H. Hill launched simultaneous assaults down the Williamsburg Road. Somewhere in the early morning hours of May 31, however, Longstreet decided on his own initiative (and without informing his commander) to move his division south to the Williamsburg Road behind Hill, rather than abreast of him. The ensuing logistical nightmare, as Longstreet's and Huger's troops competed for the use of an inadequate, single-plank bridge, delayed the opening of the Confederate attack for more than six hours, while Johnston was left—according to G. W. Smith—"anxiously awaiting the development of affairs upon our right." Smith made it abundantly clear in the first draft of his battle report that Longstreet had either misconstrued or disobeyed orders.[15]

But Johnston considered Longstreet his most valuable subordinate and moved to protect the Georgian from censure. He prevailed upon Smith to eliminate several key paragraphs from his report, and so Davis did not see them. In his own report, Johnston adopted the position that it had always been the plan of battle for Longstreet to deploy on the Williamsburg Road. If the president recalled Smith mentioning Longstreet's wayward actions on the evening of May 31 (a contention which rests only on Smith's postwar testimony), the apparent unanimity between the three reports probably convinced him that he had misinterpreted Smith, or that the exhausted Kentuckian had misrepresented events in the heat of battle.[16]

The Seven Days Battles further cemented the credibility of Johnston's report by augmenting Longstreet's prestige and destroying what remained of Huger's credibility. After the war, it became evident that Johnston and Longstreet had victimized Huger at Seven Pines, but Huger's lackluster performance under Lee reinforced their case. By early August, when Huger saw the reports condemning him for his conduct in the earlier battle, Lee had already found him wanting and begun the process of shipping him out of the Army of Northern Virginia. Davis, who had considered Huger a liability since the South Carolinian's earliest days of command at Norfolk, supported Lee.[17]

In contrast, Longstreet's undeniable tactical abilities were earning him the sobriquet at "Lee's War Horse." During the Seven Days, the massive Georgian had been entrusted with control of two divisions; by the time the campaign against Maj. Gen. John Pope opened in August, he led half the army. During the bloodiest day of the war, at Sharpsburg, Longstreet held the critical center of Lee's position against everything the Federals could bring against him. These events led to his promotion soon thereafter, when he became the ranking lieutenant general in the Army of Northern Virginia. Longstreet's unfortunate predilections toward army politics, self-aggrandizement and ignoring orders he did not like appeared to lie dormant during this period.

The only two reports from Seven Pines that might have cast some doubt on this picture were those of Maj. Gen. D. H. Hill and Brig. Gen. Cadmus Wilcox. Hill's report was important as that of the commanding general of the division that did most of the fighting on May 31. If Davis had carefully examined the report, he would have discovered that it did not concur with many of Longstreet's assertions. Wilcox went even further, suggesting that Huger's culpability for the failure to win a decisive victory had been tremendously exaggerated. Hill's report was undated, but its context makes clear that it was written far too late to have been read by Davis at the same time as the others, and Wilcox's report, coming as it did from a junior brigadier whose command did not even make it into the fight on the first day, probably never crossed the president's desk.[18]

Additionally, there was a concerted effort by Johnston's circle of supporters to portray the Battle of Seven Pines as the initial successful action in the campaign to push the Yankees away from Richmond. Headed by Congressmen Louis T. Wigfall and Henry Foote and Senator John Yancey, a loose association of administration opponents seized on Johnston as a useful tool in their pillorying of Davis's conduct of the war.[19] Improbable as it now seems, they were able to build—in the eyes of many—out of Manassas, Williamsburg, and Seven Pines a tactical record for Johnston that they considered to rival or surpass that of Lee. In early November, for example, a Richmond *Examiner* editorial noted that Johnston was about to report himself fit for duty, and that he should of course be returned to the head of the Army of Northern Virginia; Lee, editor John Daniel argued, was a gallant soldier who had done his best, and deserved to be elevated to Secretary of War in order to let the Confederacy's premiere tactician take the field in his stead. A sympathetic piece in the January 1863 edition of the *Southern Literary Messenger* reiterated the praises of Johnston as the foremost tactician among senior Confederate generals.[20]

Certainly it would not do to suggest that Jefferson Davis based his opinions on those of his administration's critics, although he did in fact read the *Examiner* on a regular basis. What is just as unlikely, however, is that Davis could have been unaffected by the general public acclaim for Johnston, especially given that he seemed to have in hand the evidence to prove that Johnston had done no worse—if not substantially better—in his first battle than Robert E. Lee. It would have been difficult to counter arguments that the general deserved his chance for a second day of battle.

Finally, there was Johnston's insistence that only darkness and his wounds had prevented his culmination of a total victory despite the lengthening odds against him. For Davis, this claim had an eerie resonance with his personal beliefs about the Battle of Shiloh, in which his friend and military idol. Gen. Albert Sidney Johnston, had fallen. One of Davis's most cherished misconceptions throughout his life was that by failing to continue the assaults Sidney Johnston had intended for the evening of April 6, 1862, second-in-command Beauregard had squandered a once-in-a-nation's-lifetime opportunity to push the Union Army of the Tennessee into its namesake river. Had Sidney Johnston survived his wound, the defeat at Shiloh on the second day would hardly have disqualified him for a return to command in the president's eyes. He was prone to see Johnston at Seven Pines in almost exactly the same light, especially as Gustavus Smith proved himself less and less capable as a field commander.

Furthermore, it is worth noting that, throughout the war, Davis was exceedingly reluctant to punish his generals for fighting battles, no matter how ill-advised or how badly managed. He turned a deaf ear to the cry for Lee's hide after Pickett's Charge, supported Bragg through Perryville, Stone's River, and Chickamauga, kept John B. Hood at the helm of the Army of Tennessee when Atlanta fell and even tied to find a corps command for John C. Pemberton after Vicksburg. Nor was it a coincidence that Beauregard lost his command in the west after relinquishing Corinth, Mississippi, without a battle. Because it was an implicit element of Davis's grand strategy for winning the war that Confederate armies had to take the offensive from time to time, he recognized that risking an attack meant risking failure or defeat, and he realized that even the most skillful of generals could not hope for an unbroken string of successes. He needed generals who would fight, and Seven Pines suggested that—earlier quarrels notwithstanding—Johnston would do so. Otherwise, there would have been no reason for including in Johnston's powers of command in Department No. 2 the specific right to step into any battle at any time and supersede either Bragg or Pemberton at his own discretion.

But if Davis's perceptions of Seven Pines as a positive factor prompted him to employ Johnston in a critical post, there remains the question of all the other influences suggesting animosity between the two men. They had quarreled over Johnston's rank, his administration of the army, state brigades, the withdrawal from Manassas in March and the subsequent withdrawal from Yorktown in May. Surely these issues had not been summarily forgotten or dismissed by the stiff-necked Confederate president, known for his ability to hold a grudge far longer than Lee held Petersburg.

Here again, the uncertainty principle as a metaphor for describing human behavior works better than the laws of motion or thermodynamics. Davis had reasons to dislike and distrust Johnston, and Davis was a tenacious disliker and distruster, but it would be asking too much to believe—especially in the summer of 1862—that these feelings never wavered. We may suspect that on any given day, after Seven Pines and prior to the great swirling controversies of Vicksburg and Atlanta, positive thoughts about Joseph Johnston strayed into the head of Jefferson Davis.

For all the rancor over the question of Johnston's rank, to give but a single example, Davis acted to bury the issue rather than animate it. In March 1862, he even made a pass at defending Johnston, in a mild sort of way, when rumors circulated that the general had threatened to resign in a huff over his lack of seniority.[21] Nor was Davis so set in following his own counsel that he did not take into account the opinion of others; during the summer of 1862 men the president respected—Braxton Bragg, Robert E. Lee, Leonidas Polk, and George Wythe Randolph—all had occasion to speak favorably of Johnston.

Substantive differences over strategy were significant, however, as was Johnston's apparent propensity for keeping his own counsel to the point of leaving the government in the dark while he conducted operations. Johnston's most critical failure as a commander was his inability to temper what he considered to be the dictates of military strategy with an understanding of political realities. He remained an unabashed advocate of merciless concentration of force throughout the war, even when it would have been political, even national, suicide for Davis to adopt such a course. His insistence on massive reinforcement of his western command in December 1862, without regard for the costs of yielding precious territory in other parts of the diminished Confederacy and with the cavalier comment that he could "beat the enemy here, and then reconquer the country beyond it," is but a single example of Johnston's political naiveté.[22]

Yet when examining how Davis received Johnston's ideas we must once again return to the atmosphere in mid-1862. During February and March in the concentration of forces leading to the attack at Shiloh, the president proved more than able to stomach the gamble of surrendering territory for the opportunity to strike a decisive blow. That the Confederates lost the battle did not convince Davis that the strategy had been erroneous, nor was he as deaf to Johnston's pleas in April to strip the defenses of the Atlantic coast in favor of Virginia as the general believed. From the time Johnston's army arrived at Yorktown to the opening shots at Seven Pines, Davis allowed seven brigades containing 30 infantry regiments, two infantry battalions, and three field batteries to be transferred into the Richmond area from the Carolinas and Georgia.[23] When McClellan's army retired to Harrison's Landing in July, the president considered the risk amply repaid by the rewards. Later in the war, as the agitations of Beauregard, Johnston, Longstreet and others grew more strident for hugh strategic concentrations that the Confederacy's deteriorating transportation system could never have supported, Davis became increasingly hostile toward such grand plans, but in 1862, this plainly was not the case. Far less distance then separated the strategic views of the two men than is usually supposed.

There still remains to be considered Johnston's frugality with the written word, particularly with those words addressed in the direction of his civil and military superiors. Johnston's reticence became legendary in Richmond long before the war ended and played a major part in his personal debacles at Vicksburg and Atlanta. Nonetheless, great care should be taken in extending the full force of Davis's suspicions and frustrations in this regard back into 1862, despite the testimony of his unsent 1865 memorandum or his postwar writings.

In fact, the secretive manner in which Johnston operated during the remainder of the war has caused historians to treat his conduct during the Peninsula campaign in much the same way that Huger's poor performance under Lee allowed him to be made the scapegoat for Seven Pines. During the 16 days that Johnston defended Yorktown, he addressed no fewer than 14 letters to either Lee or the secretary of war. His longest silence of the period came between May 2-5, during the immediate hours of the retreat from Yorktown and the battle of Williamsburg, and there is circumstantial evidence that the general attempted at least in that span to telegraph a report to Richmond. It should also be noted that a careful examination of the letters received in the offices of the secretary of war and the adjutant and inspector-general during that period reveals that almost no mail from Johnston's army managed to make it through to Richmond. Certainly Johnston should have made communicating with higher headquarters a greater priority, but the slip here was not nearly so great as it is often presented as being.[24] Without foreknowledge of campaigns to come, no one could reasonably have drawn significant enough inferences from the lapse to disqualify him from a future command.

Nor had Davis or his representatives lack for occasions to consult directly with the general as his army neared Richmond. Face-to-face meetings occurred with Johnston on May 14, 17, 18 (or 19), 23, 27 and 30.[25] The tendency of historians to dismiss these meetings as unproductive or inconclusive is reflective of their willingness to accept postwar testimony—especially by Davis—which should always be reviewed with extreme caution. Contemporary records suggest that, while Davis did not always agree with the manner in which Johnston managed his army, neither he nor Lee disagreed profoundly with the strategy Johnston pursued in his step-by-step retreat toward Richmond. Following the May 14 meeting, Davis wrote Johnston that "if the enemy proceed as heretofore indicated, your position and policy, as you stated it to me in our last interview, seems to me to require no modification. . . ."[26] The letter hand-carried to Johnston from Davis on May 17 as he crossed the Chickahominy, indicates that he understood the general's intent after the Federal attack on Drewry's Bluff to offer McClellan a chance to expose his army to attack while moving toward the James River, when "the opportunity desired by you to meet him on land will then be afforded."[27]

Contrary to what is often suggested, there is substantial evidence that Johnston communicated to Richmond on both May 28 and 30 his intent to launch an attack the following morning. On the first occasion, the general spoke to Davis directly, which accounted for the president's anxious visit to the field on May 29. A day before the Battle of Seven Pines, Johnston informed Col. A.L. Long, Lee's military secretary, of his plan to strike.[28] Since Lee was serving at the time as the *de facto* commanding general of the Confederate Army and therefore was Johnston's direct military superior, this certainly would have satisfied protocol for keeping the government up to date. Jefferson Davis had little cause to complain about Johnston's willingness to communicate during the defense of Richmond.

More to the point, Davis had little cause in November 1862 to think twice about appointing Johnston to command the western theater. Johnston's record in command was solid enough, and, as we have seen, there were numerous reasons why it appeared to shine more brightly then than now. His shortcomings, while already evident to some degree, remained in the president's eyes at the level of unfortunate quirks rather than disabling liabilities. His political naiveté in allowing himself to be the stalking horse for administration critics definitely angered Davis, yet this could not be compared with the offense the president took at Beauregard's constant harping or the difficulties that Bragg's knack for creating contention brought into the Confederate White House. From the perspective of the day, and leaving all that came after out of the picture, if asked in November 1862 which of his generals had the ability to conceptualize a campaign, lead an army, inspire his troops, and fight a battle, Davis would have limited the list to two: Lee and Johnston.

This conclusion requires a retreat from the standard interpretation of the Davis-Johnston feud—the mechanistic idea that the two men were locked into an inevitable spiral of a degenerating relationship. It suggests instead that historians should remain far more uncertain that the feud had even expanded before 1863 beyond the stage of understandable friction between two stiff-necked conservatives who found themselves thrown together in the attempt to carry off a revolution. If Jefferson Davis was still able, in the middle of the war's second year, to view Joseph Johnston as a major Confederate asset, then the possibility should be considered that the two men were not role-players in a Greek tragedy, condemned by *hubris* to destroy themselves and their nation, but two capable, albeit combative, personalities for whom the future was still an open question.

"What Men We Have Got are Good Soldiers & Brave Ones Too"

Federal Cavalry Operations in the Peninsula Campaign

Throughout the morning and early afternoon the young colonel paced the area around the cavalry bivouac, becoming more and more anxious as the sounds of battle increased. He sent offers of assistance to officers as they moved to the front, and as the sounds of the battle grew more ominous he finally went himself to personally offer his assistance, and to observe the battle that he had only heard throughout the morning. Between 2 p.m. and 2:30 p.m., a staff officer galloped out of the trees, saluted and said, "Colonel Stuart, General Beauregard directs that you bring your command into action at once and that you attack where the firing is hottest."[1]

The troopers first went into position on the right of the Southern line but Col. James Ewell Brown "Jeb" Stuart opted to move to the left from where he would have an easier approach to the Union flank. Here he received a dispatch from Brig. Gen. Thomas J. Jackson directing that his cavalry protect both flanks of Jackson's line. Stuart split his 300 men, sending half to watch Jackson's right flank while he led the rest toward the left. As he emerged from a skirt of woods he saw a line of troops moving ahead of him. After momentary confusion as to whose troops they were the young colonel ordered his men to charge when he saw that the men ahead were carrying the U.S. flag.

The impact of the Southern charge stunned the Federal line. After a very brief stand the Federals ran for a tree line which offered protection from the cavalry. Seeing that another charge was impossible Stuart withdrew to cover Jackson's flank. While neither side suffered heavy casualties in this brief skirmish, the thought of the charging "Black Horse Cavalry" was never very far from the minds of the young, inexperienced Union soldiers throughout the remainder of that hot afternoon of July 21, 1861. The mere mention of cavalry, much less the sight of men on horseback, even Federal cavalry, was enough to panic untrained soldiers. Later that afternoon, as the army started to retreat, officers used the fear of cavalry to keep their men from straggling. Once it became clear that the Federal army was in full retreat the threat of the cavalry became reality as Stuart was again unleashed. While he dogged the main column and snapped up prisoners, another column of troopers, led by Col. Richard C. W. Radford caused havoc along the Warrenton Turnpike near Bull Run.[2]

None of this is meant to suggest that Southern cavalry was responsible for the victory at Bull Run that day, but the impression they left throughout the North brought the issue of cavalry, and the need to raise this very expensive arm of the army, to a national debate.

Following the American Revolution the fledgling government of the United States disbanded all cavalry units because of the expense to maintain them and only raised units as needed and disbanded them when the crisis passed. As one historian explained it "the history of Cavalry for the fifty years prior to 1833 is one of feeble beginnings and sudden retrenchments, depending upon the moods of legislators. . .and upon the nation's economy." In addition to the expense of raising and maintaining cavalry there were several other arguments against the mounted arm. Because the cavalry was never around long enough, or raised in sufficient force to earn an enviable record, it was not seen as the important or elite force that it would later become. Furthermore the largely wooded terrain of the eastern United States was seen as restricting or preventing the movement of large bodies of mounted troops.[3]

The mounted arm was re-established by act of Congress in March 1833 when one regiment of dragoons was authorized. While there was no difficulty raising the authorized companies other problems developed; there was no means of training the men as there were no experienced cavalry officers in the army nor was there a manual of cavalry tactics. In 1835 the army instituted a cavalry school, under the command of Capt. Edwin V. Sumner, at Carlisle Barracks, Pennsylvania as a means of addressing some of these training issues.[4]

The Mexican War, while a training ground for many officers who would rise to a position of command early in the Civil War, saw little mounted action. The majority of the officers who saw action with the dragoons would command infantry units during the Civil War, and handle the cavalry as they had seen in Mexico. As one historian explained:

> For the men in Mexico who were to take a commanding part in the Civil War, the Mexican War taught few positive lessons about Cavalry. Either through ignorance or indifference, the men in command made slight use of Cavalry, and that use was not the best. No one was interested enough to concentrate the regular Cavalry, and much reliance was placed upon mounted volunteers.[5]

A number of mounted volunteer units were raised during the war with Mexico, almost all from the Southern states, and instead of being organized into a useful command they were scattered across the western frontier. Their level of training and discipline, as well as their equipment or lack thereof, left a poor impression of volunteers in general. One who looked with disdain on the concept of a volunteer army was George B. McClellan, and while his attitude would improve toward the close of the war he recognized that "it is barely possible to make a decent soldier even of Infantry in 5 years, much less. . .Dragoons."[6] This estimate of 5 years, while extreme for both branches, especially in terms of the infantry, may well have affected McClellan's thinking on the Peninsula, but it

most certainly was an overriding concern that governed military thinking at the outbreak of the Civil War.

For the most part officers too young to have seen service in Mexico
would become the effective leaders of the mounted arm during the Civil
War. A number of these men, Jeb Stuart and John Buford for example,
would miss the war and graduate from West Point without having received any formal instruction in cavalry tactics. The men who graduated
in the late 1840s and early 1850s learned the rudiments of mounted
service on the plains where the dragoons saw hard service at widely
scattered outposts. When they saw combat it was generally at a company
or squadron level. Many of the young firebrands who were leading the
cavalry at the close of the Civil War, received the benefit of cavalry
instruction at West Point, and then learned under the tutelage of the now
experienced officers coming back from the frontier. That was generally
not the case with the officers who were in command of cavalry units or
who, as corps or division commanders, were in a position of control over
the cavalry, during the Peninsula Campaign. While many of these officers, men like Philip St. George Cooke and Edwin Sumner, had been in
the mounted service since the early days in the 1830s, and had developed the concept of American cavalry, or more correctly dragoons, their
views and opinions were outdated by the 1860s. Unfortunately many
seemed unable or unwilling to modify or adapt lessons learned over the
last 30 years. They had seldom seen cavalry used in regimental much
less brigade strength and therefore had no concept of how to use the
regiments that would be under their command; herein lay one of the
obstacles to an effective cavalry force in The Army of the Potomac. But
before these issues surfaced other obstacles would re-surface.

At the outbreak of the war there were five regiments of mounted
troops in the army, with three different titles; two dragoon regiments, a
regiment of mounted rifles and two cavalry regiments. With slight differences in dress and armament there was little difference in function.
They still served in widely scattered outposts, seldom at anything beyond company size and, generally, still reflected the armies desire that
the men be capable of fighting on either foot or horseback. All of these

units would be designated as cavalry in August of 1861. The majority of the officers and men in these regiments would stay with their units after the firing on Fort Sumter, but it would take many months before the scattered companies could be pulled together, forcing the army to rely on volunteers.

While McClellan once thought that it would take five years to train a cavalryman the accepted axiom was that it took two years to properly train both man and mount. Gen. Winfield Scott, the man to whom Lincoln would turn for much of the early policy on the war, firmly believed that the war would be one of short duration, certainly much less than two years. In addition, the old sticking points of cost and terrain convinced him that cavalry would play no part in the conflict. Many valuable months would be lost before Southern troops would force some change to this view of the war and the role cavalry could and would play.[7]

One final obstacle that would hamper the development of the cavalry, and hinder it on the Peninsula, was that the manuals then in use in the army were predicated on European thought and tactics, developed generally by Napoleon and put into practice across open country. Most important, the last man to write a treatise on the use of cavalry was George B. McClellan.

In March 1855, Secretary of War Jefferson Davis sent a three member military commission to Europe to observe the latest weapons and tactics being developed during the Crimean War. Captain McClellan, an engineer only recently transferred to the 1st Cavalry, was the youngest member of the commission. His lack of experience with the cavalry was a concern to "be regretted" as one officer put it. After a year abroad the three officers began writing their reports with each focusing on their own area of expertise which for McClellan was the engineers and the cavalry. The result was a new cavalry manual and a study published under the title The Armies of Europe. This work covered most every aspect of the cavalry including methods for transporting horses aboard ship. It did not, however, reflect any predilection on the part of the author to use the cavalry as an offensive weapon.[8]

McClellan opened the section on the cavalry of the United States by observing that:

> the nature of cavalry service in the United States being quite different from that performed by any in Europe, we ought not to follow blindly any one system, but should endeavor to select the good features, and engraft them upon a system of our own.

He went on to advise "that we need only light cavalry in the true and strictest sense of the term." He added, "Everything in reference to heavy cavalry, lancers, hussars, &c., should be omitted."[9]

While he would not follow many of his own recommendations, (arming the 6th Pennsylvania Cavalry with lances being one example), other suggestions with merit, such as establishing a cavalry depot and school of instruction for officers and recruits would be adopted, but not until the mid-point of the war. This concept would insure uniform training at all levels, something that was sadly lacking in the early years of the war. He also suggested that a general, with a cavalry background, be appointed to oversee all aspects of the cavalry arm. The real issue, however, was would McClellan take heed of his own counsel and shake off the outmoded, or inapplicable, tenets of European thought concerning the use of cavalry and develop his own.

The argument over the necessity of cavalry in the coming conflict was not limited to the Government. With no cavalry heritage to draw from in the United States, newspaper editors looked to the cavalry heroes of Europe as they entered the debate. A thoughtful editorial in the New York *Times* of June 1, 1861 recognized a number of important points concerning the need for a well trained mounted force in the Federal armies. The writer suggested that:

> Foot to foot. . .few would hesitate to say that the North, with its superior weight and strength and stamina, must last longer than the South and conquer in the end. But, should a fight between the two be prolonged. . .the South has one reliance in reserve of which the North is almost destitute. . .a well-trained cavalry. . . .Cavalry is the right hand of active, open warfare. Without cavalry the great army of the Union. . .is crippled and imperfect.

After an accurate assessment of the Southern advantages in this regard, the writer concluded with this impassioned plea:

Let this matter be looked into directly. . . .we have no desire for gorgeous troops of Life-Guards and Cuirassiers; but we must have serviceable bodies of horsemen. . . .who shall meet the horsemen of the South in equal shock, and save our infantry from annihilation, as did the Scot's Greys for Wellington at Waterloo.[10]

Would the young general take heed of his own counsel or would 'The Young Napoleon' let the heroes of Europe govern his thought as did the writer of this editorial? Just three days after Southern troopers instilled a dread of the "Black Horse" into the Federal infantry at Bull Run the same editor, presumably, wrote a follow-up column, stating that:

In the commencement of this campaign we urged upon the authorities the necessity of organizing an efficient corps of cavalry for the Army. We were met by the assertion that cavalry had ceased to be regarded as essential to military operations. . . .In fact, we were told that cavalry was obsolete in modern military science. . . .It would almost seem that we are doomed to learn wisdom only from the lessons of disaster. . . .Still it is encouraging to know that we do progress. . . .[11]

One day after the defeat at Bull Run, General McClellan was summoned to Washington from his fields of success in western Virginia. Since early that spring his voice had been among those raising the steady call for more cavalry. He had, while in western Virginia, taken as his personal escort a battalion of horsemen from Illinois known as Barker's Battalion, after their commanding officer Maj. Charles W. Barker, but who became known later as McClellan's Dragoons.[12]

On August 2, McClellan presented to President Abraham Lincoln a "Memorandum for Consideration." In it he called for an Army of Operations to include 28 regiments of cavalry totaling 25,500 troopers. Under increasing pressure government officials dropped their opposition to increasing the size of the mounted arm and soon men were rushing to enlist in the cavalry.[13]

Brig. Gen.
George Stoneman

Generals in Blue

On August 17, McClellan was given command of the newly formed Department of the Potomac and authorized to organize the troops who would form The Army of the Potomac. Three days later he announced the names of the officers who would form his staff and the positions that each would hold. Among these was Brig. Gen. George Stoneman as chief of cavalry. By doing so he had fulfilled one of the precepts from his treatise on the cavalry, that being to appoint a general of cavalry to oversee that branch of service.[12] George Stoneman and McClellan had been graduated from West Point in the class of 1846, but while McClellan joined the engineers, Stoneman's first commission was with the 1st Dragoons. By the outbreak of the war, Stoneman was senior captain in the 2nd Cavalry, and his old classmate McClellan sought his service in July 1861 in western Virginia. "In heaven's name," McClellan pleaded to the war department, "give me some General Officers who understand their profession. . . .Give me such men as Marcy, Stoneman, Sackett, Lander etc & I will answer for it with my life that I meet with no disaster." Later when Gen. Scott proposed transferring Stoneman to serve with Maj. Gen. John C. Frémont, McClellan wrote a strong endorsement of Stoneman's fitness for his current position:

I sincerely doubt whether [Stoneman] is exactly the right man for the particular place [Frémont's chief of staff], although he is invaluable in the duty to which I have assigned him. . . .It would *very* [McClellan's emphasis] seriously impair the efficiency of this army were he to be removed from it.

The following spring, this endorsement aside, McClellan made it clear that the position of chief of cavalry was strictly an administrative post, without command authority unless specially ordered.[15]

On August 23, the same day that he presented Stoneman as cavalry chief to the army, McClellan noted to his wife the swelling ranks of horsemen in his army. "There were only some 400 cavalry at Bull Run—I now have about 1,200, & by the close of the week will have some 3,000." Soon enlistment posts and training depots would be overwhelmed as young and old rushed to join the cavalry, and overburdened the ability of the country to supply and equip them.[16] On September 8, McClellan began to address some of the problems facing his burgeoning army, the artillery and cavalry in particular. He again showed his bias against volunteers and gave some insight as to how he would put these men to use in the coming campaign. As for the Regulars the 'Young Napoleon' appeared to have in mind the formation of his own Old Guard unit similar to that relied on by Napoleon.

In regard to the composition of our Active Army, it must be borne in mind, that the very important arms of Cavalry and Artillery had been almost entirely neglected until I assumed command of this Army, and that consequently the troops of these arms, although greatly increased in numbers, are comparatively raw and inexperienced, most of the Cavalry not being yet armed or equipped.

A week later he explained:

As to the regular Cavalry—I have directed all of it to be concentrated in one mass that the numbers in each company may be increased & that I may have a reliable & efficient body on which to depend in a battle. For all present duty of cavalry in the upper Potomac volunteers will suffice as they will have *nothing to do but carry messages & act as videttes*. [emphasis added]

Within a week the young army commander recognized the fact that the swelling ranks of volunteer cavalrymen had overwhelmed the ability of the army to supply them. Retrenchment began to set in, again.

I respectfully request that no more Cavalry regiments be authorized in any part of the country. Those already authorized cannot be armed and equipped for several months & they will be all that will be required this winter.

In response the secretary of war ordered that cavalry units not fully mustered be consolidated, and that any who objected be discharged. This edict quickly reached the recruits, in some cases with demoralizing consequences as the issue was not quickly resolved. What was forgotten in the rush to relieve logistical burdens and cut cost was the old training axiom that it took two years to make a good cavalryman.[17] McClellan sought a means to pluck out and retain the best recruits and transfer to the infantry or discharge those who did not measure up to the standards of the cavalry, as a way to reduce the size of the mounted force already with the army. Again he showed his bias toward the Regulars as he suggested that all interested volunteers be allowed to transfer to the regular regiments. He suggested that all volunteer officers be brought before an examining board to determine their fitness for command; and to avoid "injustice or mistake" he recommended that all volunteer regiments be inspected as a means of determining which were retained and which disbanded.[18]

In an age when men enlisted in certain units to be with friends and neighbors, and when the state banner meant as much to morale as the national flag, the idea of forcing men to transfer to other branches of service or to regiments from other states was bound to be unpopular. The proposal that all officers face an examining board had merit, however. A writer for the Rochester *Daily Union & Advertiser* wrote "The idea of disbanding any available cavalry force, is. . .simply preposterous. . . .The want is of experienced and efficient cavalry officers. . . ." The mounted arm, by its nature, drew more than its share of "fops" and men of social position who had no business leading men into combat, and these men needed to be weeded out and quickly. Unfortunately many would survive until the rigors of the coming campaign gave them reason to resign.

At the same time McClellan requested competency examinations, he considered a proposal for an accelerated training program at West Point to help meet the need for proficient officers. He thought that by eliminating all but military subjects in their training the academy could turn out good infantry officers in two months and fair cavalry officers in just four months.[19]

That the role to be played by the cavalry, at least the Federal cavalry, was still very much in question in early 1862 is further suggested by two editorial columns in the Northern press. In an accurate but limited "Argument Against Cavalry" the writer urged that modern weapons had made the soldier on horseback obsolete. Certainly the rifled weapons of the 1860s had made a mounted charge against well formed infantry "madness", but there the argument ended, as if the cavalry had no other role. Apparently no thought was given to mounted reconnaissance, raiding or any other aspect of mounted service.[20]

In an equally shortsighted column in the Rochester *Daily Union & Advertiser*, the writer saw no point teaching cavalrymen to ride to battle and fight on foot, the very tactics that would have the greatest success by the war's end. Instead, the writer argued, the cavalry should be light cavalry in the truest sense of the term and only natural riders should be accepted, not those taught to ride in a riding school (presumably this included regimental instruction camps). It was also suggested that cavalry officers should select the natural horsemen from infantry regiments and transfer them into the cavalry, replacing them with men from the mounted regiments who did not measure up. Again, the morale, the heart and desire of the young men who would be spending long wearisome hours in the saddle, on patrol, picket and in combat do not seem to have been considered. Instead, the writer determined by observation alone that 50 percent of new recruits would never become good cavalrymen, and thus should be transferred.[21]

Eight months into the conflict, then, there was in the North still no sense of what the cavalry was all about. The issues of recruiting, training and equipping the mounted arm were no more resolved than the issues of how, where or why the cavalry was to be used. The Peninsula Campaign would serve as the start of a year-long learning process for the officers and recruits as well as for the administration and the war department, to include ordinance, quartermaster and logistics officers. An important issue as a result of this debate was the morale of the recruits. Nothing made this more apparent than the question of disbandment.

The 9th New York Cavalry

By late 1861 the authorized strength of the armies had been realized and on December 3, 1861 General Orders No. 105, brought an end to all new recruiting. It allowed for men in regiments not fully mustered to be transferred to other regiments or branches of service to the advantage of the army. The same day a telegram was sent to the governors of 22 states advising them that incomplete cavalry regiments would not be completed. Units that could be consolidated into a complete regiment would be received, while all others would be mustered out of service. The governors were further advised that the government wished to turn some of the mounted regiments into infantry or garrison artillery.[22]

Two days later the Paymaster-General, in reply to a request from Senator Henry Wilson of Massachusetts, issued a report with suggestions for reducing the enormous expense of the army. He was especially critical of the mounted arm, citing the number of regiments, special pay allotments for cavalry officers and the cost of forage. In response Senator Wilson issued a bill before the Senate that would reduce the size of the mounted arm to 50 regiments. Another senator proposed that the force be limited to 20 regiments. While these bills would eventually be tabled, a number of regiments would go through some turmoil as a result of the reduction in force. New York, with the largest number of authorized regiments, would lose one regiment of horse, the 7th, while the 9th would, to the great disgust of the men, go to the Peninsula as infantry and artillery.[23]

Rumors of disbandment quickly reached the ranks, where the men were left to wonder how they would be affected. For most the answer would not come until the beginning of the campaign. Daniel Peck, a teenager in the 9th New York Cavalry, expressed the hope of many a young cavalryman when he told his sister "We are not to be disbanded nor likely to be as I know of." But unlike some he was already planning which infantry units he was willing to join.[24] On March 8 any hopes the men had that their regiment would not be affected were dashed. They were marched to the colonel's tent where an order from their namesake, General Stoneman, was read asking for 150 volunteers to join the artillery. Initially only a few stepped forward but by later that day about 100 men had answered the call. The following afternoon the situation began taking an ugly turn. It was reported that Stoneman had determined that the entire regiment would join the artillery, with the first battalion leaving on the 10th. The men then learned that their colonel had misrepresented their response to Stoneman, telling him that the entire regiment had volunteered to go. Sergeant James Burrows noted, "a great deal of dissatisfaction is manifesting itself in all the companies at the move." Burrows, in a letter to the Fredonia *Censor*, stated that Stoneman himself came to their camp on the 9th and expressed his gratitude at the "patriotic spirit" shown by the men. As if to counter that Pvt. Nelson Taylor told his father:

> . . .I for one will not take any other kind of arms unless I am forced in to it and I will be [kept] under [arrest] some time before I will do it then. . .if ever there was a mad lot of men it is in this Camp. . . .[25]

The regiment was broken up by battalions: The 1st Battalion was transferred to the artillery, the 2nd and 3rd Battalions were sent to the infantry. A member of the regiment, writing for the Jamestown *Journal*, reported that:

the morning of March 10th found us marching into Dixie with Austrian rifles in our hands and forty rounds of ammunition in our cartridge-boxes: the four or five months drill we had in the 'school of the trooper dismounted,' and manual of the carbine made us tolerable good foot soldiers.[26]

Sergeant Burrows was less circumspect as he described the events of March 10, during the march from Washington to Alexandria.

[The men] were very much dissatisfied at being forced into artillery and were on the point of rebelling then. But finally. . .we got started and marched for Long Bridge, more like a mob than anything else, there being scarcely a show of order.

The rebellious troops located the artillery reserve on the morning of the 11th. Burrows continued his explanation.

We were then distributed about four to a gun. We do not have much to do, but it is understood that in case of our coming into action we are to ride the horses which are attached to the pieces.[27]

By mid-March the army was concentrated around the port city of Alexandria awaiting transport to the Peninsula. The 1st Battalion arrived on the 14th, followed the next day by the 2nd and 3rd Battalions. Those with the infantry were assigned to guard the ammunition train. Sergeant Burrows, with the artillery and now in charge of battery and forage wagons, predicted the "Onward to Richmond" move. He also assured his mother that "The story about our being disbanded is all nonsense."[28] The issue of disbandment was a matter of great concern for numerous regiments. With the release of the December 3, order the 1st Michigan Lancers, a unit not fully recruited, became concerned but then received reassurances that they were exempt from the order. By late February, all reassurances aside, the regiment was ordered to be disbanded and the men were mustered out on March 20. Numerous other regiments, including the 6th Ohio and 3rd West Virginia, were also not fully mustered or completely mounted and were therefore subject to transfer. Both of these units would survive.[29]

As early as February 8, rumors of dissolution had been "rife in [the] camp" of the 6th New York. Colonel Tom Devin, of the 6th, made two trips to Washington, the week of March 16, to plead for horses and to check on the fate of his regiment. By the 31st of March when the 7th New York was disbanded the 6th had received their marching orders for the Peninsula and could breath a little easier. But while the men of the 9th would also sail with the fleet their future, as well as their reputation, was still much in doubt.[30]

The 1st Battalion began embarking on the 28th and were caught on the river when a blinding snow storm struck on the 29th. The berthing arrangements were uncomfortable at best as the men bedded down in the hold of the transports. The ships reached Fort Monroe during the evening of the 30th, were pulled into shore by a tug on the 31st but would not disembark until the April 1. The other two battalions left Alexandria on the 1st and arrived at Fort Monroe on the 4th.[31]

Although the regiment was now with the army, its organization was still in doubt as shown by the reports in the local papers. The official version appeared in the Jamestown *Journal* of April 4.

> Gen. Stoneman visited [the regiment] recently and urged them to undertake an honorable service in the outgoing expedition. . . .This service. . .would secure them the first mounted regiment hereafter. . . .The organization of the Cavalry, therefore, has not been broken up, as stated in our papers at home; they are only on detached service. . . .[32]

A letter dated April 5 to the same paper shows that the situation had changed, at least unofficially:

> I regret to state. . .what is now beyond denial, that the 'Stoneman Cavalry' are to be disbanded. . . .The Secretary of War has already issued the order. . . .They will probably have an opportunity to enlist in another capacity, if they desire, but I understand the Secretary of War as holding that they *cannot be compelled into the army in any other shape* (emphasis in original).[33]

A follow-up editorial appeared in the paper of April 25.

[The] greatest apprehension prevails among some of the officers that the
regiment is coming to disorganization and disgrace—Disgrace in some
quarter there certainly will be, and retribution too. Why is it, and who is
working out the astounding cheat and wrong, that these men are continued
in the service, when the order for their disbanding was issued on the 29th of
March. . . .If they are drawn into the fight at Yorktown and killed, it will be
adding murder to insult. . . .[34]

On April 17, General McClellan glossed over the feelings of the
men in an attempt to retain the regiment with his army. He claimed the
order disbanding the regiment had never reached his headquarters, and
requested that such order be suspended as the men "do not desire to
leave the field of battle." By way of reply Stanton explained that they
had been disbanded when it was learned they "had been fraudulently
imposed on by their officers to enlist [in the artillery and infantry]." He
suspended the order and gave McClellan the discretion to retain or discharge them.[35]

That the reputation of the men and the regiment was suffering was
confirmed by Charles Wainwright, an intolerant man, serving as chief of
artillery attached to Brig. Gen. Joseph Hooker's division. He concluded,
"The Ninth New York Cavalry has proved good for nothing, is not to be
mounted and all the officers are to be mustered out." This proved of
personal benefit as he was in need of another horse and was able to take
his pick of the, now unnecessary, regimental horses.[36]

The rumors of dissolution continued to sweep through other cavalry
regiments moving to the Peninsula. Thomas Kelley, of the 8th Illinois
Cavalry, seemed more than willing to be discharged when he advised his
wife that "we will not be in the service many months longer now for
there is an awful sight of Cavalry in the Army of the Potomac." In a
follow-up letter, written aboard a transport anchored off Yorktown he
was hopeful but cautious about his prospects. "Gen Sumner said that all
Volunteer Cavalry would probably be discharged before the middle of

June but may be he does not know any better than any of us but I hope he does."[37]

At the same time the men of the 9th New York continued along toward their uncertain future. By early May men who had been arrested for refusing orders were returned to the regiment, with the exception of the ringleader who had escaped. On May 11, McClellan attempted to embarrass the troopers into a less hostile attitude toward their situation. He advised, by General Orders, that all the cowards would have their names posted before the entire army and made public, before being discharged; and then called on all honorable men to stay with the army for the coming battle.[38]

In a letter home dated May 6, Daniel Peck explained the latest confusion concerning the future of his regiment:

> The Regiment was ordered to Washington to be equipped. They then had orders to go to Albany to be Discharged. What is to be then I do not know and have not seen any of the Officers in ten days. . . .We get so many orders that we don't know anything definite.

Or as Nelson Taylor put it, "we have Orders one day they [countermand] them the next." Not until May 20 was there official word from McClellan that the regiment was being ordered to Albany for discharge. He felt that to discharge the men in the vicinity of the army would be bad for morale.[39]

By the end of May the situation was finally resolved through the intervention of three members of Congress from New York. After word of McClellan's order of May 11 reached Washington, Senator Preston King, along with Congressmen R.E. Fenton and Augustus Frank went to Stanton to protest the treatment of the regiment from their home districts as well as the tone of McClellan's order. As a result on May 14 Stanton ordered the regiment to be mustered out of service and on the 22nd the men left White House Landing by ship bound for Washington. There the men remained while a final decision was made on their future. On June 21, Stanton decided that the regiment would be mounted and retained as cavalry. The first weapons they received were the sabers turned in by the men of the 7th New York Cavalry when they were disbanded in March. It would be another year before the regiment was completely mounted and see action in regimental strength.[40]

One can only wonder about the effect this treatment had on the young men who had enlisted "like wild fire" in 1861, with the fervor of young patriots and with a desire to be "respectable troopers." By late May many felt "They had been made a cat's paw so long that they distrust everything relating to the War Department."[41]

To the Peninsula

On January 17, 1862 Assistant Secretary of War John Tucker was queried by McClellan as to the possibility of moving a large portion of the army, to include 10,000 horses, by water. One of Tucker's concerns, given the timetable for the campaign, was outfitting the transports needed for the horses. He felt that open schooners and barges would best serve the purpose but that each would need to be outfitted with some means of protection for the animals and their forage. Just over a month after being given his final orders Tucker had chartered 389 steamers, schooners and barges and the army, to include 14,592 animals, was on the Peninsula.[42]

As of March 14 much of McClellan's cavalry was in western Fairfax County, toward Manassas. General Stoneman, with ten squadrons of cavalry, was enroute to the Rappahannock River in an effort to drive any Southern troops, still in Prince William and Fauquier counties, across the river. Other units, under Hooker's command, were stationed in eastern Maryland. Three days later the army began embarking for the Peninsula at Alexandria. By that time the army counted 24,110 cavalry, but of this total five regiments and an additional 18 companies were attached to Brig. Gen. Nathaniel Bank's Fifth Corps, in the Shenandoah Valley, and the 3rd Indiana which was attached to the defenses of Washington. All or part of 15 mounted regiments and three unattached companies or squadrons would set sail for the Peninsula over the next month.[43]

All things considered the massive undertaking went smoothly enough, although a couple of late winter storms made life miserable for the troops. A reporter for the Jamestown *Journal* described the scene near the wharf in Alexandria as the First Battalion of the 9th New York embarked:

> Part of Hunt's Battery was shipped to-day, and files of Cavalry stood in close order along [King] street, waiting for their turn in the movement. The storm pelted them and they look dreary enough. I have never felt so much sympathy for our soldiers as I have since seeing their exposure and weariness here.[44]

When McClellan wrote his treatise on the cavalry he described, in some detail, how the armies of Europe transported animals aboard ship, and as already mentioned this was an early concern as ships were chartered at the outset of the campaign. However other concerns, such as cost, practicality and the overall speed with which the army needed to be moved overrode the protection of the animals. Generally, the horses were picketed on the top deck with no protection from the elements and unable to lay down or move around. Some of the ships carried a full squadron while the 8th Illinois required as many as 24 transports. The men, generally, were assigned below deck where they slept on the coal ballast and were deprived of the means to make coffee or cook their meals. Sidney Davis of the 6th U.S. Cavalry described the uncomfortable journey.

> The ballast of coal on which we were obliged to lie was a bed full of ugly points that were sure. . .[to] keep one constantly turning from side to side to ease one's misery. Then the horses on deck were continually tramping heavily. . .making one feel as though they would probably come through the flooring upon him; this was another condition not conducive to peaceful slumber.[45]

Once the ships arrived at Fort Monroe the infantry had preference at the docks over the cavalry. For that reason, and others, many mounted units were aboard ship for up to six days, and some as long as 10 days to two weeks. This was especially difficult on the horses. The 1st New York reported that a number of horses died and that all showed detrimental effects from the journey. In some cases the horses were pushed overboard and made to swim ashore while those that made it to a dock still had difficulty getting across the rickety gangways. Once ashore the horses immediately began to work the muscles that were cramped and swollen, as described by the historian of the 1st New York. "As boys let loose from a day's confinement in school, they manifested the appreciation of their freedom by rolling in the sand, capering about and cutting up all the antics possible."[46]

While troops continued to arrive and move up the Peninsula toward Yorktown the cavalry spent much of their first month training. One of the first mounted regiments to arrive, the 3rd Pennsylvania, was involved in the advance on Big Bethel on April 4 and Cockletown on the 5th, losing two men captured. On the 4th, Col. William Averell, leading the Pennsylvanians, was dispatched to Ship Point to ascertain the nature of the defenses but found the enemy garrison gone. He then moved to within a mile of the earthworks fronting Yorktown on the evening of the 5th to take no further offensive action until early May. As the historian for the regiment noted they drilled twice a day, at squadron and regimental level, and otherwise "[kept] up our masterly inactivity."[47]

With the army now laying siege to the historic village of Yorktown, many of the young cavalrymen looked to the army's youthful commander for a dramatic victory, as explained by a trooper from the 8th Illinois:

> McClellan . . .has a chance, . . .to retrieve the glorious reputation gained by him in Western Virginia, and which he has in measure lost amid the red tape in Washington. . . .But. . .he must sink the McClellan of Washington, and re-assume the McClellan of the Western Virginia campaign.[48]

Williamsburg: May 4, 1862

In the early morning of May 4 McClellan was able to trumpet to Secretary of War Edwin Stanton "Yorktown is in our possession," and shortly thereafter he followed up by advising "I have thrown all my cavalry and horse artillery in pursuit, supported by infantry." Brig. Gen.

George Stoneman, commanding a small division, was charged with the pursuit. Brig. Gen. Philip St. George Cooke led the 1st and 6th United States Cavalry along with Capt. Horatio Gibson's Company C, Third United States Artillery. Brig. Gen. William H. Emory led the 3rd Pennsylvania, Major Barker's McClellan Dragoons and Capt. Henry Benson's Battery, 2nd United States Artillery. Capt. James M. Robertson's Batteries B and L, Second United States and Capt. John C. Tidball's Light Battery A, 2nd United States Artillery accompanied the column. In addition, Stoneman was promised the support of General Hooker's infantry.[49]

Just beyond the works at Yorktown the column was held up when a torpedo, buried in the road by retreating Confederates, went off mortally wounding one of the Dragoons. A number of these land mines had been placed in fields, houses and along the main roads toward Williamsburg with deadly results for the infantry and signal corps as well as the cavalry.[50]

Covering the Confederate withdrawal was the cavalry brigade commanded by Brig. Gen. James Ewell Brown "Jeb" Stuart. He had deployed his four regiments in a line along Skiff's Creek in such a way as to allow the Southern infantry to easily pass through them. From east to west he placed the 4th Virginia near the Yorktown and Williamsburg Road along with the 3rd Virginia and a section of guns. Near Blow's Mill, in the center of the line, Stuart held the Wise and Hampton Legions and to the west he posted the Jeff Davis Legion at Lee's Bridge over Skiff's Creek. The 1st Virginia was above Stuart's line near the York River.[51] Stoneman moved out between 11 o'clock and noon along the Yorktown Road and expected his infantry support to follow by a forced march. Stoneman was to cooperate with Brig. Gen. William French Smith's division, moving from the lines at Lee's Mill, in an attempt to cut off the troops retiring along the Lee's Mill Road. When Smith's soldier's found the works at Yorktown abandoned that morning, he pushed one squadron of the 5th United States Cavalry, led by Capt. William P. Chambliss, across the Warwick River at Garrow's Ford to scout the line of advance. Once across the river Chambliss turned to the west scouting the rear of the abandoned works until he struck the road to Williamsburg.[52]

Moving into an open field Chambliss spotted an enemy cavalry picket with what appeared to be a column of infantry in support. He also received information from a citizen that a strong force of infantry and artillery was posted to block the road a few miles ahead. Expecting to be attacked Chambliss fell back to a strong position across the road and refused his line to the right. When no attack was forthcoming he continued his advance until he reached Brig. Gen. John Magruder's former headquarters at Lee's Hall. Here he again found a strong delaying force in works crowning the hill. At a disadvantage because his men were armed only with pistol and saber the captain ordered detachments to flank the position from both sides, forcing the enemy to retire.[53] Shortly thereafter he met the advance of Brig. Gen. Winfield Hancock's brigade. At Hancock's direction Chambliss sent a detachment to Skiff's Creek to protect the bridge but found it in flames. The troopers exchanged some shots with the men of the Jeff Davis Legion who had just fired the bridge. One of the men involved in this affair was Lt. George A. Custer who was instrumental in putting out the flames before the structure was destroyed. Chambliss pressed ahead until he received orders from Smith to halt. By not pressing the pursuit it was hoped that Stoneman would be able to cut off the Southern rearguard and defeat it with the aid of Smith's infantry.[54]

Passing the obstructions at Yorktown that morning Stoneman sent out Capt. William T. Magruder's squadron of the 1st United States Cavalry as an advance guard. Some seven or eight miles out they were fired on by enemy pickets. The men of the 1st Cavalry were quickly supported by Capt. John Savage's squadron of the 6th United States Cavalry and a section of Gibson's Battery, ordered up by General Cooke. A few shells reopened the road and the advance continued for another two miles.[55] After this initial skirmish Stoneman directed General Emory to move across to the Lee's Mill Road, taking with him the McClellan Dragoons, the 3rd Pennsy lvania and Benson's Battery. As this column, led by the squadron of dragoons, moved down a narrow path through dense woods it was struck by Col. Thomas F. Goode at the head of 100 men of the 3rd Virginia Cavalry. The dragoons were thrown into confusion and fell back rapidly, losing two killed and four wounded. As they cleared the road Benson's guns fired a couple of rounds of canister into the Southern column bringing it to a halt. The skirmish moved off the road into the trees as the 3rd Pennsylvania took up the challenge from the Virginians. Colonel Averell dismounted a squadron on either side of the road and forced Goode's men to retire but not before the Southerners had taken a standard. The Virginians, accompanied by Stuart, retired toward the James River and fell back to the Williamsburg line by way of Allen's Wharf. Emory pushed on to the Lee's Mill Road where he bivouacked for the night.[56]

After ordering Emory to the left Stoneman pressed ahead. Moving out of the woods into an open field his troopers were again brought to a halt by a mixed force of artillery, cavalry and infantry behind a fortified line 800 to 900 yards to their front. The enemy works were a series of 11 small redoubts and the much larger Fort Magruder in the center of the position. The line ran from College Creek across the face of the Federal advance to Cub Dam Creek and Queen's Creek. The strongest work by far was Fort Magruder which commanded the junction of the Lee's Mill and Yorktown Roads. The parapet was six feet high and nine feet thick. It was surrounded by a water filled ditch nine feet deep and nine feet wide. The ground in front of these works was cut by numerous smaller creeks and tributaries and also held a couple larger ponds, which made difficult going for the troopers. Fort Magruder was occupied by Brig. Gen. Paul Semmes' brigade, of Brig. Gen. Lafayette McLaws' Division and supported by Capt. B.C. Manly's North Carolina Battery. They would later be supported by Brig. Gen. Joseph Kershaw's Brigade.[57]

When Manly's guns opened the Regulars were again aided by Lieut. William Fuller's section of Gibson's battery. Fuller moved off the road to the right while a second section went into line on the left. As the Southern resistance intensified, Cooke ordered Gibson to move forward, about 400 yards, to a more open position from where both the guns and his cavalry could effectively meet an attack from the enemy. To support

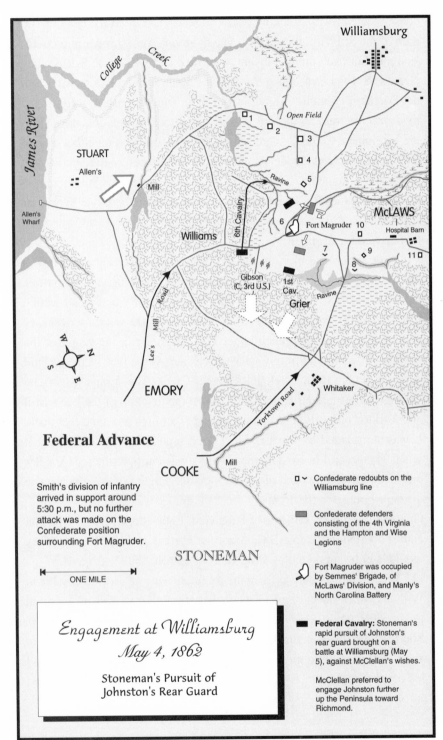

Williamsburg

College Creek

James River

STUART

Allen's

Open Field

1

2

3

4

5

Mill

Allen's
Wharf

6th Cavalry

6

Ravine

Fort Magruder 10

McLAWS

Hospital Barn

Williams

Gibson
(C, 3rd U.S.)

1st
Cav.

7

8

9

11

Grier

Ravine

Lee's Mill Road

N
W   E
S

EMORY

Yorktown Road

Whitaker

Federal Advance

COOKE

Mill

Smith's division of infantry
arrived in support around
5:30 p.m., but no further
attack was made on the
Confederate position
surrounding Fort Magruder.

STONEMAN

◄————►
ONE MILE

□ ↘ Confederate redoubts on the
       Williamsburg line

      Confederate defenders
      consisting of the 4th Virginia
      and the Hampton and Wise
      Legions

ᗡ Fort Magruder was occupied
    by Semmes' Brigade, of
    McLaws' Division, and Manly's
    North Carolina Battery

*Engagement at Williamsburg
May 4, 1862*

Stoneman's Pursuit of
Johnston's Rear Guard

Federal Cavalry: Stoneman's
rapid pursuit of Johnston's
rear guard brought on a
battle at Williamsburg (May
5), against McClellan's wishes.

McClellan preferred to
engage Johnston further
up the Peninsula toward
Richmond.

Mark A. Moore

the guns Cooke ordered Lt. Col. William Grier, commanding three squadrons of the 1st Cavalry to form in column along a ravine on Gibson's right. Grier was well liked by his men who referred to him as "Old Billy Grier, the bueno commandante." Cooke also sent Maj. Lawrence Williams with four squadrons of the 6th Cavalry to move around the left of the line by a sheltered road through the woods.[58] Major Williams believed that he had been ordered to attack the enemy's left flank or a battery on the extreme left of the enemy line. As his column exited the thick woods they saw Fort Magruder off to their right front, and a line of abandoned redoubts to their left. The open field was cut by a narrow ravine that slowed the troopers approach, as they could pass no more than two abreast, but which provided the only avenue across a marsh. Once through the ravine Williams reformed the men about 100 yards from the fort. To this point their approach had gone undetected as the gunners within the fort were occupied with Gibson's Battery and the 1st Cavalry to their front.[59]

Williams stated that he sent a platoon to scout the moat around the fort but a trooper in the ranks stated that the entire regiment moved in column to the ditch and moved along it to the rear of the fort where they were brought to a halt by a fence. Sidney Davis was so baffled by their casual approach that he thought the post must have been manned by Union soldiers. It was not until some of the men began tearing down the fence and one of the officers gave orders on what they should do once in the fort that Davis realized the true nature of his predicament.[60]

At the point the men were about to charge into the fort General McLaws ordered the 4th Virginia Cavalry along with the Wise and Hampton Legions out to challenge them, convincing Major Williams to fall back to the wood line. By now Manly's gunners had also turned their attention to the column of troopers making for the tree line. As the retiring Federals reached the deep ravine they were forced to slow, allowing the enemy cavalry to close on the rear squadron led by Capt. William Sanders.[61]

The cry of "Cavalry coming!" was sounded up the line but the lead companies had apparently moved into the woods and did not participate

in the battle developing at the marsh. Those men near the head of the
ravine plunged through the swamp in an effort to reach the high ground
on the far side, while those at the rear of the column began taking
artillery fire from the fort as well as pistol and carbine fire from the
enemy troopers. Once Sanders got his men across the marsh he ordered
"Sixth Cavalry—right about wheel!" and led them, at a charge, into the
ranks of the Wise Legion led by Lt. Col. James L. Davis. Sanders was
aided by a portion of Capt. J. Irvin Gregg's squadron which had already
cleared the marsh but returned to aid their comrades. This charge drove
the Confederates back and to their left toward Gibson's guns. The Confederate attack convinced Stoneman, who now realized that the promised infantry support would not be forthcoming, to order Gibson to
withdraw his guns. His teams, badly depleted by losses during the battle,
were unable to pull one of the guns and three caissons out of the rain-
soaked roads before the advancing enemy forced him to abandon
them.[62]

Grier and his Regulars covered Gibson's withdrawal. Suddenly Grier's last squadron, Companies I and K, was charged by the same troops
who had attacked the 6th Cavalry moments before. The 4th Virginia may
have been at the front of the gray column as their regimental standard
was captured in this melee and Col. Wickham seriously wounded by a
saber thrust in the side. The standard was officially listed as captured by
Pvt. Samuel Caskey, Co. I, 1st Cavalry. However, Gibson claimed that
the flag was seized by Pvt. John Thompson of his battery, but lost when
Thompson was sabered by a trooper in the 1st Cavalry (hopefully by
mistake in the confusion). During the combat Col. Grier was wounded
and his horse killed. Federal losses were listed as 35 killed, wounded
and missing in addition to the cannon and caissons. Southern losses were
not tabulated but Capt. William Newton of the 4th Virginia was captured
and 15 dead or wounded were noticed around the ravine after the fight
with the 6th Cavalry.[63]

Once he pulled back, Stoneman determined that there was nothing
further that he could accomplish as his infantry support was not forthcoming. About 5:30 p.m., Smith finally arrived and was ordered by

Sumner to attack as soon as his division was formed. After scouting the difficult ground over which the attack was to be made Smith, along with Hancock, decided to call off the attack.[64] In the much larger battle of May 5 the cavalry would contribute little. Stoneman's command was broken up into small detachments, as it would be for much of the coming campaign. No modern history has given credit to the cavalry for what they accomplished on the 4th. Many are critical of Stoneman for being too slow, yet McClellan felt that there never would have been a fight at Williamsburg if not for the aggressive pursuit of his cavalry—an intriguing comment since he meant it as a criticism of his cavalry and their pursuit. What Stoneman knew of the defenses fronting Williamsburg, the vigor with which he pushed his command and his objective was much debated by both sides during and after the war. The last Southern troops left the Warwick line in the early morning and the Federals were aware of the evacuation by daylight. Yet according to Governor William Sprague, who advanced with Stoneman, nothing was done until 10 a.m. and then only after a number of generals went to McClellan and urged action. According to Sprague, the cavalry started by 11 a.m. Furthermore Stoneman, according to Alexander Webb had only "vague, if any knowledge" of the Williamsburg defenses when he set out yet he pushed his column until he struck the line anchored by Fort Magruder. The speed of the pursuit was affected by McClellan's inaction, Southern obstructions and Stuart's delaying actions none of which Stoneman could control.[65]

McClellan's comment that the May 5 battle was "an accident brought about by the rapid pursuit of our troops" was clearly meant as a criticism of his cavalry, a duplicitous statement that he maintained for life. It was clear that he did not wish to confront Johnston's army again on the lower Peninsula, and he was late arriving in front of Williamsburg on the 5th because he preferred to make his next move by water and was working to get it underway from Yorktown. This alone was the reason that Stoneman was not ordered to pursue until late morning.[66]

Once McClellan ordered his cavalry to pursue Johnston's army he was forced to maintain that it was a vigorous pursuit meant to overtake the fleeing army. Governor Sprague claimed that Stoneman received a dispatch from McClellan at about 1 o'clock urging him to "push on with all speed." McClellan himself later stated that the "general instructions given to the troops. . .were to overtake the enemy and inflict as much damage as possible," but then explained:

> I think if our cavalry had been a few hours *later*, (author's emphasis) probably no fight would have occurred there. That action was brought on, I think, by that fact that our cavalry caught their rear-guard, and forced them to bring back their troops.[67]

Skirmishing toward Richmond

Immediately following the Confederate evacuation of the Williamsburg line several Federal cavalry units were again sent in pursuit while others were sent to a multitude of points along the York and James Rivers. At first glance some of these moves appear random, but in reality McClellan was moving small detachments up the Peninsula along the rivers while Stoneman's column moved up the center. The most dramatic infantry move was the advance of Franklin's division by boat up the York River to West Point. One cavalry unit, the 1st New York, accompanied the expedition. The men were ordered to have their horses saddled prior to embarking the night of May 5 and "were at it all night, and many a curse was pronounced upon the enemy for getting us into such trouble." They left Yorktown early the next morning arriving off West Point at 4:00 p.m. but did not debark until the following day. They did not participate in the fighting at Eltham's Landing on the 7th, but began advancing along the Pamunkey River on the 9th reaching Cumberland on the 13th and White House on the 15th.[68]

Other units were sent to scout Jamestown Island and Mulberry Island along the James River and Barrett's Ferry at the mouth of the Chickahominy River. Their mission was to reconnoiter former Southern strong points, and open communications with the navy. In an attempt to cover as much ground as possible some regiments were broken up by

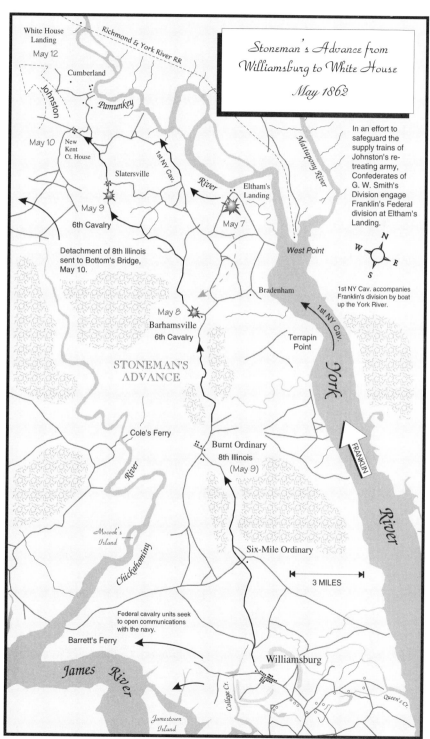

Stoneman's Advance from Williamsburg to White House

May 1862

In an effort to safeguard the supply trains of Johnston's re-treating army, Confederates of G. W. Smith's Division engage Franklin's Federal division at Eltham's Landing.

1st NY Cav. accompanies Franklin's division by boat up the York River.

White House Landing
May 12

Richmond & York River RR

Cumberland

Johnston

Pamunkey

May 10

New Kent Ct. House

Slatersville

1st NY Cav.

River

Eltham's Landing

May 7

Mattapony River

West Point

May 9

6th Cavalry

Detachment of 8th Illinois sent to Bottom's Bridge, May 10.

Bradenham

1st NY Cav.

May 8

Barhamsville

6th Cavalry

STONEMAN'S ADVANCE

Terrapin Point

York

Cole's Ferry

Burnt Ordinary

8th Illinois

(May 9)

FRANKLIN

River

Mocock's Island

Chickahominy

Six-Mile Ordinary

3 MILES

Federal cavalry units seek to open communications with the navy.

Barrett's Ferry

Williamsburg

James River

College Cr.

Queen's Cr.

Jamestown Island

Mark A. Moore

battalion, squadron or company and dispatched to widely scattered points.[69]

On the night of May 5, while the army was delayed by rain-soaked roads, Stoneman set out at the head of a mixed brigade of infantry, cavalry and artillery. His command included the 6th Cavalry and 8th Illinois as well as Robertson's and Tidball's Batteries. The 2nd Rhode Island Infantry and 98th Pennsylvania Infantry rounded out his brigade. Gov. Sprague later testified that Stoneman's advance made 15 to 20 miles the first day out although still much hampered by a lack of accurate maps. In speaking of their advanced position Sprague voiced frustration with the overall situation. Being 15 to 20 miles from the army "would seem to exhibit either too much risk on the part of the advance, or too much delay on the part of the army to come up to its support." The troopers skirmished at Barhamsville on the 8th and at the small crossroads hamlet of Slatersville on the 9th where the 6th Cavalry lost 20 men killed or wounded, in "two very handsome charges."[70]

About 80 men of the 6th Cavalry led Stoneman's advance on the 9th, with the infantry in supporting distance. Stoneman's other mounted unit, the 8th Illinois was 10 miles behind near Burnt Ordinary. About 3 o'clock in the afternoon the men of the 6th charged an enemy force, near Slatersville, and drove it from high ground into some woods off the road. The infantry and Robertson's Battery had just occupied the hill when three squadrons of the 1st Virginia Cavalry supported by artillery and infantry advanced from the woods. The 2nd Rhode Island, as well as the carbineers of the 6th Cavalry, deployed as skirmishers while the 98th Pennsylvania went into line of battle behind their artillery and the cavalry. The Southern force seemed bent only on delaying the Federals and allowed themselves to be distracted by the activity of the Union skirmishers to their front while four companies of the 6th Cavalry moved, unnoticed, around to their rear. Once in position the Regulars charged "cheering vociferously", and drove the Virginians from the field.[71] Stoneman continued his advance on the 10th reaching New Kent Court House at noon and pushed on to the Pamunkey where he bivouacked that night. At the same time a detachment of the 8th Illinois was sent

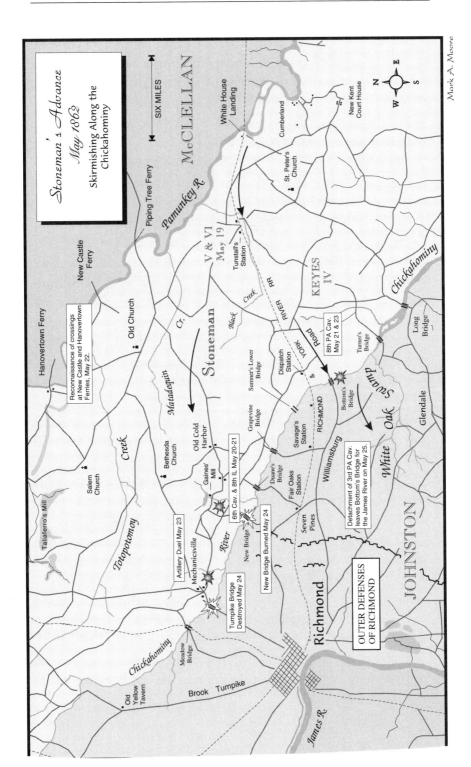

Stoneman's Advance
May 1862
Skirmishing Along the
Chickahominy

Mark A. Moore

toward Bottom's Bridge on the Chickahominy. On the 11th the command rested as much as possible during the day and made a night march to White House arriving on the morning of the 12th. When questioned about the resistance encountered by the army during the advance from Williamsburg McClellan replied that it was "Merely cavalry affairs. There were some sharp cavalry affairs. . . ."[72]

Once the army resumed the advance, hampered by their lack of maps, the army and corps commanders began to realize the need for and value of the mounted arm. The lack of a strong force was beginning to be felt and McClellan and others began their call for more horsemen. Unfortunately their reasons for requesting these men often had little to do with aiding the advance toward Richmond. On the 8th Brig. Gen. Samuel Heintzelman requested and received a company of the 5th Cavalry for headquarters escort duty. Within an hour of their arrival he was informed that they could not be spared and the troopers were sent back. On the 9th, while Stoneman was engaged at Slatersville and with the mass of the army still lingering around Williamsburg, Brig. Gen. Erasmus Keyes was whining about whose command the 8th Illinois belonged to, his or Stoneman's. On the 10th McClellan started his call for "two or three more" regiments as he was "overworking" those with the army. Silas Wesson spoke for the men in the saddle when he noted in his diary "Skirmishing every day is our work now. It keeps us busy."[73]

The 5th Pennsylvania Cavalry was one of the few regiments to arrive after the start of the campaign, not sailing for the Peninsula until May 8, but once it arrived the majority of the regiment would be assigned to duties that kept it away from the army. Immediately four companies were detached and held at Yorktown for scouting duty north of the York River. Six companies would make their headquarters at Williamsburg, for the remainder of the summer, where their colonel David Campbell was appointed military governor. The last two companies, I and K were started toward West Point and the army on May 15.[74]

Garrison and constant scouting duty could be both dangerous and comfortable as explained by a corporal, from the 5th Pennsylvania, to his hometown newspaper:

We have a great deal of picket duty to do. The Guerrillas are thick about here. . .I would rather go into a battlefield than go to Yorktown alone; when a party of one or two men go they are killed.

The trooper then explained the more comfortable aspects of garrison duty. "We have secesh tents, and good secesh furniture in them. . . .Most of us here have hair [mattresses] and feather pillows to sleep on, so I guess we can get along this summer." A month later, as the army moved closer to the bloodletting of the Seven Days, another soldier in the regiment expounded on the regiment's comfort. "We have but little sickness, and our horses are in good condition. . . .We have a Printing press in town. . .and will shortly have a paper of our own."[75]

On May 16, four days after his cavalry secured the railroad crossing at White House, McClellan arrived and established his headquarters there. At the same time General Joseph Johnston withdrew his army to the south side of the Chickahominy River. McClellan now had a decision to make concerning his route of advance and his line of communications and supply. He could advance along the Pamunkey to the north or follow the James River to the south. The issue was settled, unsatisfactorily by the general's view, when Stanton sent reinforcements via a land route from Fredericksburg, thus tying McClellan to the Pamunkey.[76]

Moving behind a cavalry screen that stretched from New Kent Court House north to Cold Harbor McClellan pushed the V and the VI Corps to Tunstall's Station, six miles northwest of White House on the 19th. The next natural obstacle facing McClellan was the Chickahominy River and therefore much of his attention was directed to the bridges over that stream and others that lay across his path. Names such as New Bridge, Bottom's Bridge, Long Bridge and Meadow Bridge now figured prominently in many dispatches as well as the day to day activity of the cavalry. At times the Confederates were assisted by a Union bureaucracy that slowed and frustrated the Federal advance. The historian of the 8th Illinois Cavalry reported that Stoneman's advance was held up for three days when the bridge over Black Creek was burned by retreating troops. "Red tape" forced the cavalry to wait while engineers surveyed the site and then sent their estimates back to White House. Frustrated with the delay Colonel Farnsworth asked for and received Stoneman's permission to rebuild it without the engineers. After only two and a half hours a bridge was fashioned that allowed the advance to continue.[77] On the 20th, a scout by the 6th Cavalry and the 8th Illinois to New Bridge resulted in a skirmish near Gaines' Mill. One press account claimed, rather boldly:

> Stoneman stirred [the enemy] up with a long pole several times, harassed their rear all day, and kept them constantly in line of battle. This work was mainly done by the Sixth Regular Cavalry, whose appetite for active life and adventure is now daily fed by the service which they perform so admirably.

The historian of the 8th Illinois was not as impressed with the ability of the Regulars, referring to them as a "new regiment" whose mistakes were the cause of their losses in the skirmish on the 20th. Another of Farnsworth's men claimed "all the prisoners we have taken say they fear us worse than the regulars."[78]

By the 21st Stoneman's cavalry was within sight of the spires of Richmond. That morning the cavalry commander, accompanied by McClellan's aeronaut Professor Thaddeus Lowe, ascended in a balloon to observe the city and the Southern lines. Launching from near Gaines' Mill and rising to a height of 400 feet they were able to observe, not only the buildings of Richmond but enemy camps as well as the arrival and departure of trains from the Southern capital. That morning another brief skirmish at New Bridge cost the 6th Cavalry one killed, one wounded and two horses killed.[79]

To the south elements of General Keyes IV Corps, accompanied by the 8th Pennsylvania Cavalry scouted toward Bottom's Bridge, resulting in skirmishes on the 21st and 23rd. Ever mindful of the Pamunkey on his right McClellan ordered a reconnaissance of the crossings at New Castle and Hanovertown Ferries on the 22nd. Colonel Richard Rush led his Lancers on an uneventful circuit of those crossings that afternoon.[80]

General Stoneman pushed his advance toward Mechanicsville on the 23rd and engaged the enemy in an artillery duel there before being relieved by supporting infantry units. Darkness brought an end to the fighting which resumed in the morning when Brig. Gen. John Davidson's brigade drove the Confederates across the Chickahominy. To prevent a Southern excursion across the river, Company I, 8th Illinois Cavalry, was sent to destroy the turnpike bridge. Arriving at the river, four men volunteered to chop the supports from under the span which was done while under fire the entire time. At the same time other elements of the 8th moved three miles upstream where they destroyed a vital Virginia Central Railroad bridge and sections of track.[81]

Four miles south of Mechanicsville another dramatic skirmish flared up along the Chickahominy near New Bridge when a Federal infantry force, supported by a squadron of the 2nd United States Cavalry, approached the river crossing to cover a party of engineers surveying the bridge site. The cavalry made one charge in an attempt to cut off an enemy force from the river. This was unsuccessful and the bridge was burned preventing the troopers from continuing the fight once the foot soldiers waded the stream. First across the river however was a young cavalry lieutenant named George Custer. His actions drew the attention of all who observed him and prompted McClellan to personally thank him. The general recalled the young officer as "slim, long-haired and carelessly dressed" but was so impressed that he offered Custer a position on his staff that he accepted and retained until McClellan was relieved.[82]

On the 25th a detachment of 12 men of the 3rd Pennsylvania Cavalry, under the command of Second Lt. Frank Davis, left the regiment near Bottom's Bridge and moved toward the James River in an attempt to communicate the location of the army to the gunboat fleet. Following a circuitous route of about 25 miles Davis led his command to a point on the river above City Point. Here he left his men, boarded a small boat and rowed out to the *U.S.S. Galena* where he delivered a brief message to the ship's captain. He then rejoined his men and rode back to Bottom's Bridge having successfully completed "his errand in a style so handsome, and surmounted such difficulties," that he earned the personal thanks of the commanding general.[83]

Hanover Court House: May 24-29

On the 17th McClellan was informed that reinforcements in the form of General McDowell's I Corps would move south from Fredericksburg in an effort to bolster the attack on Richmond. Until those troops arrived McClellan had to be mindful, as he moved to cross the Chickahominy, to protect their line of approach from the north. McDowell had advised McClellan on the 22nd that he hoped to be on the road in two days. Word of a heavy enemy force gathering near Hanover Court House, directly astride McDowell's route, mandated yet another cavalry reconnaissance on the 24th.[84]

A scouting force spearheaded by the 6th Pennsylvania Cavalry left Hanovertown that morning moving toward Hanover Court House. As these troopers pushed northward, they destroyed several ferry crossings along the Pamunkey. Increasingly strong enemy pickets along the route convinced Colonel Rush that the rumors were true however, and he returned to Old Church reporting that 3,000 to 5,000 troops were in the area. The following day fresh rumors of 17,000 troops at Hanover prompted McClellan to order General Cooke to send out another scouting force from Cold Harbor. The orders were typical McClellan, urging the old trooper to travel light, take plenty of cartridges, and make a thorough sweep of the area but at the same time stressing extreme caution.[85] The 1st Cavalry along with the McClellan Dragoons left Walnut Grove Church early on the 26th, aided by the 5th New York Infantry and Rush's Lancers moving from Old Church. These troops marched to within three miles of Hanover Court House before returning with reports that 5,000 to 6,000 troops were believed to be in the area. On the right the infantry led by Col. Gouverneur Warren engaged some enemy pickets along the Pamunkey and one company of the lancers, led by Lt. Charles Leiper, made what may be one of the few charges with the lance during the war, driving a cavalry picket back on their infantry supports. A bridge over the Pamunkey was torn down before the troops returned to Old Church.[86]

That same day McClellan ordered Fitz-John Porter to advance in the morning with 12,000 men including a large force of cavalry on Hanover Court House, clear out the enemy force believed to be in the area and to do as much damage as possible to the railroad and river crossings. As Porter moved north from New Bridge Warren's mixed brigade would again advance along the line of the Pamunkey from his camp at Old Church. Before the expedition was over the infantry would bear the brunt of the fighting but the lasting benefit to the army was achieved by the cavalry. Porter marched at an early hour behind a cavalry screen provided by Brig. Gen. William Emory's 5th and 6th Cavalry and a battery of horse artillery. At every crossroads enemy pickets were run off and scouts sent out to develop the enemy position. Near the junction of the Ashcake Road and the road to Taliaferro's Mill the cavalry began skirmishing with the lead elements of the 28th North Carolina. They continued to challenge the Southerners until relieved by the 25th New York Infantry. While directing the battle that quickly developed around Slash Church Porter ordered his cavalry west toward the rail lines. The battle turned quickly, if briefly, in Porter's favor at which time he immediately ordered Emory's cavalry in pursuit of the fleeing enemy. The troopers pushed their pursuit five miles from the battlefield, gobbling up many prisoners, when a fresh Southern force was detected coming in on Porter's rear, necessitating the recall of the cavalry, which was by now well scattered.[87]

A squadron of the 5th Cavalry, commanded by Lt. Abraham Arnold, was dispatched toward Ashland and soon ran into elements of the 4th Virginia Cavalry screening a larger infantry force moving in on Porter's left flank. The warning allowed Brig. Gen. John H. Martindale to deploy his brigade in time to meet the attack. The fact that Porter ignored the reports of a flanking force until it was almost too late left his command, for a time, in a very precarious situation. A poorly coordinated attack by the Southern flanking force allowed the Federal troops time to recover and again turn the battle in their favor.[88]

To the north Col. Warren's force was delayed by swampy roads and the necessity of having to rebuild a couple of bridges before they reached the field. He arrived just as the enemy gave way and ordered the 6th Pennsylvania Cavalry in pursuit. Moving three miles beyond the battlefield they scooped up a large body of prisoners and attempted to destroy a bridge over the Pamunkey but were recalled before the task was completed. As the Regulars arrived back on the field one noted the "inspiriting" sight presented by the Lancers, who had returned moments before. "On the left stood, formed in a long line across the field, the Sixth Pennsylvania cavalry, then armed with lances. . .and making a fine display, reminding me of the engravings I had seen once of the Mexican cavalry at the war of 1848."[89]

Stoneman's command did not participate in the fighting at Slash Church but was active along the railroad. They captured and burned a southbound train of the Virginia Central and tore up some track. Moving 10 miles to the west, near Ashland they destroyed a bridge on the Richmond and Fredericksburg line. About 4:00 p.m., Lt. Col. William Gamble led 300 men "duly provided with crowbars, sledges, axes, etc." to within a mile of the bridge when they ran into a mixed force of cavalry and infantry supported by artillery deployed to cover the span. Gamble dismounted two companies as skirmishers who opened a brisk fire at long range while he moved the other troopers so as to make a show of great force. The Southern force was convinced to retire at which time the troopers turned to the task at hand with "vim and readiness." An officer of the regiment recalled that "the rails were flung into the mud-bottomed creek, the bridge we burnt to ashes, several culverts were destroyed, and then we leisurely returned to camp."[90]

The infantry spent the 28th gathering in their wounded and burying the dead while the cavalry deployed to complete their mission of destruction. Emory, supported by the 17th New York Infantry, set out to burn the bridges over the Pamunkey and South Anna Rivers. He ordered the 6th Cavalry and five companies of infantry toward the bridges with the 5th Cavalry detailed to protect them. Capt. Charles Whiting led three squadrons of the 5th Cavalry toward Ashland Station to occupy the enemy troops there, while Capt. James Harrison chased a retreating infantry force toward the Pamunkey, eventually capturing 96 of them.

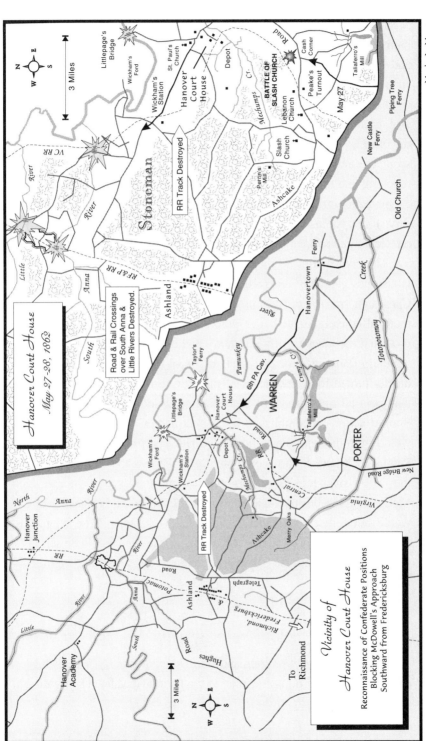

Mark A. Moore

Hanover Court House
May 27-28, 1862

Road & Rail Crossings over South Anna & Little Rivers Destroyed.

RR Track Destroyed

BATTLE OF SLASH CHURCH

May 27

Stoneman

Vicinity of Hanover Court House

Reconnaissance of Confederate Positions Blocking McDowell's Approach Southward from Fredericksburg

RR Track Destroyed

WARREN

PORTER

6th PA Cav.

Meanwhile the 6th Cavalry, under the command of Maj. Lawrence Williams, burned four bridges including a 500-foot span of the Richmond and Fredericksburg Railroad over the South Anna River. A 200-foot span on the same line was burned the next morning.[91]

On the 29th, Capt. Chambliss, with two squadrons of the 5th Cavalry, was ordered back to Ashland Station to again insure the safety of the 6th Cavalry. As he approached the station he deployed his men to scout the area, determined that the enemy force was not as strong as reported, and ordered a charge that easily carried the town. He reported capturing ten prisoners, a field hospital and a large quantity of commissary stores. He also determined that an enemy force of 6,000 had retired on Richmond an hour previous.[92]

The contribution of the cavalry in the expedition to Hanover Court House has generally received little notice in accounts of the Peninsula Campaign, yet at no other time in the campaign was the cavalry used more effectively or to better purpose. Deployed on both flanks they protected the advance of the infantry and developed the presence of the Southern flanking force on the afternoon of the 27th. They were immediately turned loose in pursuit of the retiring infantry and most importantly cut all lines of supply and communication north from Richmond. Similar actions accomplished by a much larger, veteran, cavalry force would grab dramatic headlines in the latter part of the war, but on the Peninsula, where Stuart would shortly embarrass the Federal troopers, they were over-looked or forgotten by most everyone. Indeed even McClellan placed little value on the destruction of the bridges. One who would not forget was General "Stonewall" Jackson whose attempt to unite with the Army of Northern Virginia in late June would be seriously delayed, in part, because of the destruction wrought by the Federal cavalry.[93]

The Seven Days

After the constant probing and skirmishing of the last weeks of May early June would bring some relief to the Federal cavalry. The fighting at

Seven Pines did not involve any notable cavalry action, other than for the men serving as couriers and escorts. Three companies of the 8th Illinois were in the thick of the fighting as escorts to General Keyes. Two of the companies lost all their belongings when their camps were overrun on the 31st.[94] A trooper in the 2nd United States Cavalry had earlier remarked that "escort duty may sound very pretty, [but] as applied to us it signifies perpetual motion." The perpetual activity of the last few weeks took a steady, debilitating toll on the animals. Not only were they often moving through the thick mire of rain-soaked roads but they often went for days without unsaddling or proper forage. Capt. August Kautz noted "our horses are falling away very fast. They will not last long, with the treatment they have had for some days."[95] On June 3 General Keyes was again complaining about the lack of cavalry afforded his command, and the reader of his dispatch might question his priorities. "Sumner has ordered all my cavalry to his headquarters. . .leaving me only a few [three companies] of the Eighth Illinois for orderlies and messengers. My corps now has an extensive front to guard, and cavalry is absolutely necessary." The high command, taking their example from McClellan, was enamored with the showy troopers around their headquarters instead of around their army. On June 8, an entire company of the 3rd Pennsylvania escorted a Mexican general while he observed the army.[96]

Further evidence of McClellan's appreciation for the ostentatious is offered by a member of his headquarters escort in the 2nd Cavalry:

> I was detailed to take charge of an escort to a flag of truce sent by General McClellan. . . .Ten of the finest-looking troopers were selected and mounted on bay horses picked for the occasion, and attired in holiday garb, with a brand new white flag, carried by. . .a stalwart and handsome dragoon. . .[the Southern] riders' sombre-hued garb contrasted ill with our bright and "natty" clothing.[97]

The men who drew picket and scouting duty saw little relief. Thomas Kelley was frustrated with the constant duty but proud of his regiment. "[W]e are on Picket duty and scouting all the time and I tell you we are a pretty tired looking set of fellows and our Horses look [pretty] well jaded."[98] The consequences of McClellan's mismanagement and misplaced priorities struck home on the morning of June 13 when General Stuart led 1,200 troopers around the right of the Union army. The loss and embarrassment suffered at the hands of Stuart's men quickly led to speculation as to who was responsible. The men of the 8th Illinois, who manned the picket line north from the Chickahominy maintained that Colonel Farnsworth and Stoneman had repeatedly warned of a gap in the line on their right toward the Pamunkey, and that they had been reassured by Cooke that the gap would be filled.[99]

Cooke had been directed to send two squadrons to Old Church on May 31 but again the manner in which the order was written may have left the old general wondering as to his priorities. The better part of two paragraphs were used to explain that these troops were responsible for guarding Southern property in the area, including the home where Mrs. Robert E. Lee was staying. It was at the end of the message where he was advised "to watch well the movements of the enemy."[100]

The fact was that the area immediately south of the Pamunkey was not unguarded but was covered by pickets as well as daily patrols. Two of these patrols, one under Lt. Edward Leib of the 5th Cavalry as well as a patrol of the 6th Cavalry, first observed Stuart's command near Hanover Court House on the morning of the 13th. But neither was strong enough to have influenced Stuart. Direct, or tactical, responsibility rested on the shoulders of Philip St. George Cooke. Cooke was burdened by his pre-war experiences. His two largest campaigns on the frontier, the Sioux Expedition of 1855 and the Mormon War of 1857, had taken months and in the case of the former over a year to organize. In neither case was an immediate response necessary or possible and so the army methodically gathered together the far-flung dragoons as well as the provisions for a long march. This was not the case on the Peninsula yet Cooke reacted in the same methodical manner, even admitting that he retired to his tent for a cup of coffee during a critical period on the afternoon of the 13th. When told that his men needed food and forage he ordered them back to their camps until supply wagons came up. Emlen

N. Carpenter of the 6th Pennsylvania was understandably critical of Cooke just days after the raid. "Gen. [Cooke] did not attach much importance to the [first reports] thinking it was only a foraging party. . .never dreaming in his listlessness that [Stuart] would have the audacity to attack him. . . ." Carpenter, who felt deeply the sting and stigma attached to the Federal cavalry after the raid continued. "The whole affair was a. . . disgraceful failure on the part of Cooke to prevent it, Gen. Cooke is an old man & has not the vim necessary to manoever against [Stuart]. . . .I hope he will do better next time. . . ." As the record will show Cooke would be more aggressive the next time but with deadly results.[101]

Late on the 15th of June two battalions, one each from the 8th Illinois and the 6th Cavalry, were directed to move on the rail lines at Ashland again. Marching independently of each other the volunteers arrived well ahead of the Regulars. They took the town by surprise but reported that a "brisk skirmish ensued" when they entered. The troopers then proceeded to burn supplies, tear up track and cut telegraph lines, all before 6 a.m. They had covered two miles of the route back when they came upon the Regulars who "looked not a little chagrined when they found the object of the expedition was accomplished."[102]

On June 16, Colonel Averell took two battalions of his 3rd Pennsylvania across the Pamunkey River to investigate rumors that Jackson was moving to strike the right flank of the army. He was to attempt to make contact with General McDowell as well. Moving from Fair Oaks to White House they boarded transports to be ferried across the river, an operation that took the better part of the evening. Once across they were joined by three companies of the 17th United States Infantry. At dawn the troops marched toward King William Court House, a distance of 28 miles, arriving at 10 a.m. After a short rest the expedition continued north to Ayletts on the Mattapony River. Two squadrons of cavalry charged into the town capturing several prisoners, including 15 termed political prisoners. Once the town was secured the cavalry moved out to picket the roads while the infantry set about burning supplies and destroying bridges and ferries, a process that took less than an hour. Unsure if the telegraph operator had sounded the alarm prior to the town's capture Averell insisted on a rapid return march and had the foot soldiers ride with the cavalry. When this proved to severe they dismounted and continued on foot as quickly as possible, reaching the Pamunkey at 2 a.m. on the 18th. They bivouacked for the night under cover of several gunboats, having marched 78 miles. Averell later remarked that this was "the last extension of our hands toward McDowell, for Jackson came sooner. . . ."[103]

On June 25 McClellan issued another cry for fresh troops including "a couple new regiments of cavalry." Just the day before, the 4th Pennsylvania Cavalry had arrived at White House, but concerned with his line of retreat McClellan immediately ordered one battalion of the fresh regiment to strengthen the garrison at Yorktown. Here the troopers would remain until the end of the campaign.[104] On the same day that McClellan issued his latest call for more men, Sgt. Maj. David Ashley, 6th New York Cavalry, brought his parents up to date on the strenuous activities of his regiment over the last week. Rushed up to the area of Tunstall's Station in the wake of Stuart's raid, the New Yorkers arrived too late and soon settled down to foraging patrols.

> . . .have been much engaged, Foraging for my own benefit, and patroling [sic] for my own satisfaction. . .within 4 days I have picked upwards of 20 quarts of Beautiful Blackberries. . . .Yesterday one of my Roommates brought in 4 chickens 3 Geese & 1 Turkey — and as there is plenty of stray cattle about we have plenty of fresh meat making it much more pleasant than when we were to the front.[105]

Certain activities obviously came naturally to the young troopers.

As the campaign drew toward a climax the cavalry picket line generally followed the line of the Chickahominy River to the Virginia Central Railroad and then across to Hanover Court House. With rumors of Jackson's arrival escalating and with all of the army south of the Chickahominy, except Porter's V Corps, patrols were pushed out almost daily to check the upper crossings of the Pamunkey. Reacting to information supplied by a deserter McClellan ordered Cooke toward the Pamunkey on the 23rd and again on the 25th. In the second order he urged that all roads be obstructed, and all bridges, except those needed for retreat, be burned. Furthermore, he stressed that the road to Pole Green Church be closed.[106]

The Battle of Oak Grove, the first of the Seven Days, was initiated by General McClellan but he would not arrive on the field until afternoon, accompanied by his escort consisting of the entire 1st New York Cavalry, minus four companies serving as escorts elsewhere. With their duty completed the men stood in line of battle a short distance behind the battle line where they helped keep stragglers and shirkers from fleeing the ranks.[107]

The only cavalry skirmish of note occurred near Ashland where a patrol from the 8th Illinois ran into a screening force from the Jeff Davis Legion and the 4th Virginia Cavalry covering Jackson's advance from the valley. The Federals pushed through the pickets as far as Ashland Station where they reportedly observed the men of "Jackson's Grand Army" and claimed to have pushed the Southern pickets back a mile and a half, killing four or five in a "brisk" skirmish. The Federals cut the telegraph lines before retreating in the face of a charge by a company of the 4th Virginia. Lt. Col. Will Martin, of the Jeff Davis Legion but commanding both units that day, reported that the telegraph was immediately restored. Jackson had hoped to camp that night along the railroad at Ashland, but was slowed by "boggy roads, high, bridgeless streams, and reports of Union cavalry." With the exception of an advance guard his command camped west of Ashland.[108]

Lee and Jackson planned to launch a coordinated attack early on the morning of June 26, against the precarious right flank of the Federal army, near Mechanicsville. In a meeting with Lee on June 23 Jackson believed that he could be ready to attack on the morning of the 25th but attempts to move his army by rail had already proved difficult as a result of the Federal bridge burning expedition in late May. Lee allowed him an extra day to move into position, and set the hour of the offensive for early morning on the 26th. Hoping to be under way at 2:30 a.m. the men moved slowly and were soon six hours behind schedule. Jackson's orders were to move toward Pole Green Church from where he would communicate with his supporting units before launching his attack. Cooke's patrol of the previous day now paid its dividend to Porter and the men of his corps as the obstructed roads and burned bridges, as well as confusion over the location of the church itself, set the timetable back even further. When Jackson had not arrived by mid-afternoon an impatient General A.P. Hill launched the attack without him.[109]

The freshest mounted force in the Army of the Potomac was the 4th Pennsylvania, led by Col. James H. Childs. Companies E and F were picketing the line near Meadow Bridge in front of Maj. Roy Stone's 13th Pennsylvania Infantry, known as the Bucktails. Childs' troopers would claim the honor of firing the first shots of the battle when Hill launched his attack. As the attack developed Stone bolstered the cavalry line with three companies of his Bucktails before they were forced to withdraw. Once pulled off the line Childs' formed his regiment in line of battle behind the infantry awaiting further orders, which never arrived.[110]

On the right of Childs, the picket line was manned by the 8th Illinois, from Atlee's Station to Shady Grove Church. Undoubtedly the men from Illinois felt they had fired the first shots and may have suffered the first casualty as well. Maj. Daniel Dustin and Capt. Rufus Hooker had just completed a tour of their pickets when they rode out along the road to Hanover Court House. About a mile beyond the lines they were fired on and Capt. Hooker was struck in the pit of his stomach. He maintained his saddle until near their lines when Maj. Dustin helped him to the ground, tied his horse to a tree and rode for help. Before he could be recovered "the enemy came on in force and no one could get back [to] him."[111]

Farnsworth strengthened his pickets with an additional two companies of the 8th Illinois while detaching another company with orders to obstruct the roads in the face of the enemy. Company B was ordered to ride out the road to Pole Green Church and soon brought word of troops moving against Porter's line by that avenue. A soldier correspondent gave the following account of the regiment's resistance:

> We deployed in every field, and remained as long as possible. . . .On reaching Shady Grove Church we became more consolidated. . .we manoeuvered [sic] until three o'clock. . . .At every defile we felled trees across the [road to Meadow Bridge] so that they were impeded. . . .

The men continued skirmishing throughout the afternoon and bivouacked for the night at the intersection of the road to Old Church and the Pole Green Church Road.[112] General Emory's Regulars manned the picket line to the right of Farnsworth's regiment along the Totopotomoy Creek, east of Pole Green Church. The troopers kept active throughout the day, scouting as far as the South Anna River, destroying bridges and blocking roads before being ordered to Old Church where they spent the night in the saddle without food or forage.[113]

By late afternoon McClellan was already planning a retreat to the James River. Porter would pull back to cover the bridges over the Chickahominy while the supply base at White House was moved to the James. In addition to removing an immense quantity of food, forage and armament from White House Porter needed time to get his own supply wagons across the river. By dawn on the 27th his corps was arrayed behind Boatswain's Creek covering four key bridges across the Chickahominy. To his front was the home and mill owned by Dr. William Gaines.

Throughout the afternoon the Federals staunchly withstood several assaults, until dusk when Lee ordered a general attack along the entire line. Under the renewed pressure Porter's line began breaking on both flanks. Supporting the Federal line were a number of reserve artillery batteries that became a natural target for the Confederates as they pushed the Federals aside. In planning a large scale, fixed battle, such as Gaines' Mill the antiquated thinking of the senior officers in the Federal army usually relegated the cavalry to positions in the rear of the battle line. Here they were expected to stand, under fire, protect the artillery and prevent stragglers from fleeing the field. Porter would not break with tradition on June 27. The consequences would be dramatic, deadly and controversial.

Porter placed Cooke's command, consisting of 220 men in six companies of the 5th Cavalry, 125 men in four companies of the 1st Cavalry and 250 men in six companies of the 6th Pennsylvania, on the left of his line. An additional 39 men of the 6th Cavalry served as a Provost Guard. Just 634 men were all that remained of the Reserve Cavalry Division. To their right was the 4th Pennsylvania and to their right the 8th Illinois. The orders to Childs and Farnsworth were clear, support the artillery and drive any shirkers back to the battle line. The orders given to Cooke became a matter of controversy in light of the events at the end of the day. In 1864, General Wesley Merritt, who was at the time of Gaines' Mill a captain in the 5th Cavalry, wrote:

> There are a thousand and one misrepresentations in regard to the operations of the cavalry at Gaines' Mill, arising from statements of persons who were ignorant of the facts or circulated falsehood maliciously.[114]

Porter stated that Cooke was to "watch our left flank, and, should the opportunity occur, to strike the enemy on the plain. He was told that he should do nothing on the hill," behind which he was initially placed. The "plain", which is more accurately described as the bottom land of Boatswain's Creek, varies from 300 to 800 yards wide and deemed "suitable for cavalry. . . ." Cooke deployed his men, behind the hill, in squadron formation, double rank, in close column of regiments. From left to right were the 6th Pennsylvania, the 1st Cavalry and the 5th Cavalry on the right.[115]

When the left of the Federal line began to waver some of the reserve batteries limbered up and retired. Others opened fire on the brigade led by Brig. Gen. George Pickett, as it emerged from a wood line on the extreme left. When the battery officers again wavered Cooke rode up and told them he would support them with his troopers, who were then masked from the enemy by the brow of the plateau. Cooke immediately moved his troops to the left of the batteries, onto the plain, but after surveying this ground he ordered them back to their first position behind the hill. This was the decision that infuriated Porter and one that Cooke never seriously addressed in his later writings, saying only that the posi-

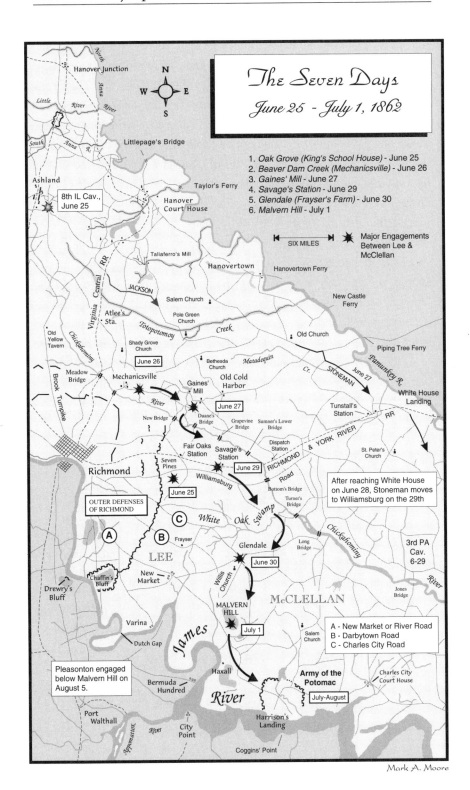

The Seven Days
June 25 - July 1, 1862

1. *Oak Grove (King's School House)* - June 25
2. *Beaver Dam Creek (Mechanicsville)* - June 26
3. *Gaines' Mill* - June 27
4. *Savage's Station* - June 29
5. *Glendale (Frayser's Farm)* - June 30
6. *Malvern Hill* - July 1

SIX MILES | Major Engagements Between Lee & McClellan

8th IL Cav., June 25

After reaching White House on June 28, Stoneman moves to Williamsburg on the 29th

3rd PA Cav. 6-29

A - New Market or River Road
B - Darbytown Road
C - Charles City Road

Pleasonton engaged below Malvern Hill on August 5.

Army of the Potomac
July-August

Mark A. Moore

tion on the plain did not allow him to "*face* the enemy" (Cooke's emphasis). Here they remained until Pickett's men were within 100 yards of the guns where canister fire began to slow their momentum. The cavalry's position was now vulnerable to enemy fire and casualties began to mount. The rate of fire from the batteries was also slowing due to rising losses and Cooke saw only one option. Believing that the enemy was on the verge of breaking under the rain of canister Cooke saw the classic opportunity to unleash his troopers. The shock of a massed cavalry charge would win or at least save the day. Cooke, however had misjudged the stamina of Pickett's Virginians. Strangely, Cooke ordered only Capt. Charles Whiting's 5th Cavalry to make the charge, to be supported if needed by the 1st Cavalry. The 6th Pennsylvania was to support the guns however some of the lancers would join in the attack. Drawing their sabers the regulars went to the gallop as quickly as possible, owing to the short distance they had to cover, but were still unable to reach the enemy in "full career." Their line was struck by heavy fire from their right front that immediately destroyed their cohesion. All but one of the officers went down in this first volley. A few of the men rode through the enemy ranks while others turned to the right and retreated as quickly as they came.[116]

Charles Fenton James, 8th Virginia Infantry, described the reaction of the infantry:

> We. . .were starting up the last hill in the face of the artillery fire, when the cry was heard, Cavalry! Cavalry! . . .There was no panic and no sign of wavering. The foremost boys simply stopped and waited for those behind to close up and fall into sort of a line. On came that splendid body of regular cavalry at breakneck speed, while our boys calmly waited until they were within about seventy five yards, and then there shot out from that ragged line a continuous sheet of flame, emptying many a saddle and hurling back the charging squadron in wildest confusion.[117]

The 5th Cavalry lost one officer killed and five officers wounded, including Capt. Chambliss, who had been at the forefront of the advance since Yorktown. In addition to the officers three troopers were dead, 25 wounded and 24 missing with 24 horses killed. Southern losses were negligible.

Opinions as to the value of the charge were generally divided along service lines. Those in the cavalry saw a gallant sacrificial charge, in the style of Napoleon, that was not appreciated by the army or the nation. Lt. Arnold believed that a follow-up charge by the remainder of the division would have wrecked the Confederate right. But the men of the 1st Cavalry saw nothing but futility and death in such an attempt and did not support the assault as ordered. Those in the infantry saw a blunder that resulted in the loss of numerous cannon and came near to wrecking the army.[118]

The charge and its effect on the battle, which in fairness was negligible, became a source of bitter acrimony between Cooke and Porter. Porter saw in Cooke a scapegoat for his own generalship and an easy target as Cooke had violated his orders by operating on the hill. An infantry officer wrote that Cooke was thought of as a "'back number'— a gallant old man, but too old to learn modern ways or cope with new conditions." Writing after the war Wesley Merritt confirmed this opinion even as he defended his former commander. "General Cooke was par excellence a cavalry officer, drawing his inspirations from the history. . .of the Great Frederick and the First Napoleon. He insisted on the mounted charge. . .[and] was opposed to fighting on foot. . . ." At his own request Cooke was relieved on July 5 and ordered to Washington.[119]

As Porter's entire line gave way Brig. Gen. George Morell suggested another cavalry charge to Col. Childs who had his men formed and ready before Cooke put an end to the idea. When night fall brought an end to the blood letting the cavalry served as policeman, directing the retreating troops over the bridges, rounding up stragglers and were generally credited with being the last off the field. As Porter fell back across the Chickahominy a squad of the 8th Illinois was sent north to warn Stoneman that he was in danger of being cut off. Farnsworth sent another squadron to Dispatch Station to guard the hospital and supplies until morning.[120]

Late the next morning this squadron was attacked by Southern cavalry. Thomas Kelley described the events of the day.

> . . .our boys. . .charged on them driving them back 3/4 of a mile we then left videttes to watch their movements & came & cleared 2 [hospitals] of 260 sick burying one man & taking & destroying by fire the [hospital] stores & [hospitals] then holding in check for 2 hours and 40 minutes. . .to enable our sick soldiers to walk 4 miles to Bottoms Bridge. . . .[121]

On Thursday morning, the 26th, General Stoneman moved toward Old Church at the head of another mixed force that included the 2nd and 6th Cavalry, the 17th New York and 18th Massachusetts Infantry and some artillery. His orders were to guard the line of the Richmond & York River Railroad until the supply depots along the line could be removed or destroyed. About 1 p.m. on the 27th, he received orders to fall back to White House. Arriving there on the 28th, he immediately ordered the destruction of the remaining supplies. When this was completed the infantry embarked on transports for Yorktown.[122] The 11th Pennsylvania Cavalry had been posted at the huge supply base since early June enjoying relatively easy duty. With the exception of a brief scare during Stuart's raid these troops had seen little campaigning. The Pennsylvanians paid the price for their easy duty when Stoneman ordered his command, now including the 11th, to make a night march toward Yorktown. The unseasoned troopers were a hindrance to the column. This was not only the first long march these men had made, but also the first night march and "it occasioned no little trouble to keep the men on the move and the column closed up." The troops halted at Slatersville for breakfast and reached Williamsburg that afternoon. After the difficult march and a couple days of bad weather these garrison troopers again settled down to duty that was "easy and free." Stoneman led the remainder of the column to Yorktown and then Fort Monroe.[123]

The cavalry would not participate in the fighting at Golding's Farm on the 28th or Savage's Station on the 29th. Picket duty along key roads or guarding vital bridges combined with the usual escort assignments was the extent of their involvement in these affairs. Silas Wesson spoke

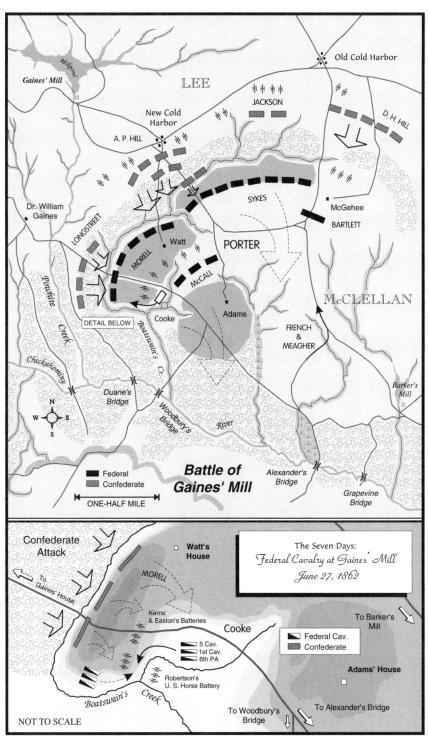

Battle of Gaines' Mill

The Seven Days:
Federal Cavalry at Gaines' Mill
June 27, 1862

Mark A. Moore

for men of both armies when he noted in his diary, "retreating all night
and fighting all day. I wonder when this thing will stop."[124]

On the 29th, a routine patrol flared into a deadly skirmish involving
the 3rd Pennsylvania and the 1st North Carolina Cavalry. Three companies of the 3rd Pennsylvania, along with a couple infantry companies
and two guns, were ordered to picket Jones Bridge on the Chickahominy. As they neared the junction of the Charles City and Quaker
Roads just north of the Willis Methodist Church, scouts detected a column of Southern cavalry. This was the 1st North Carolina Cavalry followed by the 3rd Virginia, on orders to develop the Federal picket line.
The Federals left a squad near the intersection as bait for an ambush they
established down the trail. The two guns were rolled into the road while
the cavalry deployed to charge the column. When the unsuspecting Tarheels moved within range the troopers left as bait fired a volley and fell
back drawing the Carolinians after them. "Yelling and screaming like
Indians" the Confederates pursued at a full gallop. Two hundred yards
from the guns the Federals quit the road and the guns belched fire into
the face of the tightly packed column. Staggered by the artillery the
Confederates were charged by the squadron of Pennsylvanians and
driven in disorder back whence they came, leaving over 60 casualties in
the road. The Federals lost one killed and five wounded. One of the
surviving Tarheels remarked that "we unfortunately Lost a [heap] of our
men," while an officer saw the disaster "as a wholesome lesson in making mounted charges."[125]

During the afternoon Maj. Alfred Pleasonton, commanding the 2nd
Cavalry and the McClellan Dragoons, was ordered to the James River to
open communications with the gunboat fleet and to scout a location to
establish the army. Reaching the river at 5:30 p.m. near Carter's Landing
the major and several other officers set out in small boats to locate the
navy. Soon ships arrived to cover the landing. Early the next morning
the sick and wounded began arriving and were placed aboard for transport to better facilities.[126] Throughout the day on the 30th, while the
armies battled near Glendale, the cavalry continued to cover the retreat
to the James. Guarding key bridges, protecting wagon trains of supplies

and wounded as well as facilitating the flow of traffic were the order of the day for the cavalry. With the exception of the 4th Pennsylvania, which was under fire most of the day, the cavalry did not directly participate in the battle of Glendale.

That evening, with most of the army near the James, it became necessary to send couriers to attempt to contact generals Heintzelman and Franklin who had not been heard from as they covered the retreat. Lts. Walter Newhall and Charles Treichel from the 3rd Pennsylvania were volunteered. Newhall, with two orderlies was ordered to contact General Franklin at White Oak Bridge. Locating the general, who was already falling back from the crossing, Newhall delivered his message and started back. Moving in the dead of night he rode into an enemy encampment where he was challenged twice but escaped. He reached McClellan's headquarters, delivered the news and as a reward was asked to ride back with a second message for Franklin. He traveled alone, was often fired upon and chased after Franklin throughout the morning. Newhall arrived back at McClellan's tent to discover Franklin had arrived. In "an act of signal daring" the young officer had ridden 64 miles in full darkness over unfamiliar ground and in almost constant contact with the enemy.[127]

The cavalry would play no dramatic role in the battle at Malvern Hill but after the constant activity of the last weeks the mounted arm was in poor shape and, like the army, more than a little dispirited when it reached Harrison's Landing. "No sign of rest, no let up in the fighting" wrote Silas Wesson. "I am so sleepy I cannot eat and so hungry I cannot sleep. My horse has worn his saddle for a week. He is tired and sleepy too." Just days later he noted "Chaplain Matlock is going [on a leave of absence]. He can be spared well enough for we have no time to pray." Many of the officers, including Col. Farnsworth, took furloughs — a privilege not extended to the men in the ranks.[128]

The events of the last week and the retreat to the James were a bitter disappointment to the common soldiers who had slogged through rain, mud and swamps, and generally fought very well. The dejected men performed their normal duties, however, their comments carried a hard edge like those by Capt. August Kautz. July 1: "Kept standing to horse for some time as Emory marched off without giving orders. When we joined him he kept us standing to horse till sundown. . . .Two squadrons left out on picket for what object it is difficult to conceive." July 2: "The General [Emory] is grossly neglectful of us."[129]

A correspondent writing for the Chicago *Tribune* observed a scene that "defies all description" at Harrison's Landing on July 2.

> [The men] looked more dead than alive; they were covered to the crown of their heads with mud. . . .Whole regiments were immersed to their knees. . .scraping off the dirt. Cavalrymen went out so far, trying to get a "clean wash," that the water reached their saddles, while they vigorously scraped themselves and their weary steeds, many of the men had not had a dry biscuit for twenty-four hours.[130]

The transfer of General Cooke to Washington on the 5th prompted a reorganization of the mounted arm that was announced in orders dated July 8. Removed along with Cooke was General Emory, another aging veteran whose leadership during the campaign was uninspired at best. Overall command of the cavalry would rest with George Stoneman. Colonel Averell was given command of the first brigade, consisting of his 3rd Pennsylvania as well as the 4th Pennsylvania and the 1st New York. His immediate assignment was to cover the right wing of the army. Col. David M. Gregg was given command of the second brigade, including his 8th Pennsylvania, the 8th Illinois and two squadrons of the 6th New York, with responsibility for the left wing of the army. Five squadrons were assigned to the corps commanders as escorts and the 6th Pennsylvania was broken up to serve as guides for the corps commanders. The Regulars were to be consolidated and detailed to unspecified duties. The total strength of the Federal cavalry was listed as 6,978 men present and absent, with about only about 4,700 men ready to take the field.[131]

The following day Kautz reported that the 6th Cavalry was detailed to Colonel Gregg's brigade and that Averell had also petitioned for the unit. The Regulars were proud of their traditions and service and wanted no part of the volunteers. Kautz reacted sharply. "This is the most un-pleasant stroke of all. After having adhered to the Regular service so long to be made a Volunteer of, in spite of myself. I am resolved now to get out of it."[132]

With the entire army now encamped along the water at Harrison's Landing the health of the men and horses became a concern. The horses were particularly bothered by the flies, to the point that many died from exhaustion. An officer in the 2nd Cavalry wrote how he was "watching my horses as they keep up a perpetual dance around the trees to which they are tied, in a vain endeavor to escape the murderous assaults of the flies."[133]

Another officer in the 4th Pennsylvania reported that much sickness prevailed. "The. . .shores were covered with dead horses which festered and [putrefied] there half in the water half on land. On the surface of the river was a scum of refuse hay and oily fragments of decomposing animal matters. . . ." Later in the month Kautz noted "The horses are dying very rapidly from some unknown cause. They stop eating for a day or two then go down and never get up again."[134]

Although the campaign was essentially over, the army would not quit the Peninsula until late August. Until then the cavalry continued to watch over the army. Daily patrols often led to brief skirmishes where men whose names are lost to history died in small numbers on back trails and roads on the outskirts of the army. Most of these patrols were directed toward the river crossings over the Chickahominy. Others were to points south as McClellan pondered his options, including with-drawal. The patrols often ended where Stuart's troopers wanted them to end as they effectively screened their army and thereby limited McClel-lan's knowledge of Lee's movements and intentions. McClellan used his cavalry as a barometer by which he measured the offensive activity or the lack thereof of the enemy, advising his wife in late July that "Secesh is very quiet of late — scarcely even a cavalry skirmish. . . ." He advised Halleck on the 30th, "The Cavalry scouts are daily extending their beats & meet with less resistance. . . ." He went on to mention "I am very weak in Cavalry. . . .I feel the want of it very much," but less than two weeks earlier his quartermaster had reported "We have too much cavalry. . . ."[135]

What McClellan's troopers were not able to tell him was that General Lee was slowly withdrawing his army from the Peninsula to meet a new threat posed by Maj. Gen. John Pope and his Army of Virginia. Pope, in an effort to relieve pressure on McClellan was threatening the rail lines around Gordonsville. Jackson was ordered to Gordonsville on July 13 and a week later Stuart's cavalry pulled back to Ashland. If his cavalry was not reporting this movement Pope's was, but McClellan was not disciplined to act offensively.[136] On the night of July 31 Lee determined to threaten McClellan's communications and further confound him by shelling his camps. Five batteries opened shortly after midnight with most of the damage occurring in the cavalry camps before Federal gunboats silenced the enemy guns. Three horses were killed in the camp of the 3rd Pennsylvania while the 4th Pennsylvania lost four men and six horses. The 6th Pennsylvania lost one man killed while the 6th Cavalry had several wounded, three killed and one horse killed. Based on McClellan's report most, if not all, of his losses were suffered by his mounted arm.[137]

On August 2, 300 troopers from the 3rd Pennsylvania and the 5th Cavalry supported by an infantry contingent crossed the James River at Coggins Point, to drive enemy troops out of the area. Colonel Averell skirmished with Southern cavalry near Sycamore Church and burned their camp and supplies before recrossing the river.[138] The same day, in a last effort to maintain his army on the Peninsula and to retake the offensive McClellan ordered General Hooker to retake Malvern Hill. General Pleasonton's (he was promoted on July 18) cavalry brigade, including two batteries of horse artillery, accompanied the command. The expedition got underway early on the 3rd but was forced to return after blundering onto the wrong road. They got underway again the following afternoon and moved as far as the junction of the Quaker Road and the Charles City Road.[139]

Shortly after the cavalry led the column out the next morning they were fired on by videttes of the 1st North Carolina Cavalry who fell back before the advance along the Quaker Road. When Pleasonton approached Malvern Hill his skirmishers were brought to a halt by a line of infantry supported by the Fauquier Artillery. Pleasonton brought up his two batteries, engaging the enemy guns until Hooker arrived. Once Hooker deployed his infantry the Southern force fell back, under cover of their guns, along the New Market or River Road.[140]

Pleasonton was ordered to pursue and he ordered out the 8th Illinois and the 8th Pennsylvania. Pushing two miles up the New Market Road through deep woods the cavalry entered a clearing. Drawn up across the clearing was the rearguard, including the 8th and 17th Georgia Infantry and the Fauquier Artillery. The Southern gunners opened fire on the head of the column and were answered by the horse gunners. Under the cover of his guns Pleasonton ordered the 8th Illinois to charge the Georgians. Leading his regiment Lt. Col. Gamble went down at the first fire with a shell fragment in his chest. The Southern fire emptied several more saddles before the soldiers fell back.[141]

Pleasonton stated that he again pushed his troopers in pursuit but undoubtedly they were much more cautious this time, settling for a few prisoners before returning to Malvern Hill. Earlier that morning Lee had ordered up two brigades of infantry to bolster the defense of the hill. These troops arrived too late to participate in the action but their pickets regained as much ground as possible before nightfall.[142]

That evening, the 6th Cavalry picketed the New Market Road with the support of two pieces of artillery. Just before dark a squadron of the Regulars moved beyond their own picket line on a final reconnaissance of the road. The rattle of steel and the creak of leather alerted the Southern pickets of their approach and the infantry delivered a full volley into their ranks. The troopers unleashed a volley of their own before retreating for their own lines, having lost six men killed.[143]

On the morning of the 5th Colonel Averell was dispatched toward White Oak Swamp bridge to watch the northern approaches to Malvern Hill. He had 400 troopers from the 5th Cavalry and his 3rd Pennsylvania along with one battery. They arrived near the bridge about 10:30 a.m. to find it guarded by two companies of the 10th Virginia Cavalry. Carelessness on the part of the Southern pickets allowed the Union troopers to advance undetected to a point closer to the bridge than the Virginians. Cut off from the bridge the Confederates were further disturbed when the majority of their weapons failed to fire due to bad caps and damp powder. Forced to fall back across the swamp the two companies lost 28 men, the majority captured. Learning of a larger body of Confederates nearby Averell also withdrew reporting the loss of only two horses.[144] The Federals vacated Malvern Hill, for the second time, on August 7, as McClellan was ordered to withdraw his army to Aquia Landing. Pleasonton was directed to cover the approaches to Harrison's Landing from Haxall's Landing, due south of Malvern Hill. Under the protection of several gunboats the troopers maintained strong pickets on all roads until the army vacated the landing. On August 16 Pleasonton began falling back to Charles City Court House and then to Barrett's Ferry, at the mouth of the Chickahominy River. Large numbers of stragglers were corralled along the route, most of whom were evacuated aboard gunboats at the ferry. On the 19th the troopers marched to Yorktown.[145]

Thomas Kelley of the 8th Illinois declared "our retreat (or evacuation) was well managed not a man lost or a single cent of Property fell into their hands it was a clean thing. . . ." As the men waited for transports to take them north Kelley told his wife "we are [pretty] well drudged out for we have been in active service ever since we came on the peninsula & I tell you both ourselves and horses [need] rest. . . ."[146]

The cavalry embarked between August 11 and September 3. Much of the delay was necessitated by a lack of transports for the horses. On the 12th, McClellan advised of "a vast deficiency in horse transports," noting there were only enough to carry 1,000 horses. At that time a total of 6,000 horses were with the cavalry division that listed 5,853 troopers present for duty. Two regiments, the 5th and 11th Pennsylvania would stay behind at Williamsburg and Suffolk. The remainder of the horsemen would arrive at Alexandria by September 4.[147]

On August 29, McClellan, now at Alexandria, issued a now familiar refrain: "I am now terribly crippled by the want of cavalry."[148] Thomas

Kelley noted similar thoughts concerning his regiment but from a different perspective:

> . . .we [were] a crack regt when we [were] full & I would like to see them all together as we [were] when we left Washington for Alexandria but that never can be some have gone to another & better world and others are disabled for life. . .what men we have got are good soldiers & brave ones to [sic] . . . .[149]

The mounted arm reported the loss of 234 men during the Seven Days, however a tabulation of their actual losses for the campaign, while certainly much higher, would be difficult to accomplish with accuracy.[150] On September 3, while many of the troopers were still aboard ship, enroute to Alexandria, the Northern press again raised the issue of the need for an effective cavalry force. In a brief column the editors of the New York *Times* concluded:

> We take it that the War Department has at length found out the mistake [of not having an effective mounted arm], and if Stuart and his men have been influential in opening their eyes, let us be thankful for it.[151]

More than a year after the Battle of Bull Run, Jeb Stuart and his troopers were again the spark for the Northern debate over the need for cavalry. Now they were also the standard by which this force would be judged.

For far too long the effectiveness of the Federal cavalry on the Peninsula has been measured against two events, neither positive: Stuart's ride of mid-June and the charge of the 5th Cavalry at Gaines' Mill. Many historians would have the reader believe that the Federal cavalry played no other role in the campaign. The question then is whether or not these two events are a fair measuring stick by which to judge the Federal cavalry. Furthermore, was the Southern cavalry already that dominant over its Northern counterpart?

Certainly the South bore a great advantage in the quality of its early mounted force. The South saw the need for and the advantage of a strong cavalry force immediately. The fact that the agrarian Southern society bred quality horses and horseman was an early advantage. That these men brought their own mounts, well-bred and properly broken, was a benefit that would become a burden by 1863. But the Southern cavalry was hampered by many of the same problems as the Federal cavalry. Numerically the Southern mounted force was never greater than McClellan's, and it was only very late in the campaign that it would achieve some measure of parity. In April, Stuart's brigade numbered just three regiments with an effective strength of 1,289. The need for cavalry in The Army of Northern Virginia, during the Peninsula campaign, was just as great as in The Army of the Potomac.[152]

The terrain and climate of the Peninsula held no advantage for the South. It was not cavalry country. The poorly constructed, narrow roads made movement difficult through the prevalent heavy woods, swamps and deep ravines. Moreover, the Southern troopers were not much more familiar with the area than were their Northern counterparts.[153]

For most of the cavalrymen, North and South, this campaign was their first taste of combat and the grueling hours of constant picket duty. One of Stuart's staff officers referred to cavalry service in the early part of the campaign as odious. But because the men were still new to the miseries and horrors of combat the eagerness of their youth saw them through the campaign. The "glory" of the cavalry aside the young men in the natty blue uniforms were just as dedicated, just as willing to give their lives to their country as were the men in the somber gray uniforms. Neither had a particular advantage in weapons or equipment at this point in the war either. What then was the difference?[154]

The difference was in the officer corps, the men in positions of authority over the mounted arm, the men who set the tone for how the service would be used. The difference, first and foremost, was George McClellan. While much younger than most of his senior officers, McClellan did not bring young ideas to the cavalry. Although he had for a short time been a member of the 1st Cavalry, he did not have a cavalry background. Any knowledge he might have acquired in his study of European cavalry was illusory. His treatise was filled with minutiae on the daily activities and maintenance of cavalry units. Other sections, such as his detailed explanations of how to transport horses aboard ship proved impracticable. Whatever else it was, his book of observations on European cavalry was not a study of tactics or operations. His cavalry manual dealt almost entirely with non-offensive aspects of mounted service: organization of the regiment, placement of the officers and non-commissioned officers while on the march, guard details etc. The work was not one to lead readers to suppose McClellan had a new vision for the cavalry. After the war an officer opined that "McClellan. . . destitute of experience, was dominated by theory." Another wrote that his "one idea of the shortcomings of the cavalry was that it was not large enough." Yet he continually divided it among his infantry commands "[subverting] its true value, bringing sarcasm and ignominy" down on the shoulders of the men who rode in the ranks.[155]

McClellan's oft-stated disdain for volunteers made clear early on that volunteer cavalry units did not hold his trust. He believed in the two-to-five year rule for cavalry and thus had little, if any, faith in the men who made up the bulk of his mounted arm. He did appreciate the Regulars but when these units arrived they were understrength, poorly armed and no better prepared for the coming campaign than were the volunteers. While he expressed a desire for the Regulars to set an example for the volunteers he often used the men for his personal escort, where only he derived any benefit. Of his three senior cavalry officers he picked the two oldest for brigade commands and initially put his youngest, George Stoneman, in an administrative position with no authority over the others. Though he professed great faith in Stoneman's abilities, he gave command of his Regulars to one of the older men in the army, Philip St. George Cooke. It was Stoneman, however, who would achieve the most success in the campaign and the only one of the three who remained with the army at the close of the fighting, by which time younger officers, leading volunteer units, were demonstrating their talents and rising to brigade command. The cavalry was clearly a young man's service—a service where men unburdened by outdated methods of operation, practiced on vastly different terrain and with the ability to quickly adapt to ever changing circumstances would achieve fame. The service also needed men with the stamina to spend long hours in the saddle, as Stuart had demonstrated in June.

Problems of vitality aside, the Federal cavalry fought harder and achieved more on the Peninsula than it has been given credit for. Were Federal troopers better than their counterparts? Absolutely not—nor did they accomplish all that they might have. But for men who only months before may not have known how to saddle or ride a horse, the Northern cavalryman's accomplishments are worthy of some admiration. Williamsburg, Hanover Court House and Willis Church are just a few reminders that the men in the short blue jackets with the yellow or orange piping did not always embarrass their country or their army. Jeb Stuart and his troopers were the standard by which these men would be judged, and embarrassing days still lay ahead, but the Northern horsemen were learning, and their defeats seldom came from lack of desire or want of valor.

Once the administration and the military allowed these men their proper place in the army, they would establish the standards by which others would be judged.

A Report of Medical Personnel and Activity at Savage's Station During and After the Seven Days Battles

Edited by William J. Miller

John Swinburne was born in Deer River, New York, May 30, 1820. Twenty seven years later, he took a medical degree from Albany Medical College and opened a practice, which, by the time of the outbreak of the Civil War, was reputedly the largest and most prosperous in New York's capital city. He offered his services to New York authorities, and they directed him to assume control of medical arrangement's at the camp of rendezvous and instruction for volunteer soldiers in Albany. At the outset of the spring campaigns in 1862, he applied for and received from Gov. E. D. Morgan an appointment as a volunteer surgeon. He joined the Army of the Potomac on the Peninsula, was instrumental in establishing and running the hospital at White House Landing, and assisted in treating the wounded from the Battle of Seven Pines.

Convinced he could better serve the sick and wounded if he had more control over policies and practices, he returned to New York, spoke to the governor and received authority to return to the Peninsula as "medical superintendent of New York State troops." Though the position was nebulous in that it gave Swinburne no real authority and did not define his duties, he was invested with considerable power in that his appointment came from the governor of the most powerful state in the

Dr. John Swinburne
circa 1885

Union. Both Secretary
of War Edwin M. Stan-
ton and Surgeon Gen-
eral of the Army
William A. Hammond
endorsed Swinburne's
appointment and di-
rected Dr. Charles S.
Tripler, medical direc-
tor of the Army of the
Potomac, to do all possible to assist Swinburne. The earnest Dr. Swinburne arrived at Dr. Tripler's tent on the Chickahominy River just six
days after receiving the letter of appointment from Gov. Morgan in
Albany.

One observer wrote that Swinburne was untiring in his labors after
the Battle of Gaines's Mill, "making in one day twenty-six exsections of
the shoulder and elbow-joints, a number of amputations, and extracting a
double handful of bullets. He had a barn and two sheds assigned him,
and never left the operating-room while the wounded were being
brought in. During the lulls, he ate his hard-bread and hominy, and drank
his coffee, from off the operating-table."[1]

Dr. Swinburne's report of his tenure at Savage's Station and the
surrounding country in June and July 1862 is important because it details
the degree of suffering of casualties of the Seven Days Battles, it illustrates the crucial role that civilian volunteers, like Swinburne, played in
helping the wounded, and it confirms the humanity of Robert E. Lee and

other Confederate military men, who cooperated with Northern medical personnel to save Northern lives.

The pamphlet bearing Dr. Swinburne's report, a copy of which rests in the library of the U.S. Army Military History Institute in Carlisle, Pennsylvania, begins with Swinburne's letter of appointment from Gov. Morgan.

Report of Dr. Swinburne,
Giving an Account of his Services on the Peninsula

STATE OF NEW YORK.
EXECUTIVE DEPARTMENT,
Albany, June 12, 1862.

Sir: Doctor John Swinburne, of this city, proceeds to Washington to-day, by my request, with directions to place this letter in your hands.

I have become satisfied of the importance of having a medical gentleman of high professional standing in the immediate vicinity of the army of the Potomac to give general personal attention to the soldiers from this State. As a large portion of General McClellan's army is from this State, it seems proper that we should have one or more representatives there to alleviate, as far as possible, the sufferings of the sick and wounded. I well know how solicitous you have been about those whom the exigencies of the service throw upon the medical department, and how wise and generous your arrangements are for them. The whole country approves your course in this regard. But you may well know that our people, who are so willing to respond to the call of the Government, feel the deepest solicitude about our volunteers, and especially so in view of the impending battle.

I would therefore respectfully and earnestly request that Dr. Swinburne may be permitted to go to the army of the Potomac to co-operate with the Government, as medical superintendent of New York State troops.

Dr. Swinburne has already spent four weeks at White House, as a member of the corps of Volunteer Surgeons, returning day before yesterday, and for the past year has had general charge of the Military Hospital of this city. No Surgeon in the State enjoys a more deserved reputation, and from his urbanity and uniform courtesy, I am sure that no misunderstanding can occur between the United States authorities and himself.

I am with much respect,
Your ob't servant,
E.D. Morgan, *Gov. of New York*

Hon. E. M. Stanton, *Secretary of War,*
Washington City, D.C. [addressee]

Referred to the Surgeon-General with recommendation that some suitable arrangement may be made, agreeable to Dr. Swinburne, so as to secure his services.
Edwin M. Stanton, *Secretary of War*
June 14

*   *   *

"COPY."
SURGEON-GENERAL'S OFFICE,
Washington, June 14, 1862.

Sir: I have this day entered into a contract with Dr. Swinburne (the bearer) for Medical and Surgical services with the army of the Potomac.

He has a letter from Governor Morgan, addressed to the Secretary of War, upon which you will find an endorsement by the Secretary, which will explain to you the status that it is desired Dr. Swinburne should occupy.

You will, as far as the exigencies of the public service will allow, afford to Dr. S. the means to carry out the wishes of Governor Morgan and Secretary Stanton.

Very respectfully,
Your ob't servant,
(Signed) William A. Hammond
Surgeon-General, U.S. A.

Surg. C.S. TRIPLER, U.S.A.
Medical Director, Army of Potomac
Before Richmond, Va. [addressee]

*   *   *

STEAMER ELM CITY,
July 29, 1862
Wm. A. Hammond
Surgeon General, U.S.A.

Sir: Your instructions to me of the 14th of June were handed to Dr. Tripler, Medical Director, Army of the Potomac, on the 16th. On the same day I received Special Order 182.

Sec. 9. Acting Assistant Surgeon John Swinburne will report to Surgeon J.J. Milhem [sic], U.S.A. Medical Director 3d Army Corps,[2] for special duty at Savage's Station. * * *
By Command
MAJ. GEN. MCCLELLAN.
Signed,
Seth Williams, *Asst. Adj't Gen'l.*
(Copy.)

*   *   *

Dr. Swinburne's Report

I immediately complied, and ascertained that Dr. Milhem [sic] had received no instructions in regard to my duties.

Hearing nothing further of said special duty, on the morning of the 18th I called on Dr. Tripler, who informed me that I was to establish a general hospital for the sick and wounded at Savage's Station, Va., of which I was to take charge. I was to make requisitions for all articles and material necessary for the construction and furnishing of such hospital. On the same morning I sent in requisitions for approval of 75 hospital tents, 1,500 stretchers, and other things in proportion.

Late in the afternoon of the 19th, the requisition was returned, duly approved. On the same morning, I visited the White House and superintended the filling of said requisition.

On the 21st instant, the requisition not arriving, sent a special messenger to the White House, he returned on the same evening with 15 hospital tents and 20 stretchers.

On the 22nd I made a requisition on Dr. Tripler for a detail of 100 men, and a team for transportation. The requisition was partially complied with. I received 30 men; many of whom did not make their appearance until the 25th. I received no team whatsoever. With this limited force, we put the outhouses in as good order as possible, put up the tents, and converted our tents into 15 more; making accommodations for about 600 patients in all. On the 24th Dr. Vollum (Med. Insp. Army)[4], visited me, and proposed to send me all the tents and accommodations he could. On the 26th I received 150 old tents, which were intended to be used for the roofs of temporary buildings for hospital purposes. Finding the number of sick increasing rapidly (being sent from division hospitals), I was obliged to cut poles, and put up shelter with these A tents as best I could. Before night they were full, and many were left without shelter. On the same afternoon many wounded were brought in from the right wing of the army, fed and immediately transhipped [sic] to the White House, agreeable to orders. Those received during the night and the following days remained, with the exception of the few who were able to walk; these moved on to the James river with the army.

The following days (Friday, Saturday, and the Sabbath), we received about 1,500 wounded. In my surgical labors, I was assisted by Doctors O. Munson,[5] J. Underwood,[6] C. J. Volees, Edmeston, Clark,[7] Page, Hogan, Newell, Dueling, W. A. Smith, J. S. Smith,[8] Fox, Sutton, Dongal, Perkins,[9] Middleton and Nordan. Subsequently, Drs. Faulkner,[10] Philips, Russell,[11] Potter,[12] Bromley, Phillips,[13] Millner,[14] Marsh and Schell,[15] arrived from other hospitals with their patients and assisted me. Drs. Tripler, Greenleaf,[16] Smith,[17] McClellan[18] and Milaan, assisted me very materially in the necessary surgery, and the general management of the hospital during the great and important crisis.

Late Saturday afternoon I was informed by Dr. Tripler that it would be necessary for me to remain there, inasmuch as in the course of a few hours the enemy would have possession, and that I must provide myself with food for at least one week; that he would give me an *ad libitum* order on the Commissary for stores to that end, which he did; that he would also give me a letter from Gen. McClellan to the commanding officer of the confederate forces, explaining my position and his pleasure with regard to the wounded and sick, which you will find (Doc. 1).

In reference to the difficulty which now remained, to procure the transportation of food and hospital stores from the general commissary stores, I was unable that evening to obtain any detail, either of men or wagons, to make this transfer. Notwithstanding, I continued these efforts until 12 o'clock at night, and renewed them again at 4 o'clock in the morning. At 7 a.m., I had made but little progress. During Saturday evening, or early Sunday morning, I called on the proper authority (Gen. Williams), and begged that the general commissary stores should not be destroyed; or, that I should be supplied with sufficient quantity before such destruction should take place.

Early Sunday morning I was rudely upbraided by Assistant Adjutant-General McKelver,[19] of Gen. Heintzelman's staff for not having already supplied myself with proper hospital stores. I applied to Quartermaster Wicks, in accordance with Special Order No. 186 (Doc. 2), who not only neglected to furnish the transportation, but insulted me in the grossest manner, as he had on a previous occasion; the facts of which were simply these: After receiving my tents, and some other portions of my requisition, I found that portion which called for shovels, spades and axes had

not been complied with, and that my detail of 30 men were waiting for them. In order to accomplish my labors, I borrowed a few
from Quartermaster King which belonged to Quartermaster
Wicks, but which he (King), had mistaken for his own.

Quartermaster Wicks treated me very unkindly at this time,
and compelled me to return the few that I had, and keep my detail
waiting nearly two days before I could obtain my tools on requisition. Finding it necessary to have operating tables, of which my
hospital was entirely destitute (notwithstanding the requisition for
such), and finding that Quartermaster Wicks alone had tools necessary to make them, I applied to him for them, and, after allowing my carpenter to make one table, he ordered them taken from
him; and when spoken to in reference to this course, he answered:
"The instruments are mine, and I have a right to do with them as I
have a mind." And when told the use of the instruments was not a
personal favor, but necessary for the wounded, he then ordered
me out of his tent, hoping I would never "come back again," with
many unpleasant expressions. I simply said I would return as
often as my business called me there.

But to Captain McKelvey[20] [sic] and the other members of
Gen. H.'s staff, I am indebted for many attentions.

During the forenoon of Sunday, I succeeded in coaxing and
hiring a few men to take up a small quantity of commissary
stores. About noon the ever generous General Sumner appeared
on the ground, who after hearing all the facts, sent a detail of one
hundred men and supplied us pretty bountifully with food, still we
had no sugar nor tea which could have been procured by transportation at a distance of less than one-fourth mile, and was of course
destroyed with the rest of the commissary stores. In this way the
day was consumed. General Sumner also saved me fifty hospital
tents which would have otherwise been destroyed, and hence
would have caused much suffering, inasmuch as there was then
several hundred wounded lying on the ground without shelter, and
these tents were required for that purpose. The next morning the

enemy took possession, carried off our nurse and labor detail, and caused otherwise much confusion, so that the doctors were converted into nurses, &c., instead of exercising their proper vocation. In this way their valuable time was consumed instead of attending to the necessary and proper surgical operations suitable at this period after injury. We were thus employed in performing duties which would otherwise have devolved upon cooks, nurses, hospital stewards, &c.

Sunday evening the forces of General Sumner were drawn up in battle array. Opposite to them and at right angles with the houses (hospital), were the forces of the enemy. Obliquely from the house (hospital), and nearly on a line was placed a Confederate battery, the first shell from which burst directly over the hospital, wounding one man slightly and frightening the other very much. The second shot burst just over the tents, killing one man by decapitation, and perforating the tent in many places. I then sent out a flag of truce with the following communication:

GEN'L HOSPITAL, SAVAGE'S STATION,
June 29, 1862.
To Commanding General
Confederate Forces.

This is a hospital which contains 2,000 sick and wounded, some of them being your own—one Col. Lamar of Georgia.[21]

Very respectfully,
John Swinburne,
Surgeon In Charge.

He replied as follows:

The hospital will not be fired into unless undue advantage is taken of its flag,

A. Conrad, *A.A. Gen'l Confed. Forces.*

*   *   *

Soon after I received a peremptory order from Gen. Sumner "to come to (his) headquarters immediately," with which order I complied and received a gentle but decided reprimand, for presuming to send out a flag of truce without his order. Soon after a battle ensued from which we received about 35 wounded, many of them mortal.

On Monday and Tuesday we were engaged in systematizing and making general arrangements for the comfort of the patients.

On Tuesday Gen. Stonewall Jackson, C.S.A., sent a messenger to ascertain our wants and necessities,—I returned with the messenger and had a conference with Dr. Maguire,[*] medical director Jackson's army;[22] he informed me that we (the surgeons) were not prisoners of war—that we were free to go wherever we deemed our services requisite among the sick and wounded.

He gave me a pass to visit the various hospitals where our wounded were situated and learning that many of our wounded were lying on the battlefield of Monday, I returned on Wednesday with three ambulances loaded with food and two surgeons, Dr. Edmeston of the 18th New York, and Dr. Underwood, Volunteer Surgeon, Massachusetts, leaving them at points where their services were most needed. I visited the battlefield of Monday and found many of our wounded still on the field and uncared for. I called on Dr. Mott medical director of Gen. D. H. Hills, C.S.A.,[23] who detailed Dr. Page, surgeon, C.S.A., who with a corps of detailed men removed all he could find to suitable places, (small houses in the neighborhood), these were attended principally by our own surgeons, of whom there was a very efficient corps.[**]

---

[*] Swinburne's note: "I believe it is to Dr. McGuire that we are indebted for establishing the precedent which exempts physicians from the ordinary usages of war."

[**] Swinburne's note: "The names of Kilton, Robinson [possibly Dr. Joseph W. Robinson of Hornellsville, New York. See William W. Potter's memoir, edited by John Michael Priest, *One Surgeon's Private War*, pp. 20-21, 38], McNeill, Donnelly, Ritinger, Osborne, Fossard, Collings, Cogswell, Underwood and my friend and fellow townsman, Edmeston, were among the number I now remember as efficient laborers."

On visiting the battlefield of Tuesday, I found the house and bar of Dr. _____,[24] contained several wounded who had no medical attendance or food. I called on Gen. McGruder, C.S.A.,[25] who after a hearing of the facts in the case, sent some of our own men to attend them as well as rations. In conversation with him in reference to paroling our wounded, he also suggested that I should communicate the facts of our situation and necessities to Gen. Lee, commander-in-chief, C.S.A., with which request I complied, & c., of which the following is a copy:

GEN. MACGRUDER'S [sic] HEADQ'RS
Crew's House, Va., July 3, 1862.

Gen. R.E. Lee:
Sir: I am left here by order of Gen. McClellan [a copy of the order had already been sent him], to look after the welfare of the sick and wounded and since there are numbers of them placed in temporary hospitals extending form Gaines' House to the James river, a distance of about fifteen miles, and inasmuch as it is impossible for me to oversee and ensure proper attention as to medication, nursing and food, I would therefore propose that some suitable arrangement be made either for concentrating them at Savage's and other stations, that these ends might be obtained, or what would be still more agreeable to the demands of humanity, namely, the unconditional parol [sic] of these sufferers.

From what I learn of your ideas of humanity, I feel assured (even if the Federal Government do not recognize the principle of mutual exchange) that this rule will not be extended to the unfortunate sick and wounded. The real prisoners of war should be treated as belligerents—while humanity shudders at the idea of putting the wounded on the same footing. Your surgeons have performed miracles in the way of kindness both to us as surgeons, as well as to the wounded. If this proposition does not meet with favor, I will, with your permission, communicate with the Federal Government, that some basis of transfer may be arrived at. The majority, in fact all the medical directors of your army with whom I have conferred, fully agree with me as to the humanity of carrying out this proposition. My object in asking an immediate, unconditional parol [sic] is, that time should be saved, and that the sufferers should be released more speedily. Hoping to hear from you soon,

I remain respectfully yours, & c.,

J. Swinburne, *Surgeon in Charge*

To which Gen. Lee returned the following answer:

HD. Q'RS, ARMY, N Va,
July 4, 1862.

Sir: I regret to learn the extreme suffering of the sick and wounded Federal prisoners that have fallen into our hands. I will do all that lies in my power to alleviate their sufferings. I will cause steps to be taken to give you every facility in concentrating them at Savage's station [sic].I am willing to release the sick and wounded on their parol [sic] not to bear arms against the Confederate states [sic] until regularly exchanged.But at present I have no means of carrying such an arrangement into effect.Certainly such a release will be a great relief to them. Those who are well and in attendance upon the hospitals, except those who were left for the purpose, could not be included in such an arrangement, but must be sent into the interior as prisoners of war until regularly exchanged.

Very respectfully your obd't servant,

R.E. Lee, General

Dr. J. Swinburne,
Acting Surgeon in Charge.

Being now nearly eleven o'clock at night I returned to Dr. _____'s[26] house and staid [sic] for the night. In the morning I visited the various farm-houses about the battlefield of Tuesday and found that all the wounded had been removed to Malvern Hill (overlooking James river [sic]) where as I learned they were well cared for. While passing Gen. McGruder's [sic] head-quarters, Dr. Guild, C.S.A. Medical Director,[27] handed me the following note:

Malvern Hill, July 8, 1862.

There are several cases which are needing capital operations, and which are of the latest date. Shall they remain there to be operated on? If so, further aid will be needed to continue the preparations for the removal of the others, as our time will be fully occupied. Can we possibly have further aid? If Dr. Swinburne can come (I hear he is in the vicinity) I would like it, or some other Federal surgeon.

I judge by this time some of them at Savage's Station must be at leisure.

Respectfully yours,
C. B. White,
Asst. Surg. U.S.A.

To Maj. Gen'l McGruder [sic], C.S.A.

In compliance with this request, I repaired to Pitt's house. I staid with Doctors White, Chamberlain and Jewett that day and part of the next, performing all the operations necessary at this period. Returning to the field of Monday, I was informed by some of the Confederates that some of our wounded were in a dense forest, near by. Upon visiting the place, I found several in the position indicated, all of whom had been fed, and water given to, by the Confederate soldiers. I caused steps to be taken to have them removed immediately to a place where they could be cared for. I again visited the neighboring hospitals, found the surgeons U.S.A. were attending to their duty faithfully, and returned the same evening to Savage's Station, where I found my patients doing well; but my nurses—what few remained—pretty thoroughly worked out. In this connection, I wish to make special mention of my volunteer corps of nurses; which consisted of Mr. Brunot, and several nurses from Pittsburgh, Pa.; Rev. Mr. Reed, Washington, D.C.; and Mr. Howell of Chicago. These gentlemen assisted in the organization of the hospital, superintending the cooking and dispensing of food, as well as all those little things which belong to a hospital steward, and the general management of a hospital. Up to this time, and for some days afterwards, the Confederate authorities had neglected either to return the nurses that they took from us at the time we became prisoners, or send us others. This neglect on their part not only increased our labors, but rendered the wounded less comfortable, and in some instances proved fatal.

On or about the 8th of July the Confederate authorities arrested the Rev. Mr. Reed, and, without making any specific charges, took him to Richmond. On the 9th I made a special requisition on Gen. Winder (Provost Marshal Gen. of Richmond),[28] in accordance with Gen. Hill's directions, for a detail of 200 of our men and rations for the same, to act as nurses, and for other purposes. About this time I visited Malvern Hill, and the hospital in the neighborhood of White Oak Swamp, and found that most of the wounded had been removed either to Richmond or Savage's Station; and on my return to S.S., I found to my disgust and surprise that the Confederate authorities had arrested and carried to Richmond Mr. Brunot, his corps of nurses, and Mr. Howell, leaving us in a sad predicament in reference to our wounded. I again petitioned the officer in charge to the effect that he should visit Richmond in person, and solicit from Gen. Winder some of our men for nurses. On the 10th we received 200 men from Richmond, with whom no rations were sent. Up to this time, we had not sufficient materials for food. But now our rations being nearly out, and the Confederate authorities furnishing none, I made a requisition on the officer of the post for food. On the 12th our requisition for food was answered by sending us a limited supply of flour and poor bacon. We were compelled to make the best of our condition; and with these 200 men we commenced at once to improve the sanitary condition of the hospitals and grounds.

On the 12th we had everything in good order and our men comfortable. At this time Dr. Johnson, Med. Purveyor, C.S.A., visited the hospital. He said he supposed we had been or would soon be removed. On the evening of the 13th a courier arrived at the hospital with a message for Dr. Guild, which he red to me. It consisted in an agreement between Generals McClellan, Lee, and their medical advisers (Dr. Letterman and Guild), to the effect that we would be paroled and sent to our lines by the most direct route. [For communication, made to Gen. Lee, see Doc. 3]

Dr. Greenleaf of the U.S.A., and Dr. Guild of the C.S.A., were to arrange the time and place at which their parol should be carried into effect. On the 14th the Confederate officers informed me that an entire exchange of prisoners would take place; that an agreement between the Confederate and Federal authorities was made; that Gen. Hill of the C.S.A., and Gen. Dix of the U.S.A., were to arrange the preliminaries. On the same evening, Maj. _____,[29] C.S.A., met me with a train of army wagons, filled with sick (form a hospital situate about a mile to the east of Savage's Station), en route to Richmond. He informed me that in the morning 300 army wagons would be a Savage's Station to remove our sick and wounded to City Point via Richmond, or to Richmond, and hence down the James river on flat boats to our transports. I protested against this inhuman manner of moving the sick and wounded. I took steps immediately to ascertain the truth of the statement, and procure a more humane mode of removal, as I then supposed, to our own lines. Since what had occurred on the previous two days, I had not the remotest idea that there would be any detention in Richmond; but, on the contrary, would be placed directly on board the flat boats and sent down the James river to our own transports.

Had I supposed that they were to be detained in Richmond to receive the treatment that they subsequently did, whereby many valuable lives were sacrificed, I should have sought an interview with Gen. Lee, and thereby have prevented this misfortune.

On the 15th Major Rodgers called with a train of cars, box and platform, saying we were to be removed to Richmond, thence down the James river on flat boats to our transports. This day he removed over a thousand, including physicians and many nurses. During the afternoon, Dr. Johnson, C.S.A., called, took charge of all stores, instruments, medicines, tents &c., for which he gave me a receipt (see Doc. 4), saying the remainder would be removed the next day. On the morning of the 16th another load was removed, and in the evening a second train had just been loaded. Many of the most severely wounded placed on platform cars, when we experienced the most violent storm of wind and rain, and which continued until late in the evening; the train arrived in Richmond about 10 p.m., it still raining somewhat. Dr. Churchill, U.S.A., in charge, informed me that no one was present to receive them; no building prepared to put them in; that no food was prepared for them; no persons present to unload the wounded. The train was left outside the depot, and that he, with the limited number of nurses, succeeded in removing those from the platform cars to the adjacent sheds and depot by 3 o'clock next morning. Here these poor wounded men remained, in the rain, wet and cold, with no blankets, no food, and, I may say, no shelter; many of them lying near the rails for 40 hours. Dr. O. Munson, U.S.A., who had charge of one train, informed me that when good Samaritan women offered to supply the wounded with coffee, tea or other nourishment, that they were rudely driven away by the bayonet of the Confederate soldier. Then (under guard) he was conducted to prison, where he remained without supper or breakfast, while for dinner he simply had a little poor bacon and bread. He remained in prison until two o'clock the next day, when he was allowed to visit his patients, under guard. He found that his patients had had no nourishment; no water to wet their wounds or to drink; and that their nurses had been taken from them. The remained in this condition until the afternoon of the 17th, when over a hundred of the worst cases were sent back to Savage's Station; the residue were sent to close and ill-ventilated hospitals, and several died before removal. Those who were returned to

Savage's Station arrived late in the evening, and inasmuch as it was raining and they were in box cars, and the tents, what were left standing from the storm, were wet, I resolved to leave them where they were through the night. We therefore prepared them for supper—flour gruel, the only food we hand—and then made them as comfortable as we could. The next morning we prepared tents and moved the patients to them. Being informed that we would stay some time at Savage's Station, and that those who were taken to Richmond were still there and would not be soon removed, we again made preparations for a long stay.

I had sent several surgeons to Richmond with the wounded and learning (from Dr. Munson, U.S.A.) that about thirty U.S. surgeons were there in attendance, and were all kept in close confinement, and only allowed to see the patients under guard, and that every facility, including medicines, instruments, nurses, proper food, &c. had been removed from them, and they were then upbraided for not doing their duty. And though we had sixteen left to attend (nearly half of whom were sick) on the 350 sick and wounded at this place, I deemed it best to retain them, inasmuch as they would do not additional good, since they would be treated as the others were. (See Doc. 8)

Up to this time we had been enabled to furnish ourselves with some fresh meat and soups from some beeves which remained in charge of Rev. Dr. Marks, U.S.A., who had charge of a small fever hospital, of about 100 patients, situate about a mile east of Savage's Station, the management of which requires some little notice; and though I have not a statistical report, I think it was the best managed and disciplined hospital in Virginia. But now the remnant of our own stock, including instruments, medicines &c., having been taken by the Confederates Medical Director, under the alleged impression that we were to have been removed at the time the rest were, we were obliged to depend upon the material furnished by requisition from Confederate authorities or by purchase with our own funds. Up to this time the officers had furnished the principal portion of their own subsistence by purchase. It then became a matter of serious consideration, knowing, as we did, that the rations furnished by the Confederates consisted of flour and poor bacon only. While food, necessary for the comforts of the sick, was very expensive and difficult to obtain, and the inhabitants were unwilling to sell unless for gold, and were also instructed from Richmond not to sell to the "Yankees;" at that it was very difficult to obtain a sufficient amount of food for the officers, and at the following exorbitant prices: Eggs, $1.50 a dozen; milk, 25c to 50c pr. quart; butter, $1.25 pr. lb.; sheep, $8 a piece: other things in proportion. While at Richmond, tea sold for $10 and $16 lb.; coffee, 20c per lb.; sugar (common brown) $1.25; brown hard soap, 50c for a piece [illegible] in. square. Other things proportionally high, including bread. In this dilemma, I wrote Dr. Guild, M.D., C.S.A., our condition and wants, who answered it by sending us, the next morning, Dr. Winfield, C.S.A., Medical Inspector Hospitals Camps, &c.; and accompanying him was Col. _____,[30] an officer of Gen. Lee's staff, and sent him. In answer to the inquiry of these gentlemen as to what we were feeding our patients, I stated that flour and bacon was their food, medicine, &c.; it was all we had; that our bacon, though limited in its supply, was absolutely maggoty. This statement was confirmed by Lieut. Lacey Stewart, C.S.A., commanding post. I referred him to the wan, worn, and exhausted countenances of the patients; that what little choice stores we had were removed by their own people on the 15th inst. They left, saying they would see to it, and send us all they could; that they had been providing us with rations the same as was supplied their own men; that they would also interest Gen. Lee in our behalf. In the evening they sent us a small invoice of medical stores; the first and only supply from the C.S.A., for copy of which see Doc. 5 I will here state that nearly 100 of the patients, then at Savage's Station, had recently been brought from a hospital, situate on the battlefield of Friday, June 27, where they had lived on nothing but flour from the day of the battle up to July 16, and hence were exhausted, and many moribund when they arrived.

This hospital was under the charge of the late Dr. Milner, U.S.A., who fell a victim to cerebral exhaustion, induced by this insufficiency of food.

In reference to the removal of the wounded men to Richmond and their subsequent treatment, Dr. Winfield, C.S.A., stated that they should never have been removed until paroled., and then sent directly to our lines; that their removal was not in accordance with Gen. Lee's or the Medical Director's wishes, and intimated that it was brought about by some meddlesome parties in Richmond who wished to exercise a little brief authority. But I gravely suspected that it was more a desire to make an exhibition of the "wounded Yankees" (as they familiarly called them) than it was a meddlesome interference. Still I cheerfully and fully exonerated Gen. Lee from any part or knowledge in this transaction.

I feel assured that all the deficiencies and difficulties which we experienced were not the fault of Gen. Lee or his medical staff, since all the generals and medical officers with whom we were brought in contact were unusually attentive to the necessities of the wounded and sick; but that there was a fault somewhere there is not question, and that fault I attribute to the inhumanity of the authorities of Richmond, and this fault has been a fatal one to many of our soldiers.

In view of all the circumstances here set forth, on the 20th I summoned all the medical officers present to meet in order to devise some suitable means of sustaining and supporting the strength and thereby preserving the lives of the wounded remaining at Savage's Station. (For result of those proceedings see Doc. 6) In the afternoon I visited several farm houses in the neighborhood, found mutton and beef very expensive. From this time we made mutton soup in addition to the rations furnished, and which supply I kept up with my own funds.

This day for the first, Lt. Lacey Stewart, commanding post, succeeded in obtaining in addition to regular rations, some sugar, salt and dried apples, the first and last they furnished.*

To-day (22nd) Dr. Sutton, U.S.A., died exhausted from typhoid remittent fever (see Doc. 7, letter to Dr. Guild).

On the 23rd the Surgeons passed preamble and resolutions, and attended the funeral in a body.

On the 24th I wrote to Gen. Winder a letter in relation to our status, which will be found (Doc. 8).

I also visited some of the battle-fields and ascertained that none of our dead had been buried. They had remained as they had fallen; simply a sufficient dirt had been thrown over them to form a scanty covering, and in many instances hands and feet were still projecting and many of the bones are now strewn about the field. This was true of all the battle-fields from Gaines' Mills to James river [sic]. This, together with the unburied horses, made the atmosphere very offensive and sickening to those in hospitals. One fact is here worthy of notice: while the Confederates removed all their wounded, buried their dead men and horses in some secluded spot, they failed to bury our dead at all, and at best left them exposed for several days, a loathsome spectacle to behold, and from the fact of its occurring on every battle-field from Gaines' Mill to James river [sic], one would be led to suppose that it was done purely for effect. We noticed another fact, that our wounded were always left on the battle-field, not only till theirs had been removed, but their dead men and horses removed also. As an instance: some of the wounded of Monday (battle of White Oak Swamp)[31] were left on the battle-field until Saturday, for which I could not see any palliating circumstances, nor could the enemy render any valid excuse.

---

* Swinburne's note: "I since learned that these things were drawn for his own command, and that they generously divided them with the wounded."

On the 25th one of our surgeons, Dr. Milner, U.S.A., died very suddenly from inanition, induced by insufficient food. Upon this occasion I again addressed Dr. Guild, C.S.A., in reference to our condition (see Doc. 9), and received in answer (Doc. 10).

On the 26th the surgeons met, passed appropriate resolutions in reference to his death, and attended his funeral in a body. At the same time, I addressed Gen. Winder (see Doc. 8) and I received the following verbal answer: "He had nothing to do with us."

On the 26th, Lieut. Lacey Stewart, commanding post, went to Richmond, an din the evening returned with a train of cars, saying we must be loaded by 4 o'clock a.m., the following morning, to be transshipped to City Point the same day. The following morning, according to directions, we moved to Richmond, under the kind care of Dr. Cullen, C.S.A., and were carefully transferred in good ambulances to the Petersburg Railroad Depot, from thence to City Point, arriving at that place about 5 p.m., 27th, and were soon shipped on board our own transports. This being the last of our sick and wounded from these battle-fields before Richmond, except some few minor cases. The next day (28th) I reported to Dr. Letterman in person, who said under the circumstances I had better report to you (Surgeon General).

I herein append the names of the sick and wounded of those remaining at Savage's Station on Monday the 30th day of June, and those received at that time, and up to our departure (27th July), also the names of those who died as far as could be ascertained.

All of which is respectfully submitted,

John Swinburne,

Surgeon in Charge

P.S.—The conduct of Lieut. Stewart, who commanded the post, was such, that the Medical and Line Officers deemed it worthy a series of resolutions, commendatory of his course, which were presented to him, accompanied by an appropriate speech by Dr. O. Munson, U.S.A., on the evening preceding our departure, who, in answer, stated that during his intercourse with us he had received nothing but the most satisfactory treatment; that he should look back to that interview with more pleasure than upon any other period of his life, and that when next we met we should meet as friends.

To Generals Lee, D.H. Hill, Stonewall Jackson, McGruder [sic] and their Medical Directors, Doctors Guild, McGuire, Mott and Medical Purveyor Johnson, are we particularly indebted for many kind attentions, and I feel assured that these gentlemen saved us from many indignities, which would otherwise have been practiced upon us. J.S.

Doc. No. 1

HEADQ'RS ARMY POTOMAC,
June 23, 1862

To the Commanding General of the Confederate forces, or the commanding officers:

Dr. Swinburne, a volunteer surgeon with a number of other surgeons, nurses and attendants have been left in charge of the sick and wounded of this army who could not be removed.

Their humane occupation recommends itself under the laws of all nations to the kind consideration of the opposing forces.

It is requested that they may be free to return as soon as the discharge of their duties with the sick and wounded shall permit, and that the same consideration shown to the Confederate sick, wounded and medical officers who have been captured by our forces, may be extended to them.

A large amount of clothing, bedding, medical stores, &c., have been left both at Savage's Station and Dr. Trent's house.

By command,
Maj. Gen. McClellan.

Chas. S. Tripler,
Surg. & Med. Director Army, Potomac.

Doc. No. 2

HEADQUARTERS ARMY POTOMAC,
Camp Lincoln, Va., June 20, 1862
SPECIAL ORDER,
No. 186

12. Thirteen men of the 2nd Army Corps., ten from the 4th Army Corps, and fourteen from the 6th Provisional Army Corps, will be detailed by the corps, commanders to report to Acting Asst. Surgeon, John Swinburne, for duty at the hospital at Savage's Station.

On the requisition of acting assistant surgeon, John Swinburne, in charge of the hospital at Savage's Station, the subsistence department issue such rations, and the quartermaster's department will furnish such transportation as will be required for that hospital.

By command,
Maj. Gen. MCCLELLAN
S. Williams,
Asst. Adjt. Gen.

Doc. No. 3

GEN'L HOSP'L, SAVAGE'S ST'N, VA
July 7, 1862
Gen. Lee, C.S.A.:

Sir: Your kind favor of the 4th, which informed me of the parol [sic] of the sick and wounded, volunteer nurses, was duly received, for which please accept my kind regards. I now share you [sic] some of the circumstances which prompt me to ask an immediate removal, and enclose a letter from Dr. Skilton, in charge of Nelson and Gatewood house.

This is only a sample of the solicitations (verbal and otherwise) of the necessities of life that I am daily in receipt of, and which I am expected to furnish. I returned here yesterday and found every available place occupied during the day and night. About a hundred more wounded were brought in during the night, filling us to overflowing. Quite a change has taken place since my visit to you, induced by the crowded state of the wards, decomposing blood and filth, the sup[illegible] wounds, the exhalations from human deposits and other filth. The insufficiency of help prevent this, have rendered the place so offensive as to be almost insufferable. Typhoid fever is making its appearance among us to an alarming degree. We can accommodate no more sick and wounded, since what are here are suffering so severely from the combined influences of malaria and putrefaction. Yesterday we had a number of deaths, and mostly from typhoid fever. Four of our physicians are on the sick list, leaving us too few effective workers for our two thousand sick and wounded.

Yesterday two of our most valuable civilian nurses were stricken down, one with diarrhea, the other typhoid fever. In fact all the physicians are ready to succumb at any moment. Yesterday a Virginia gentlemen came in and said about thirty of our men were sick from [illegible] at his house, and he wanted me to give an order for their immediate removal to our place. I said I would send them food as I could, but that they could not be removed to our place, for the obvious reason we had no room, and I knew of no other place they could be removed to.

I ordered the captain of the ambulance train to transport no more to this place until further orders; but that he must concentrate the remaining portion at the Nelson and Gatewood House until I could communicate with you. Now in view of all these facts and circumstances, I do not know that I can better do than to wait the action of your authorities, which I hope, for the sake of humanity, will be very speedy. I am most fully assured that you will do all that you can; and I hope therefore that I shall be pardoned for the solicitude which I manifest, as in fact I know I shall be when you knew the condition to which we are reduced. We at this time request fresh meats for soups, stimulants, bread; and in fact there is scarcely anything we don't require, except salt meat. I cannot ask a supply of all these. I only ask you to carry into immediate effect the condition of the parol which you were kind enough to promise us on the 4th. If this is to be done, let it, in the name of Christianity, be effect without delay. Now for every 20 sick and wounded, I require a day and night nurse—equal to 400, besides cooks, water and wood carriers, stewards, and so forth; instead of which, we have not more than 150, including some of the crippled. I write this, not in a complaining spirit, but simply to give you a full knowledge of our condition.

Now in view of the suffering of the sick and wounded, I would respectfully ask as a favor (in the name of the surgeons with whom I am associated, and into whose hands our wounded have fallen), that we communicate with our Government directly at Washington, to the end that they shall ask of your authorities the parol the sick and wounded, in accordance with the contents of your kind note of the 4th instant; and also that we be transmitted directly to our lines (under a flag of truce), to the most eligible point not inconsistent with the interest of your government, and that the sick and wounded be left at Savage's Station, and there cared for, pending this favor.

I am, respectfully yours,

John Swinburne,

Surg. in Charge

(Doc. No. 4)[32]

SAVAGES STATION, VA, July 15th, 1862

Received of Dr. John Swinburne all the medicines, hospital stores, tents, &c., including the U.S. property left at Savage's Station hospital, except such as were used for the comfort of the sick and wounded.

(Signed) Jas. T. Johnson,

Surg. C.S.A., Med. Pur. Dep., N.V.

(Doc. No. 5)

Invoice of Medicines, & c., Issued to Surg. John Swinburne, U.S.A., in Charge of Savage's Station Hospital.

B.

Surg.: James T. Johnson, Med. Purveyor, C.S.A.

Camphora	lb.,	1		Opii,	lb.,	1/4
Cerate Simp.,	lb.,	1		Tr. Ferri Chlor.,	lb.,	1/2
Emp. adhesive,	yds.,	5		Whiskey,	galls.,	5
Iodine,	oz.,	1		Band'ges (rolls),	doz.,	6
Oleum Terebinth,	blts	1		Lint,	lb.,	1

I certify that the articles have been issued as above, and that they were delivered to Dr. John Swinburne, at Savage's Station.

Signed, Jas. T. Johnson,
Surg. and Med. Purveyor, D.N.V.
HD.QTS., D.N.V.
July 19th, 1862

(Doc. No. 6)

GEN. HOSPITAL, SAVAGE'S STATION, VA,
July 20, 1862

A meeting of Surgeons was held this day, for the purpose of appointing Dr. Swinburne to purchase fresh meat for the sick and wounded at this hospital; said sick and wounded now suffering for the want of these articles being unprovided for by the Confederate authorities.

The meeting being called to order,

Dr. Churchill was elected President, and J.P. Middleton, Secretary.

Drs. Schell, Nordman and Page were duly appointed to draw up resolutions, and offered the following:

Resolved, 1st, That the bacon and flour, the only food at present furnished us by the Confederate government, is totally inadequate as a diet for many, if not most, of the wounded men in our charge.

Resolved, 2d, That some strong soup, made from fresh meat, is absolutely necessary to save the lives of many of our patients; and that we hereby request Dr. Swinburne to purchase such sheep or beeves as he may deem best adapted to the case, and earnestly recommend to the U.S. Government that the purchase-money thereof be refunded.

On motion, the resolutions were adopted.

(Approved)

A. Churchill, Ch'm, and Surg. 14 N.Y.V.

P. Middleton, Sec'y, A.A.U.S.A.

H.H. Page, Vol. Surg. U.S.A.

N. Milner, A.A. Surg. U.S.A.

A. Palmer, A. Surg. 2d Me.

O. Munson, A. Surg. N.Y.V.

E.J. Marsh, A. Surg. U.S.A.

H.I. Schell, A. Surg. U.S.A.

W.A. Smith, A.A. Surg. U.S.A.

A.P. Clark, A. Surg. 37 N.Y.V.

G.F. Perkins, A. Assist. Surg. 22 Mass. V.

Wm. Faulkner, Surg. 83 Pa. V.

On motion, the meeting adjourned.

(Doc. No. 7)

GEN'L HOSPITAL, SAVAGE'S STATION, VA,
July 23, 1862
Dr. Gould:[33]

Sir—I regret, exceedingly, to again trouble you, but, under the circumstances, I must call your attention to a fact which I have before stated to you that "some of our surgeons are sick." One of them breathed his last yesterday afternoon. Some others are still sick, and all are more or less unwell. Lieut. Johnson, the commandant of this place is now very sick, as is also several of his men. Lieut. Lacey Stewart has recovered, and has gone to Richmond, to-day, to procure rations for the patients. I feel as if I could not resist, much longer, the combined influences of this pus-generating place, and the insufficiency of flour and bacon, as food. It is not, however, for myself that I am so anxious. I have, in my keeping, many valuable lives, and I feel that every exertion, on my part, is due to them, to the end that they may be spared to their families.

In view of these facts I have purchased two sheep, daily, from my own funds, and have converted them into soup for the patients, hoping that it might contribute, somewhat, to their physical force during this trying ordeal. I trust, therefore, you will continue to exert your benign influence, in behalf of suffering nature, so long as our necessities remain in the present status, or until we can all be removed to our own homes. I have to thank you for many kind attentions which I can never repay, or which, at least, I never expect to repay in the same way. So also, Gen. Lee's attentions have surprised me, since he is burdened with a thousand cares incident to a life like his. I can only attribute it to his sympathy with those in distress, whether friend or foe. Now, sir, will it be possible for me, or some one of us, to go on with these sick surgeons, who are delicate, and place them on board our transports, and so superintend the removal of our sick and wounded. I hope you will excuse this constant interruption in affairs, since my whole heart is set on getting proper food for the sick and wounded. For myself it matters little, but please don't allow us to remain in Richmond over night.

I am, respectfully,
(Signed)J. Swinburne,
Surg. in Charge

(Doc. No. 8)

GENERAL HOSPITAL, SAVAGE'S STATION, VA,
July 24, 1862
Gen. Winder:

Sir,—I address you, at this time, in behalf of the sick and wounded soldiers, now in confinement in your city and at this place. I had supposed, from assurances received from the Medical Directors and Purveyors of the Confederate Army, that we should not be retained, any time, within your lines, and hence we remained quiet, and have so continued, until forbearance ceases to be a virtue. When I send a surgeon to look after the interests of the sick and wounded, you place him in a lock-up, where he can do no good, and can only see patients under guard. Only two of these surgeons have returned, and their report is a sad one.

I send you a copy of my instructions, from Gen. McClellan, and ask you

1st. If I can visit the places where the sick and wounded are imprisoned, and again return to this place without any obstructions or delay.

2nd. Are we at liberty to return to our lines, in accordance with these instructions, of course under proper regulations which you shall specify are arrange.

3rd. Can I send or take some of our surgeons (who are ill) to our transports, that they may recuperate. If they stay here they are sure to die. Yesterday we paid the last sad tribute to a departed surgeon of our army: others will soon go unless soon relieved.

4th. Can we have rations, suitable for the sick and wounded. I am sure you do not know the limited, and in some instances the absolute bad character of the food furnished for us all. Up to three days since the only rations furnished us was flour and bacon. Yesterday we had rations sent, for three days, consisting of good flour, while the bacon and shoulders were absolutely filled with maggots.

Now if you judge this the kind food furnished your sick and wounded prisoners North, as is in accordance with the usages of war among civilized nations, you are mistaken. I have had to buy fresh meats for soups and bread to supply the deficiency, since we have no means of cooking flour suitable to the sick. Now I submit that flour and poor bacon are entirely unfit for the sick and wounded, since many have died from sheer exhaustion or starvation, and many more will die unless better fed. Many of those taken to Richmond and detained so long in the depot, without proper attention, have also died. Now, sir, all I ask is, to have the sick and wounded, who have become the recipients of my care, receive the attentions due them, as prisoners of war, agreeable to the usages of civilized people, and that the surgeons, to whose care they are intrusted, be treated, not as felons, but in accordance with the precedents which have been established, and which you publish, in all your papers, as the laws of the land. If we cannot be fed, in accordance with the common usages of war, in other words, if you have not the material wherewith to feed us, so as to keep us from starvation, I feel assured that your elevated sense of humanity will assist us to reach our own lines, where we can be attended to. I have seen and attended your sick and wounded at New York, Philadelphia, Fort Monroe, and in this hospital, and have never seen any distinction made between them and our own. Now, with the insufficient nourishment supplied us, our funds failing, what are we to do? I leave the answer to your impulses of humanity and ask you, in the name of the common obligations due from man to man, that you interpose your dictums and change the status of our condition.

I am, respectfully, &c.,

John Swinburne,
Surgeon in Charge

(Doc. No. 9)

July 26th, 1862.

Sir—Since penning the preceding note, that your people neglected to send to you, I have to announce the death of Dr. Millnor, whose demise was very sudden. He was one of our most respected brothers, and died with his armor on, and evidently from sheer starvation or exhaustion. I am down with a from of diarrhea, somewhat like cholera, stools being soapy and watery, and exhausts me exceedingly and keeps me confined to the bed—I have by the concurrence of all the surgeons present, purchased daily, fresh meat, which has been made into soup for the sick and wounded, while we surgeons have eaten bacon and shoulder, the majority of which is absolutely bad, being maggoty. Now, my dear Doctor, in the name of common professional friendship, do interpose in our behalf that we may leave this place. After the 2,000 sick and wounded left for Richmond we had 16 surgeons, two of whom have died from inanition, and several more will follow unless very soon relieved. I am certain that my strength cannot hold out long; others are complaining from nervous exhaustion. We have no soap, no candles or anything else, except flour and poor bacon. If we go to Richmond we are thrown into prison, as the rest of the surgeons have been. What is our remedy? In this dilemma, we appeal to you, since no official, outside of our profession, unless it is General Lee, would take any interest in our affairs - do come and see us that you may act intelligently, and from your own observations. I don't want to die here, and I know the other surgeons don't, and besides your assured me that we were not to be prisoners, but would be allowed to leave by application to the proper authorities, when our services ceased to be useful to the sick and wounded; and this status I claim now exists for the majority of us, and has so existed for some days, and particularly for the sick and wounded surgeons, since four of the well are amply sufficient for the labor, taking into consideration the facilities with which we are surrounded.

An early answer is solicited.

I have the honor to be,

Very respectfully your obd't servant,

John Swinburne,

Surgeon in Charge

P.S.—Will you have the kindness to submit these documents to General Lee,
  And oblige
  J.S.

(Doc. No. 10.)

CAMP NEAR GEN. LEE'S HEADQUARTERS,
July 25th, 1862

Sir—Your communication relative to the suffering condition of the Federal sick and wounded at Savage's Station, has just been received. I will at the earliest possible time submit what you have written to me to the General, and suggest that you and your sick and wounded be conveyed without delay to your own lines.

The purchase of fresh meat being indispensably necessary for the use of your hospital, is approved by me as far as my official position is concerned and I have no doubt the General himself will approve it.

I trust there will be no difficulty in your proceeding directly to City Point without hindrance or molestation, as you anticipate in your letters. I will ask the authorities to provide against such interruption in Richmond.

Very respectfully your obd't servant,
L. Guild,
Surg. and Med. Director D.N.V.

To Dr. John Swinburne, Surgeon in charge of Federal Hospital, Savage's Station.

(Doc. No. 11.)

SURGEON GENERAL'S OFFICE.
Washington City, Aug. 18th, 1862

Sir—Your communication of the 7th inst. has been received. The Surgeon General accepts your resignation, and in doing so he desires me to render you his sincere thanks, for the very faithful and able manner in which you have performed the duties to which you have been assigned.

Very respectfully your obd't servant,

By order C. H. Alden

Assistant Surgeon, U.S.A.

Dr. JOHN SWINBURNE , Albany, N.Y. [Addressee]
Official Compliment to Dr. Swinburne.

STATE OF NEW YORK,

SURGEON GENERAL'S OFFICE

Albany, August 5, 1862.

Sir: I am requested by his Excellency, GOV. MORGAN, to express his high appreciation of the service rendered by you while serving with the Army of the Potomac, as Medical Superintendent of the forces from this State, and Acting Assistant Surgeon of the United States Army, and to return you thanks for the same.

An expression thus officially made is not intended as invidious to the noble corps of Volunteer Surgeons, who so promptly and faithfully gave their time, their energies, their professional abilities, and in some instances their life, to ameliorate their sufferings of the wounded; but that the position in which you were placed by the authorities of the State, the peculiar circumstances which resulted therefrom, and the manner in which you conducted yourself, both professionally and as the representative, for the time, of your Government, call for, as it is most cheerfully bestowed, the commendation and approval, not only of the constituted authorities, but of a whole community, who have watched, with vivid interest, the responsibilities, privations and labors to which you were subjected.

As the head of the State Medical Bureau, I cannot forego the opportunity of thanking you for the bright example your labors have furnished of Conservative Surgery upon the field of battle.

Had you, merely, in the performance of your labors, done all which humanity demands, you would have merited the compliment proffered; but to that you have added the exercise of high professional skill. When in a hospital of two thousand sick and wounded, you amputated less than half a dozen limbs, but strove rather to save, by execution, you illustrated and carried out the views of the most intelligent of the profession.

Wishing you, in your safe return to your family and friends, the enjoyment of a well-merited confidence, I am, with respect, your obedient servant,

(Signed) S. OAKLEY VANDERPOEL
Surgeon General
JOHN SWINBURNE, M.D. [Addressee]

* * *

John Swinburne served as health officer for the port of New York in 1864 and was in charge of the American Ambulance Corps in Paris during the Franco-Prussian War in 1870-1871. He became mayor of Albany 1882 and a member of the U.S. House of Representatives in 1885, serving until 1887. Swinburne died March 28, 1889, and was buried in Albany Rural Cemetery.[34]

"Weather Still Execrable":

Climatological Notes on the Peninsula Campaign, March through August 1862

Occasionally, viewers of the long and varied cavalcade of military history catch a glimpse of an extraordinary commander who, with relentless determination, pursues his goals regardless of all obstacles, including, perhaps especially, the weather. Thomas J. "Stonewall" Jackson was one such general. He seems to have discounted heat and cold entirely and on one notable August 1862 march drove his columns 54 miles in two days under killing Virginian sun. George S. Patton heeded the weather in December 1944 enough to beseech the Almighty "to restrain these immoderate rains," but the general did not wait for Divine compliance. Patton pushed the bulk of his 250,000-man III Army 75 miles in less than a week over slippery roads and through snow and bitter cold to relieve the garrison at Bastogne.[1] The unofficial spokesman for this fraternity of galvanized generals might well be that extraordinary soldier of the 18th century Field Marshal Prince Alexander V.

Suvorov, who once told a subordinate general, "only women, dandies and lazy-bones need good weather."[2]

But most of history's commanders, good, bad or superb, would likely agree with British military historian and theorist Maj. Gen. J. F. C. Fuller, who wrote:

> Weather is not only to a great extent a controller of the condition of the ground, but also of movement. It is scarcely necessary to point out the influence of heat and cold on the human body, or the effect of rain, fog, and frost on tactical and administrative mobility; but it is necessary to appreciate the moral effect of weather and climate, for in the past stupendous mistakes have resulted through deficiency in this appreciation.[3]

Whether Fuller counted Maj. Gen. George B. McClellan's Peninsula Campaign among those "stupendous mistakes" we will never know, but no student of the campaign can fail to detect weather as an important theme in the letters, diaries and post-war writings of the soldiers and sailors who were there.

Drawing conclusions about the effects of the weather on the armies during the campaign has been difficult because we have lacked a broad picture of what the climate was like. Though precise meteorological data for March through August 1862 in the Virginia Tidewater is not available, participants did leave a wealth of unscientific observations of the weather, which offers a window on the physical atmosphere in which the two armies grappled.

Precipitation largely determines the comfort of humans living out of doors or under canvas, so it is not surprising that the observations presented below focus on rainfall. This is convenient in helping to answer questions about the conduct of the campaign. For example, having an idea how wet the roads were or how high the rivers might have been can tell us much about why generals moved columns as they did, why troops performed as they did on marches and on battlefields and why the armies, specifically McClellan's, seemed to sit "idle" for long periods.

This investigation into weather during the campaign begins with the goal of answering two questions: How much rain fell and was that amount extraordinary? Part 1 below, a climatological journal, presents data to help answer the first question, and Part 2, comparative historical data, place the spring and summer of 1862 in context relative to "average" weather in the Tidewater.

Part 1: Climatological Journal of the Peninsula Campaign

This journal reports at least one remark on the weather for each day of the campaign. On days when more than one comment was available, the journal presents observations from as broad an area as possible, generally one account from the area of the James River another from the Pamunkey-York drainage and a third from the land someplace in between—usually along the Warwick or Chickahominy Rivers. These multiple readings, of course, help present a broader, more accurate picture of the weather in the region on a given day. All temperatures are given in degrees farenheit.

In the interest of eliminating much repetition, abbreviated citations will refer to the following sources: Without exception, observations attributed to U.S. Navy gunboats—the *U.S.S. Chocura*, *U.S.S. Currituck*, *U.S.S. Galena*, *U.S.S. Port Royal* and *U.S.S. Sebago* inclusive—derive from the deck log of the cited ship in Record Group (RG) 24, National Archives, Washington, DC. Observations attributed to Brigadier General Samuel P. Heintzelman are recorded in his "Pocket Diary" in the Samuel P. Heintzelman Papers, Manuscript Division of the Library of Congress, microfilm reel 1, beginning on frame 736. All observations by Flag Officer Louis M. Goldsborough are recorded in his letters to his wife and daughter in the Louis M. Goldsborough Papers, Manuscript Division of the Library of Congress. Lt. Charles Haydon of the 2nd Michigan Infantry often commented on the weather in diary, and his remarks have been quoted here as reproduced in *For Country, Cause & Leader: The Civil War Journal of Charles B. Haydon*, Stephen W. Sears, ed. (New York, 1993). Observations from Pvt. Charles C. Perkins derive from his diary, part of the Civil War Times Illustrated Collection, U.S.A.M.H.I., Carlisle Barracks, Pennsylvania. Richard J. Sommers published an edited portion of Perkins's diary as "The Civil War Diary of Pvt. Charles C. Perkins, 1st Massachusetts Infantry Regiment, June 4-July 4, 1862," in *The Peninsula Campaign of 1862: Yorktown to the Seven Days*, William J. Miller, ed., 3 vols. (Savas Woodbury, Campbell, Cal.), vol. 1, pp. 143-176.

March 10: Gunboat *U.S.S. Currituck*, at anchor in Hampton Roads: "fair and clear"

11: *Currituck* in Hampton Roads: clear

12: *Currituck* in Hampton Roads: "pleasant"

13: *Currituck* in Hampton Roads: "fine pleasant weather"

14: *Currituck* in Hampton Roads: predawn "thick, rainy weather," foggy all day

15: *Currituck* in Hampton Roads: "thick & foggy"

16: *Currituck* in Hampton Roads: "fine and pleasant"

17: Peninsula Campaign Begins—Federal troops debark from Alexandria, Virginia, for Fort Monroe, Virginia, beginning the Peninsula Campaign. *Currituck* in Hampton Roads: "fine"

18*: Currituck* in Hampton Roads: "fine, pleasant all day"

19: *Currituck* in Hampton Roads: clear, rain in the evening and through the night

20: *Currituck* in Hampton Roads: predawn "unpleasant," strong winds, afternoon rain, storms at night

21: *Currituck* in Hampton Roads: "thick, foggy," rain in morning, showers and "unpleasant" throughout afternoon

22: *Currituck* in Hampton Roads: clear morning, cloudy afternoon

23: Lt. Charles Haydon, 2nd Michigan Infantry, in camp at Hampton, Va.: "cold & unpleasant" moderate rain at night; Currituck in Hampton Roads: "pleasant"

24: Haydon at Hampton: "hard frost" at night; Currituck in Hampton Roads: clear, evening squalls

25: *Currituck* in Hampton Roads: "fine & pleasant"

26: Haydon at Hampton: "light flurry of snow" at night; Currituck in Hampton Roads: cloudy, snow and rain in afternoon

27: *Currituck* in Hampton Roads: "pleasant"

28: Haydon at Hampton: "warm & fair," "rain & high wind" at night; *Currituck* in Hampton Roads: "fine and clear, beautiful blue sky"

29: Haydon at Hampton: beginning at noon, "very cold driving rain with occasional hail" throughout the day; *Currituck* in Hampton Roads: Strong winds, stormy, heavy rain in evening

30: Currituck in Hampton Roads: thick clouds, stormy, foggy

31: Currituck in Hampton Roads: "clear & pleasant"

April 1: *Currituck* in Hampton Roads: "clear & pleasant"

2: Haydon at Hampton: "cold & raw"; *Currituck* in Hampton Roads: clear morning, "unpleasant" afternoon through the evening

3: *Currituck* in Hampton Roads: "clear & pleasant," "beautiful" evening

4: Siege of Yorktown Begin—*Currituck* in Hampton Roads: cloudy, thunderstorms at night

5: Haydon near Big Bethel, Virginia: "hard shower of rain"; *Currituck* in Hampton Roads: "squally" morning, "thick & cloudy," "beautiful" afternoon

6: Lt. Col. B. S. Alexander, U.S. Engineers, at Yorktown: "It was a clear day, with a high wind";[4] Brig. Gen. Samuel P. Heintzelman, commander Third Corps, at Yorktown: rain; *Currituck* in Hampton Roads: "foggy at night

7: Haydon before Yorktown: in the morning "cold with a raw east wind," evening and throughout the night "heavy, cold, east rain"; Currituck at anchor in the York River at the mouth of Cheeseman's Creek: "unpleasant, stormy weather"; Heintzelman before Yorktown: rain

8: *Currituck* anchored in Cheeseman's Creek: "cold & rain"; Maj. Gen. George B. McClellan, commander, Army of the Potomac, before Yorktown: "Weather terrible; raining heavily last twenty-eight hours; roads and camps in awful condition";[5] Haydon before Yorktown: "very cold, the rain lacks very little of being snow"

9: Haydon before Yorktown: "storm continues with little intermission. . . .air full of fog & mist."; Flag Officer Louis M. Goldsborough, aboard flagship *U.S.S. Minnesota* in Hampton Roads: "blowing a strong gale of wind from the North + East" "overcast" "raining" "Chilly, + quite cold for the season"; McClellan before Yorktown: "weather still execrable; country covered with water; roads terrible"[6]

10: *Currituck* in Cheeseman's Creek: cloudy with rain; Heintzelman before Yorktown: drizzle; Haydon before Yorktown: snow squalls about 11 a.m., some sun in the afternoon

11: *Currituck* in Cheeseman's Creek: "clear & pleasant"

12: *Currituck* at anchor in the York River below Yorktown: "fine, pleasant weather"

13: *Currituck* below Yorktown: "fine"

14: *Currituck* below Yorktown: "pleasant"; Heintzelman before York-town: rain at night

15: *Currituck* below Yorktown: morning squalls, "pleasant" afternoon; Heintzelman before Yorktown: morning shower; Haydon before Yorktown: "warm & fine in the afternoon"

16: **Battle of Dam No. 1**—*Currituck* below Yorktown: "pleasant"; Heintzelman before Yorktown: "Beautiful"

17: Goldsborough, aboard flagship *Minnesota* in Hampton Roads: "weather delightful" "summer's temperature"

18: Currituck below Yorktown: "clear with a cool breeze"; Heintzelman before Yorktown: 84 degrees

19: Heintzelman before Yorktown: "cloudy & some rail—rain at night"; Goldsborough, aboard *Minnesota* in Hampton Roads: "weather is delightfully pleasant"

20: *Currituck* below Yorktown: "cloudy with rain, a gale at night"; Heintzelman before Yorktown: 52 degrees at noon; Haydon before Yorktown: "weather moist"

21: *Currituck* below Yorktown: "predawn drizzle, foggy, heavy rain in afternoon"; Haydon before Yorktown: "fine. . .rained horribly nearly all night"

22: *Currituck* below Yorktown: "pleasant"; Heintzelman before York-town: rain

23: Heintzelman before Yorktown: "cool night, clear & windy, rain at night"; Goldsborough, aboard Minnesota in Hampton Roads: "Sunny"

24: *Currituck* below Yorktown: "pleasant"

25: *Currituck* below Yorktown: "cloudy, rain at night"; Heintzelman before Yorktown: "cloudy and disagreeable," 48 degrees all day

26: Haydon before Yorktown: "cold, dismal, rainy day."; Gunboat *U.S.S. Galena* anchored off Fort Monroe: "stormy," 47 degrees at 1 p.m., "cold, murky weather" at night

27: *Galena* off Fort Monroe: "thick, cold weather with rain," 50 degrees 6 p.m. to 9 p.m.

28: Haydon before Yorktown: morning "fine"; *Galena* off Fort Monroe: "cloudy with a light wind," 50 degrees at night

29: Haydon before Yorktown: "fine"; *Galena* off Fort Monroe: pre-dawn fog with a light wind, afternoon storms, 62 degrees at 1 p.m., 57 degrees 4 p.m. to 9 p.m., 51 degrees 10 p.m. to midnight

30: *Galena* off Fort Monroe: "cold and stormy," 50 degrees; Heintzelman before Yorktown: "Cloudy, damp, chilly in morning, turned to rain"

May 1: Heintzelman before Yorktown: rain at night; Galena off Fort Monroe: "calm, mild weather," 60s in morning

2: *Galena* off Fort Monroe: "fine weather + very warm," 60s in morning

3: *Galena* off Fort Monroe: "light wind and pleasant weather"

4: *Galena* off Fort Monroe: cloudy and pleasant

5: **The Battle of Williamsburg**—Heintzelman before Williamsburg: rain begins about 2:30 a.m.; *Galena* off Fort Monroe: heavy rain at night, low 60s at night

6: Heintzelman at Williamsburg: "Skies Clear About Midnight"; *Galena* off Fort Monroe: pleasant with a strong wind, low 60s

7: **Engagement at Eltham's Landing**—Heintzelman west of Williamsburg: "beautiful day"; Galena off Fort Monroe: pleasant, 55 before dawn, high 60s through the morning

8: Heintzelman west of Williamsburg: "beautiful day, Roads drying fast"; Galena on patrol in the mouth of the James River: "fine weather," a strong breeze

9: Heintzelman west of Williamsburg: "beautiful day"; Galena aground in James River: "Light breezes, pleasant"

10: Heintzelman near Barhamsville: "Windy in the afternoon"; Galena aground in James River: cloudy in the morning with temperatures in the high 60s, clear in the afternoon

11: Heintzelman at Barhamsville: "cool wind in morning, afternoon rain"; *Galena* on patrol in the mouth of the James River: "clear and pleasant," high 60s in the afternoon

12: Heintzelman at Barhamsville: "Cool morning, pleasant"; Galena on patrol in the James River: High 70s

13: Heintzelman at Barhamsville: "Cool morning, pleasant"

14: McClellan near Cumberland: rain all night,[7] Zone 2 - Heintzelman at Barhamsville: "Threatening rain; *Galena* in the James River below Drewry's Bluff: rain 6 p.m. to 8 p.m.

15: McClellan near Cumberland: "Another wet horrid day!"[8] McClellan again: "very cool, wet and dreary";[9] Heintzelman near Cumberland: "Rain continues"; *Galena* at Drewry's Bluff in the James River: "slight rain," Gunboat *U.S.S Port Royal* with Galena at 6 p.m.: light east-northeast winds, rainy

16: McClellan at White House Landing: rain, Heintzelman at White House Landing: "clearing off"; *Galena* below Drewry's Bluff: "fine weather"

17: McClellan at White House Landing: "Clear and very hot";[10] Heintzelman at Slatersville: "Beautiful, clear, pleasant day"

18: Heintzelman at Slatersville: "Quite pleasant," some rain"; *Galena* in the James above Bermuda Hundred: pleasant, clear and warm

19: *Galena* in the James above Bermuda Hundred: "pleasant," a light rain in the afternoon; Heintzelman near the Chickahominy: "Beautiful morning"; Capt. J. Howard Kitching, Battery B, 2nd New York Artillery, near the Chickahominy: "raining like fun"[11]

20: Heintzelman on the Chickahominy: "Beautiful day, rain at night;" *Galena* at anchor in the mouth of the Appomattox River: "thick fog" in morning, a fine morning with temperatures in the low 70s, heavy rain in the night

21: Heintzelman on the Chickahominy: "Heavy rain"; Galena in the mouth of the Appomattox River: "fine weather" with temperatures in the high 70s

22: Heintzelman on the Chickahominy: "night quite warm"; Galena in the mouth of the Appomattox River: cloudy, low 80s

23: Heintzelman on the Chickahominy: "Pleasant day, but getting warm, 80 degrees"; *Galena* in the mouth of the Appomattox River: "fine weather," 85 degrees at 4 p.m.

24: Correspondent for the *New York Times* near the Chickahominy: "The day was charming";[12] Heintzelman near Savage's Station: rain begins at 8 a.m., continues all day; *Galena* in the mouth of the Appomattox River: heavy rain in the morning, rain in the afternoon, temperatures in the 70s

25: *Galena* in the mouth of the Appomattox River: cloudy, temperatures in the low 70s

26: McClellan at New Bridge: rain from 3 p.m. onward,[13] Heintzelman on the Chickahominy: "Heavy rain at night"; Galena in the mouth of the Appomattox: "cold, cloudy," temperature in the low 70s, rain in the night

27: **The Battle of Hanover Court House or Slash Church**—Heintzelman near Savage's Station: Clearing in morning, "Roads now Passable"; *Galena* in the mouth of the Appomattox: rain in the morning, "fine" at night

28: Heintzelman on the Chickahominy: "Beautiful day"; Galena in the mouth of the Appomattox: rain squalls in the afternoon

29: Heintzelman on the Chickahominy: "Beautiful day"; Galena in the mouth of the Appomattox: "pleasant"

30: Heintzelman near Savage's Station: "tolerably pleasant"; Galena in the mouth of the Appomattox: clear, mid 80s in the afternoon, heavy thunderstorms at night

31: **The Battle of Seven Pines or Fair Oaks**—Heintzelman on the Chickahominy: "clearing"; *Galena* in the mouth of the Appomattox: Temperatures in the low 80s in the afternoon[14]

June 1: The Battle of Seven Pines or Fair Oaks (continues)—*Galena* in the mouth of the Appomattox: light rain in the morning, pleasant, mid-80s in the afternoon

2: Heintzelman at Seven Pines: "Heavy thunderstorm at night"; *Galena* at anchor in the James River above the mouth of the Appomattox River: pre-dawn rain squalls, clear, warm afternoon, 89 degrees at noon

3: Heintzelman at Seven Pines: mid 90s, "Heavy rain all night"; *Galena* in the James River above the Appomattox River: heavy shower about 1 a.m., cloudy afternoon, 80s through the day, 89 degrees at 2 p.m.

4: Private Charles C. Perkins, 1st Massachusetts Infantry at Seven Pines: "still raining very hard"; Heintzelman at Seven Pines: rains stops at 9 a.m., high wind; *Galena* at anchor above the mouth of the Appomattox: heavy rain all morning, cloudy afternoon, mid-70s, frequent showers at night

5: Perkins at Seven Pines: "Cloudy morn but sun out occasionally"; Heintzelman at Seven Pines: not raining, but "weather's uncertain. . .I am trying to dry my things"; Galena at anchor above the mouth of the Appomattox: predawn rain, cloudy day, 75 degrees at 1 p.m..

6: Perkins at Seven Pines: pre-dawn rain, "misty"; Galena anchored in the James: cloudy, mid-60s.

7: McClellan at New Bridge: "The sun is struggling very hard this morning with the clouds";[15] Heintzelman at Seven Pines: thunderstorm about 3:30 p.m.; *Galena* anchored in the James: cloudy, mid-70s, afternoon rain squall.

8: Perkins at Seven Pines: "Cloudy & sunshine by spells today"; Galena anchored in the James: heavy rain in the morning, cloudy afternoon, 68-75 degrees, "fine evening"

9: Heintzelman at Seven Pines: "Pleasant day"; Perkins at Seven Pines: rain at night; *Galena* anchored in the James: clear, 60s in morning, low 70s in afternoon

10: Perkins at Seven Pines: "rained last night and all today"; McClellan at New Bridge: "It is again raining hard";[16] Galena anchored in the James: "cold rain" in the morning, "cold and cloudy" in the afternoon, 50s, evening rain

11: Perkins at Seven Pines: full moon; McClellan at New Bridge: weather "good";[17] Galena anchored in the James: "cold and cloudy" in morning, 70s and "pleasant" in afternoon

12: *Galena* anchored in the James: "clear and pleasant," low 80s through afternoon

13: **Stuart's "Ride Around McClellan" Begins**—*Galena* anchored in the James: "fine weather," mid-80s

14: Heintzelman at Seven Pines: "Very warm," over 90 degrees; Perkins at Seven Pines: evening "warm"; *Galena* anchored in the James: "fine weather," 85-92 degrees

15: **Stuart's "Ride Around McClellan" Ends**—Heintzelman at Seven Pines: over 90 degrees, Perkins at Seven Pines: "Very warm"; Private Wilbur Fisk, 2nd Vermont Infantry, near the Chickahominy: "heavy thundershower";[18] Galena anchored in the James: "fine" in morning, heavy rains and squalls through afternoon and evening, low-90s

16: Heintzelman at Savage's Station: 57 degrees in morning; McClellan at Dr. Trent's: "Splendid";[19] *Galena* anchored in the James: clear, mid-70s

17: Heintzelman at Savage's Station: "Pleasant morning but warm afternoon," McClellan at Dr. Trent's: "Splendid"[20]; Galena anchored in the James at the mouth of the Appomattox River: fair and clear, high 70s

18: *Galena* anchored in the James at the mouth of the Appomattox River: "pleasant", 78-81 degrees, evening squall; Capt. J. Howard Kitching, Battery B, 2nd New York Artillery, near Fair Oaks: "Heavy shower"[21]

19: *Galena* anchored at the mouth of the Appomattox: "fine," 70s

20: Perkins at Seven Pines: "fine" evening; Galena at the mouth of the Appomattox: clear, high 70s

21: Heintzelman at Seven Pines: "warm and dusty"; Galena at anchor in the James: clear, 60s

22: McClellan at Dr. Trent's: "Quite hot this afternoon";[22] Perkins at Seven Pines: "Rained a few drops" in evening; Galena at anchor in the James: "clear and pleasant"

23: Perkins at Seven Pines: "pleasant morn," in the afternoon "Little rain and much thunder"; *Galena* at anchor in the James off Haxall's Landing: clear, 84 degrees at noon

24: *Galena* anchored in the James River below City Point: at 12 a.m., "Heavy black clouds rising to Eastward," heavy pre-dawn thunderstorms, 86 degrees at noon, cloudy afternoon with some heavy rain; Heintzelman at Seven Pines: "Afternoon Thundershower"; Perkins at Seven Pines: "Rained in torrents," and "Rain in P.M. by spells, thunder"; *Galena* below City Point: heavy evening squalls, 8 p.m. to 12 a.m. (June 25) cloudy with lightning

25: **The Battle of Oak Grove**—Heintzelman at Seven Pines: "rain in morning"; Perkins at Seven Pines: "Pleasant morn"; Galena anchored in the James River below City Point: clear, low 70s

26: **The Battle of Mechanicsville or Beaver Dam Creek**—Perkins at Seven Pines: "warm day"; *Galena* anchored in the James River below City Point: "clear and pleasant"; Capt. Weidman, 4th Pennsylvania Cavalry, near the Chickahominy: "most lovely morning"[23]

27: **The Battle of Gaines' Mill**—*Galena* anchored in the James River below City Point: "light breezes, pleasant"

28: *Currituck* and *U.S.S. Sebago* anchored in the Pamunkey River off White House Landing: "fair and still" 80-85 degrees with a faint breeze. *U.S.S. Chocura* at White House, 80 degrees at 4 p.m., wind out of southwest at 3 m.p.h., barometer holding at 30.13; Weidman near the Chickahominy: "fine morning";[24] *Galena* anchored in the James River: "warm and pleasant," 85 degrees at 1 p.m.

29: **The Battle of Savage's Station**—Maj. Heros Von Borcke, C.S.A., at White House Landing: Intensely hot, "almost tropical";[25] Pvt. Joseph P. Elliott, 71st Pennsylvania Infantry near the Chickahominy: "Cloudy and Cool";[26] Perkins at Savage's Station: "Very Warm Day,"

Heintzelman at Glendale: "Torrential Rain at night"; Galena anchored in the James River: "pleasant," 86 degrees at 2 p.m., squalls at night

30: **The Battle of Glendale or Frayser's Farm**—Perkins at Glendale: "fine morning. . .warm day"; *Galena* anchored in the James River: clear by 3 a.m.; Elliott near Glendale: very hot, clear and sunny; "Clear and pleasant all day. Wind NW"[27]

July 1: The Battle of Malvern Hill—Perkins at Malvern Hill: "Splendid morning"; *Galena* anchored in James River: clear, 74 degrees at 11 a.m.

2: Perkins at Malvern Hill: "Commenced to rain about sunrise," Heintzelman between Malvern Hill and Harrison's Landing "rained hard at night"; *Galena* in the James River: heavy rain, 60 degrees all afternoon into evening

3: *Galena* in the James: cloudy, mid-60s

4: Perkins at Harrison's Landing: "Pleasant Morning"; Galena in the James: clear

5: *Galena* in the James: clear, 73 degrees at 7 p.m.

6: *Galena* in the James: clear, low 80s in afternoon

7: *U.S.S. Port Royal* off City Point: "Calm & clear. . .warm hazy weather"

8: *Galena* in the James: high 80s in a.m., 90s in afternoon

9: *Galena* in the James: mid-90s

10: *Galena* in the James: 102 degrees at 11 a.m.

11: *Galena* in the James: low 70s

12: *Galena* in the James: mid-70s

13: *Galena* in the James: clear, high 80s

14: *Galena* in the James: clear, 90s

15: *Galena* on James: 90s in early afternoon, thunderstorm in evening

16: *Galena* in the James: low to mid-90s

17: *Galena* in the James: predawn squall, 95 degrees at 1 p.m., rain squalls in evening

18: *Galena* in the James: light predawn rain, cloudy day, 70s

19: *Galena* in the James: morning cloudy, evening clear

20: *Galena* in the James: 86 degrees 10 a.m. to noon

21: *Galena* in the James: mid-80s, cloudy afternoon, evening showers

22: *Port Royal* on the James: moderate breezes from the east. cloudy

23: *Port Royal* on the James: light southeasterly winds and cloudy, slight rain in the afternoon

24: *Port Royal* on James: calm/warm, light baffling winds and cloudy

25: *Port Royal* on James: fog in morning, calm and clear in afternoon

26: *Port Royal* in the James: fog in morning, light winds and cloudy in the afternoon

27: *Port Royal* in the James: calm and clear

28: *Port Royal* in the James: light breezes and clear

29: *Port Royal* on James: light winds from southwest and pleasant

30: *Port Royal* in the James: moderate breezes and clear

31: *Port Royal* in the James: light breeze from the west with rain all day

August 1: *Port Royal* in the James: light winds and cloudy, "pleasant"

2: *Port Royal* in the James: moderate breeze from the southwest with fine weather

3: Pvt. Henry Fogle, 9th Pennsylvania Reserves at Harrison's Landing: "wet + disagreeable"[28]

4: *Port Royal* on James near Malvern Hill: light easterly winds, clear

5: *Port Royal* near Malvern Hill: clear

6: *Port Royal* near Malvern Hill: clear

7: *Port Royal* near Malvern Hill: moderate breeze from the east, clear

8: *Port Royal* near Malvern Hill: light southwesterly winds

9: *Port Royal* in the James: calm, clear and warm

10: *Port Royal* in the James: calm and warm during the day, squall in the evening, "rainy" night

11: *Port Royal* in the James: light breeze and cloudy

12: *Port Royal* in the James: light breezes and warm, squalls in late afternoon, clear at night

13: *Port Royal* on the James near Malvern Hill: moderate breezes, clear

14: *Port Royal* on the James near Malvern Hill: light winds and clear

15: *Port Royal* on the James near Malvern Hill: light winds and cloudy

16: *Port Royal* on the James near Malvern Hill: light winds, "pleasant"

17: *Port Royal* in the James: light breezes from the north and clear

18: *Port Royal* in the James: light northeasterly winds and clear

19: *Port Royal* in the James: light easterly winds and clear

20: *Port Royal* in the James: fog in the morning, light winds and clear

21: *Port Royal* in the James: moderate southwesterly winds and cloudy with rain, "Thunder and Sharp Lightning" at night

22: *Port Royal* in the James: rain squalls before dawn, heavy rain before noon, clear and breezy in the afternoon and evening

23: *Port Royal* on the James: clear morning, increasing clouds, "Heavy squall" rising at night turning to "Heavy rain with Thunder + Lightning"

24: *Port Royal* in the James: cloudy and breezy

25: *Port Royal* in the James: cloudy and clear

26: *Port Royal* in Hampton Roads: light winds and clear

Part 2: Comparative Historical Data

Was the spring and summer of 1862 abnormally rainy in the Tidewater region? The best way to determine if rain fell in unusual amounts would be to compare the measured precipitation, in inches, during the campaign with some standard amount for the region. Unfortunately, such data is not available. Though the U.S. Army recorded climatic observations at posts in the 19th century, observations made at Fort Monroe, Norfolk or other places in the Tidewater are not available for March through August of any year.[29] It is possible, however, to determine imprecisely the number of days on which rain fell during the campaign and compare that to similar 20th century records. Such figures are presented here as the best basis for comparison.

	Years	March	April	May	June	July	Aug	Six Month Total	Annual Total
	Number of Days with Precipitation[30]								
Norfolk	1949-1978	11	10	10	9	11	11	62	115
Rich-mond	1938-1978	11	9	11	10	11	10	62	113
Tide-water Region	1862	9[31]	18	15	16	7	4[32]	69	—

These figures suggest that the spring and summer of 1862 was wetter than usual, but variables prevent a firm conclusion. First, the data from Norfolk and Richmond represent measurable rainfall—about a tenth of an inch—while the 1862 figures show any observable rainfall. Furthermore, the 1862 observations were taken at random over an area of more than 1,300 square miles—a much broader area than the historical data from Richmond and Norfolk. Admitting readings from all across the 1,300 square miles of the Peninsula rather than limiting those observations to just two fixed points, increases the chance of recording rain fall on any given day. For example, a storm might pass to the north or south of Richmond and still dump rain in the James or Pamunkey basins, then continue out to sea, missing Norfolk. Such a storm would enter the record via this journal but would not be recorded in either city. Conversely, any storm that passed over Richmond would almost certainly wet the James, Chickahominy or Pamunkey basins as well. Chiefly for these two reasons, the total number of days of rain in the Tidewater in

1862 is probably somewhat inflated beside the more precise data from Richmond and Norfolk.

While the rainfall might have been average or even a bit above average over the duration of the campaign, it is easy to see why McClellan and many of his men had the impression that the season was exceptionally wet. The showers and storms came in long stretches. In April, the Federal invaders' offensive operations were hindered by seven consecutive days of rain, and a week later rain fell for five more straight days. Late May and early June 1862 seems to have been exceptionally rainy for the Tidewater, or almost anyplace in North America, for that matter. Between May 18 and June 10—24 days—rain fell on 19 days, including each of the first 10 days of June. Soldiers reported snow on March 26 and April 10 and hail on March 29. Thunderstorms were reported on April 4, May 30, June 2, 7, 15, 23 and 24, July 15 and August 21 and 23. Beyond question, large amounts of water fell on the Peninsula that spring and summer—just when the Confederate defenders needed it most.

The diarists and gunboat crews recorded the temperatures irregularly, so we can draw no valid conclusions about air temperature during the campaign. The highest temperature presented in the above journal is 102 on July 10 recorded by the watch on the *Galena* off Harrison's Landing. The men of the *Galena* also recorded the lowest temperature—47 on April 26 off Fort Monroe, though, given the reports of snow squalls, the mercury almost certainly fell below that at some point during the campaign.

Finally, while it is true that McClellan moved his enormous army to the Peninsula with only surmises about what weather to expect, he could not say that he had not been warned to expect the worst. On February 7, 1862, almost six weeks before McClellan's first troops would set sail for the Peninsula, the editor of the *Richmond Examiner*, writing, perhaps, as much for Northern eyes as for his Southern readers, held forth on the horrors of springtime in the South. The editor so accurately described the climate and foretold the difficulties the Federals would encounter that he could have been writing after the campaign as easily as before it.[33] Given that McClellan had no reliable information about the Peninsula's climate, the following article could have been a valuable intelligence report had the Federal commander been able or willing to treat it as such.

The rains and the mire which characterize the closing months of our Southern winter, and two thirds of the succeeding spring, have at length set in. McClellan's teams can now draw little more than the mere wagons they are hitched to, and his artillery is mud-bound. The grand advance is checked in mid career; and it is well for his great armies that they have not got further from water and railroad transportation that this soft weather has found them. What his generals and their soldiers see now of Southern roads and Southern rains they must expect to witness continually for four months to come; and the wisest of them must admit that the South is still master of the situation. Better that our enemy should be far from home, and carrying on a distant offensive war, than that we should be separated by like distances from our supplies; and we doubt not the judgment of a majority of the adversary troops would now vote their winter campaign a failure.

Supplies must be carried at great cost and hazard, and the larger the invading column the greater its peril. The experience of Napoleon in Russia is repeated here, and an invading army may be annihilated by hunger and the natural elements without the firing of a hostile gun.

The season for locomotion is over for a period, and the deep loams of Kentucky will be found as impassable as the red and chocolate clays of the Potomac. A truce for some months has been proclaimed by the skies, and the Yankees will find the decree compulsory. Unlike the winter of the North, which is a season of dry snow, firm roads and facile locomotion, the winter of the South is a season of rains, mud and mire, in which man and beast must have shelter and in-door quiet, or encounter pleurisies, pneumonia and diptheria, at the risk of life.

In blind disregard of the nature of our Southern seasons, he has allowed the dry season of fall and early winter to pass him by, and has been thrown upon the seasons of rain and mud, which terminate in those of malignant fevers and fatal congestions, for prosecuting his operations.

Henceforth, for four months, the very magnitude of his armies will be the chief source of his disasters. To supply with provisions and munitions the large force of Burnside, on the stormy coast of Carolina, will cause loss, delay, shipwreck and privation in continual repetition. . . .The rains will fill the swamps and turn dry land into quagmire. If his troops push their invasion into the interior, they will have to become amphibious, and borrow some of the qualities of alligators and mud turtles. Instead of marching, they will have to wade against the secessionists.

NOTES

DARK PORTENTS:

CONFEDERATE COMMAND AT THE BATTLE OF WILLIAMSBURG
Steven E. Woodworth

1. Gustavus Woodson Smith, *Confederate War Papers* (New York, 1884), pp. 46; U.S. War Department, *The War of the Rebellion: the Official Records of the Union and Confederate Armies*, 128 vols. (Washington, D.C., 1890-1901), Series I, vol. 11, pt. 1, p. 602. Hereinafter cited as *OR*; all references are to series I unless otherwise noted; Stephen W. Sears, *To the Gates of Richmond: The Peninsula Cmpaign* (New York, 1992), p. 61.

2. Sears, *To the Gates of Richmond*, pp. 47, 68-69; Smith, *Confederate War Papers*, pp. 41-42; Joseph E. Johnston, *Narrative of Military Operations* (New York, 1874), pp. 114-115; Jefferson Davis, *Rise and Fall of the Confederate Government* 2 vols. (New York, 1881), vol. 2, pp. 86-87; Joseph E. Johnston, "Manassas to Seven Pines," in Robert U. Johnston and Clarence C. Buel, eds., *Battles and Leaders of the Civil War*, 4 vols. (New York, 1884-89), vol. 2, p. 203; Steven H. Newton, *Joseph E. Johnston and the Defense of Richmond* (Dissertation, The College of William and Mary, 1989. Ann Arbor: UMI, 1991. 9102176, pp. 242-243, 246-247, 253, 255-256, 261, 263, 273-274; James Longstreet, *From Manassas to Appomattox* (Bloomington, 1960), p. 66; William C. Davis, *Jefferson Davis: The Man and His Hour* (New York, 1991), p. 414; Douglas Southall Freeman, *R.E. Lee: A Biography*, 4 vols. (New York, 1934-1935), vol. 2, pp. 21-22.

3. Johnston, *Narrative*, pp. 116, 118, 127; Johnston, "Manassas," p. 204; *OR* 11, pt. 1, pp. 455-456, 458, 469.

4. Douglas Southall Freeman, *Lee's Lieutenants: A Study in Command*, 3 vols. (New York, 1942-1944), vol. 1, pp. 175-176.

5. Johnston, *Narrative*, p. 120.

6. Mary Boykin Chesnut, *Mary Chesnut's Civil War*, edited by C. Vann Woodward (New Haven, 1981), p. 268.

7. *OR* 11, p. 1, p. 564.

8. Ibid., p. 580.

9. Sears, *To the Gates of Richmond*, p. 70-71.

10. *OR* 11, pt. 1, pp. 564, 590.

12. Ibid., pp. 564, 584.

13. Ibid., pp. 564, 580, 590-591.

14. Newton, *Johnston*, p. 345; *OR* 11, pt. 1, pp. 580, 582.

15. Ibid., pp. 571, 580, 582, 584, 587-588, 591.

16. Ibid., pp. 576, 580, 590-591.

17. Ibid., p. 582.

18. Ibid., pp. 588, 591, 595.

19. Ibid., pp. 594-596, 598.

20. Ibid., pp. 576, 591, 598.

21. Ibid., p. 576.

22. Ibid., pp. 587-588, 591.

23. Ibid., pp. 585, 591-592, 596-598.

24. Ibid., pp. 584-585, 591-592, 598-599.

25. Longstreet, *From Manassas to Appomattox*, p. 74; Newton, *Johnston*, pp. 352-353.

26. Freeman, *Lee's Lieutenants*, 1, pp. 179-180; Sears, *To the Gates of Richmond*, pp. 73-74; Newton, *Johnston*, p. 353; *OR* 11, pt. 1, pp. 536-537, 580, 602-603, 606-607.

27. Longstreet, *From Manassas to Appomattox*, p. 74; *OR*, 11, pt. 1, pp. 565, 602.

28. Sears, *To the Gates of Richmond*, pp. 75-78; *OR* 11, pt. 1, pp. 565, 577, 585-586, 588, 592-593, 595, 597, 599, 606.

27. Longstreet, *From Manassas to Appomattox*, p. 74; *OR*, 11, pt. 1, pp. 565, 602.

30. *OR* 11, pt. 1, 275.

31. Hamilton J. Eckenrode and Bryan Conrad, *James Longstreet: Lee's War Horse* (Chapel Hill, 1986), p. 52; *OR* 11, pt. 1, pp. 993-946; Hal Bridges, *Lee's Maverick General: Daniel Harvey Hill* (Lincoln, NE, 1991), p. 55; Smith, *Confederate War Papers*, pp. 169-170; Craig L. Symonds, *Joseph E. Johnston: A Civil War Biography* (New York, 1992), p. 173.

32. *OR* 11, pt. 1, 607.

33. Ibid.

34. Early asserted that the attack idea originated with Hill, but in this assertion he is alone and, it appears, was lying. In fact, no one was very anxious to claim

responsibility for this affair after the fact. The situation Early described—with Johnston, Longstreet and Hill together when approached by Early—seems the most likely harmonization of the various participants' accounts. Longstreet, *From Manassas to Appomattox*, pp. 77-78; Jeffry D. Wert, *General James Longstreet: The Confederacy's Most Controversial Soldier—A Biography* (New York, 1993), p. 104; *OR* 11, pt. 1, pp. 565, 602-603, 607.

35. *OR* 11, pt. 1, pp. 603, 607.

36. Ibid., p. 603.

37. Ibid., p. 607; Sears, *To the Gates of Richmond*, p. 79.

38. *OR* 11, pt. 1, p. 603.

39. Ibid.

40. Ibid., p. 606.

41. Ibid., p. 591.

42. Ibid., pp. 580-581.

43. Freeman, *Lee's Lieutenants*, 1, pp. 171, 189, 192; Sears, *To the Gates of Richmond*, p. 73; Wert, *Longstreet*, p. 107.

"No private can be too good for the officers and men"

THE 71ST PENNSYLVANIA INFANTRY ON THE PENINSULA

Gary G. Lash

1. Allen C. Guelzo, "The Fighting Philadelphia Brigade," *Civil War Times Illustrated*, vol. 18, no. 9 (1980), p. 13; Stewart Sifakis, *Who Was Who in the Civil War* (New York, 1988), p. 414.

2. Samuel P. Bates, *History of Pennsylvania Volunteers, 1861-5*, 5 vols. (Harrisburg, 1869), vol. 2, p. 788; Paul Fatout, "The California Regiment, Colonel Baker and Ball's Bluff," *California Historical Society Quarterly*, vol. 31 (1952), p. 230; John W. Frazier, "Colonel Baker's Regiment. How It Was Raised In Philadelphia," *Philadelphia Weekly Times*, September 20, 1879.

3. "From the Middletown Boys," *Bucks County Intelligencer*, June 25, 1862; Richard A. Sauers, *Advance the Colors*, 2 vols. (Harrisburg, 1987, 1991), vol. 1, p. 262.

4. "A. P. S., From Col. Baker's Regiment," *Bucks County Intelligencer*, July 16, 1861; Fatout, "The California Regiment," p. 232.

5. Bates, Pennsylvania Volunteers, vol. 2, p. 788; Fatout, "The California Regiment," p. 232.

6. Frank H. Taylor, *Philadelphia in the Civil War 1861-1865* (Philadelphia, 1913), p. 86.

7. Frederick H. Dyer, *A Compendium of the War of the Rebellion*, 3 vols. (Des Moines, 1908), vol. 1, p. 276; Taylor, *Philadelphia in the Civil War*, p. 86; Frank J. Welcher, *The Union Army, 1861-1865. Organization and Operations*, 2 vols. (Bloomington, 1989, 1993), vol. 1, p. 621; "A.P.S.", "From Col. Baker's regiment," *Bucks County Intelligencer*, October 15, 1861.

8. U.S. War Department, *The War of the Rebellion: the Official Records of the Union and Confederate Armies*, 128 vols. (Washington, D.C., 1890-1901), Series I, vol. 5, p. 327. Hereinafter cited as *OR*; all references are to series I unless otherwise noted; Bates, *Pennsylvania Volunteers*, vol. 2, p. 789; Welcher, *Union Army*, vol. 1, p. 622.

9. Kim B. Holien, "The Battle of Ball's Bluff, October 21, 1861," *Blue and Gray Magazine*, vol. 7, issue 3 (1990), p. 47; Bates, *Pennsylvania Volunteers*, vol. 2, p. 789; Samuel P. Bates, *Martial Deeds of Pennsylvania* (Philadelphia, 1875), p. 693; *OR* 5, p. 328.

10. Welcher, *Union Army*, vol. 1, p. 623; Bates, *Pennsylvania Volunteers*, vol. 2, pp. 789, 790; The number of casualties suffered by the 1st California at Ball's Bluff was difficult to assess. Brigade staff officer Capt. Francis G. Young wrote that he had "no means of stating accurately the number of our loss;" nonetheless, he estimated that 260 men were lost at Ball's Bluff. Lieutenant Colonel Wistar claimed that on October 22 only 270 men remained from his force of 600 he had taken to Harrison's Island. Records compiled by the Adjutant General's office list 13 killed, 40 wounded and 228 men missing, a total loss of 281. See *OR* 5, pp. 308, 326, 329.

11. Bates, *Pennsylvania Volunteers*, vol. 2, p. 790; "From the 71st Regiment. P.V.," Philadelphia Inquirer, January 22, 1862; Taylor, *Philadelphia in the Civil War*, p. 86: The author of a recent book on the battle of Ball's Bluff suggested that the 1st California was adopted by Pennsylvania when California began forming regiments on the west coast. The 1st California Infantry Regiment organized in California was raised between August and October 1861. See Byron Farwell, *Ball's Bluff* (McLean, 1990), p. 17; Dyer, *Compendium of the War*, vol. 3, p. 1002.

12. Ezra J. Warner, *Generals in Blue* (Baton Rouge, 1964), p. 56; "B.F.H.," "From Baker's California Regiment," *Bucks County Intelligencer*, January 28, 1862: "B.F.H.", a prolific letter writer, was Sergeant Benjamin Franklin Hibbs who was mortally wounded at Fredericksburg in December 1862. See Bates, *Pennsylvania Volunteers*, vol. 2, p. 810.

13. Welcher, *Union Army*, vol. 1, p. 248.

14. C. Manington, "From Baker's California Regiment," Bucks County Intelligencer, March 25, 1862; "B.F.H.," "From Baker's California Regiment," ibid., March 25, 1862; "M.W. P.," "From Baker's California Regiment," ibid., April 8, 1862; Isaac Wistar had been promoted to colonel of the 71st on the day after the Battle of Ball's Bluff. See Bates, *Pennsylvania Volunteers*, vol. 2, p. 801.

15. Welcher, *Union Army*, vol. 1, pp. 251-252: The newly formed III and IV Corps would be commanded by Brig. Gens. Samuel P. Heintzelman and Erasmus D. Keyes, respectively. The V Corps was to be composed of the divisions of James Shields and Nathaniel P. Banks and commanded by Banks. On March 15, Banks' V Corps was detached from the Army of the Potomac.

16. George B. McClellan, "The Peninsular Campaign," in Robert U. Johnson and Clarence C. Buel, eds., *Battles and Leaders of the Civil War*, 4 vols. (New York, 1884-89), vol. 2, pp. 165, 167, 168; William J Miller, "The Grand Campaign: A Journal of Operations on the Peninsula, March 17-August 26, 1862," in William J. Miller, ed., *The Peninsula Campaign of 1862: Yorktown to the Seven Days*, vol. 1 (Campbell, CA., 1993), p. 182.

17. John Burns diary, March 27, 28 and 31, 1862, United States Army Military History Institute, Carlisle Barracks, Pennsylvania.

18. Charles H. Banes, *History of the Philadelphia Brigade* (Philadelphia, 1876), p. 46; Ward, *One Hundred and Sixth*, p. 36; Burns diary, April 4 and 5, 1862.

19. William Child, *A History of The Fifth Regiment New Hampshire Volunteers in the American Civil War 1861-1865* (Bristol, 1893), p. 57; William Child, who served as a surgeon with the 5th New Hampshire. Though he was not with the 5th on the Peninsula, Child based his history on narratives and diaries of his comrades, as well as his own recollections.

20. Ward, *One Hundred and Sixth*, p. 36; Banes, *Philadelphia Brigade*, p. 49.

21. McClellan, "Peninsular Campaign," p. 171; Ward, One Hundred and Sixth, p. 39; General McClellan claimed that after the Confederates had been softened up by the siege guns, the lines would be assaulted by the infantry.

22. "A.P.S.", "From Baker's California Regiment," *Bucks County Intelligencer*, April 29, 1862; "A.P.S.", "From Baker's California Regiment," *Bucks County Intelligencer*, April 23, 1862; Carrow, *A Model Soldier*, p. 8; Ward, *One Hundred and Sixth*, p. 40; Wistar, *Autobiography*, p. 384; Banes, *Philadelphia Brigade*, p. 53; Burns diary, April 8, 9, 10 and 11, 1862.

23. Ibid., April 9 and 18, 1862; "B.F.H.", "From the California Regiment," *Bucks County Intelligencer*, October 18, 1862. Evidently those in command realized that the rubber blankets were not suitable tents so on April 18 each member

of the 71st was issued one half of a shelter tent. Certainly not as effective as Sibley tents, they were an improvement over the rubber blankets.

24. "A.P.S.", "From Baker's California Regiment," April 29, 1862; Burns diary, April 19 and 26, 1862; Ward, *One Hundred and Sixth*, p. 39.

25. Banes, *Philadelphia Brigade*, p. 57; Wistar, *Autobiography*, p. 385.

26. Wistar, *Autobiography*, pp. 385, 386: Colonel Wistar missed much of the Peninsula Campaign because of illness.

27. Ward, *One Hundred and Sixth*, p. 43; Burns diary, May 4, 1862; On the night of May 3, the Confederates vacated Yorktown and began withdrawing up the Peninsula to Williamsburg. See Miller, "Grand Campaign," p. 186.

28. Burns diary, May 5, 1862; "B.F.H.," "From the California Regiment," *Bucks County Intelligencer*, October 28, 1862; "A.P.S.", "From Baker's California Regiment," *Bucks County Intelligencer*, May 20, 1862; Ward, *One Hundred and Sixth*, p. 43.

29. Ibid., p. 43; "A.P.S.", "From Baker's California Regiment," May 20, 1862.

30. Ward, *One Hundred and Sixth*, p. 43; Burns diary, May 6, 1862; "A.P.S.," "From Baker's California Regiment," May 20, 1862.

31. Ward, *One Hundred and Sixth*, p. 47; Banes, *Philadelphia Brigade*, p. 58; Miller, "Grand Campaign," p. 187; General Franklin's division had been part of a force ordered to seize Southern batteries on Gloucester Point across the York River from Yorktown.*OR* 11, pt. 1, p. 18; Welcher, *Union Army*, vol. 1, p. 800).

32. Burns diary, May 7, 1862; "A.P.S.", "From Baker's California Regiment," May 20, 1862.

33. Ward, *One Hundred and Sixth*, p. 47; Banes, Philadelphia Brigade, pp. 58, 62; Burns diary, May 15, 1862; Joseph P. Elliott diary, May 15, 1862, United States Army Military History Institute, Carlisle Barracks, Carlisle, Pennsylvania.

34. *OR* 11, pt. 1, p. 24; Stephen W. Sears, *George B. McClellan. The Young Napoleon* (New York, 1988), p. 186; Welcher, *Union Army*, vol. 1, pp. 253, 804.

35. Ward, *One Hundred and Sixth*, p. 49; Burns diary, May 21, 1862; Banes, *Philadelphia Brigade*, p. 62.

36. Child, *Fifth New Hampshire*, p. 60.

37. Ward, *One Hundred and Sixth*, p. 49; Burns diary, May 22, 1862.

38. Ward, *One Hundred and Sixth*, p. 51.

39. Burns diary, May 28, 1862; Banes, *Philadelphia Brigade*, p. 64.

40. Child, *Fifth New Hampshire*, p. 69.

41. Ward, *One Hundred and Sixth*, p. 52; "A.P.S.", "From Baker's California Regiment," *Bucks County Intelligencer*, June 17, 1862; Welcher, *Union Army*, vol. 1, pp. 809-810; Steven H. Newton, *The Battle of Seven Pines* (Lynchburg, 1993), p. 40.

42. Ward, *One Hundred and Sixth*, p. 52; Burns diary, May 31, 1862; Banes, *Philadelphia Brigade*, pp. 64, 65.

43. *OR* 11, pt. 1, pp. 791, 792, 806; Ward, *One Hundred and Sixth*, p. 52; Banes, *Philadelphia Brigade*, p. 65.

44. Ward, *One Hundred and Sixth*, p. 52; Banes, *Philadelphia Brigade*, p. 65.

45. Ward, *One Hundred and Sixth*, p. 53; Burns diary, May 31, 1862.

46. Welcher, *Union Army*, vol. 1, p. 811; *OR* 11, pt. 1, p. 791; Ward, *One Hundred and Sixth*, p. 53.

47. *OR* 11, pt. 1, pp. 792, 806; "B.F.H.", "From the California Regiment," October 28, 1862; "A.P.S.", "From Baker's California Regiment," June 17, 1862.

48. Ibid.; Burns diary, May 31, 1862; Banes, *Philadelphia Brigade*, p. 67; Ward, *One Hundred and Sixth*, p. 54.

49. Welcher, *Union Army*, vol. 1, p. 811; "The Battle of Last Thursday," *Philadelphia Inquirer*, July 1, 1862.

50. "A.P.S., From Baker's California Regiment," June 17, 1862; "B.F.H.", "From the California Regiment," *Bucks County Intelligencer*, November 4, 1862; *OR* 11, pt. 1, pp. 792, 807; Banes, *Philadelphia Brigade*, p. 68.

51. Ward, *One Hundred and Sixth*, p. 55; Bates, *Pennsylvania Volunteers*, vol. 2, p. 791; Burns diary, June 1, 1862; "B.F.H.", "From the California Regiment," November 4, 1862.

52. *OR* 11, pt. 1, p. 758; William F. Fox, *Regimental Losses in the American Civil War 1861-1865* (Dayton, 1974), p. 278.

53. "The California Regiment in the Late Battle," *Philadelphia Daily Evening Bulletin*, June 9, 1862; "A.P.S.", "From Baker's California Regiment," June 17, 1862; "Our gallant young leader" is probably General McClellan.

54. Burns diary, June 1, 1862; "A.P.S.", "From Baker's California Regiment," June 17, 1862; "B.F.H.," "From the California Regiment," November 4, 1862; Robert K. Krick, *Lee's Colonels* (Dayton, 1992, 4th edition), p. 111: Thirty-four year old Colonel Champion Thomas Neal Davis had served in the North Carolina state legislature until he became captain of Company G, 16th North Carolina in May 1861. He had been colonel since April 26.

55. Ward, *One Hundred and Sixth*, p. 58.

56. Banes, *Philadelphia Brigade*, p. 70.

57. Ward, *One Hundred and Sixth*, p. 58; "A.P.S.", "From Baker's California Regiment," July 8, 1862 (letter written on June 17, 1862).

58. Ward, *One Hundred and Sixth*, p. 59; Burns diary, June 8, 9, 10, 13, 14,15, 17, 18, 19, 20 and 21, 1862.

59. "B.F.H.", "From the California Regiment," November 4, 1862; Ward, *One Hundred and Sixth*, p. 59.

60. Burns diary, June 10, 1862; "A.P.S.", "From Baker's California Regiment"; Banes, *Philadelphia Brigade*, p. 72,

61. "A.P.S.", "From Baker's California Regiment," *Bucks County Intelligencer*, July 8, 1862 (letter written on June 24, 1862); Elliott diary, June 15, 1862.

62. Welcher, *Union Army*, vol. 1, p. 814; "A.P.S.", "From Baker's Regiment," July 8, 1862.

63. McClellan, "Peninsular Campaign," pp. 179-180; Welcher, *Union Army*, vol. 1, pp. 816-817.

64. Burns diary, June 25, 1862.

65. Welcher, *Union Army*, vol. 1, p. 818.

66. "B.F.H.", "From the California Regiment," November 4, 1862; Ward, *One Hundred and Sixth*, p. 60; Burns diary, June 26, 1862.

67. Welcher, *Union Army*, vol. 1, p. 819.

68. Ibid.; *OR*, 11, pt. 2, p. 223.

69. Welcher, *Union Army*, vol. 1, p. 820-821; *OR* 11, pt. 2, p. 223.

70. Welcher, *Union Army*, vol. 1, pp. 820-821; "B.F.H.", "Journal of the California Regiment," *Bucks County Intelligencer*, November 18, 1862; Command of the 71st Pennsylvania passed to Lt. Col. William G. Jones of the regular army on June 16. John Burns declared that the new regimental commander was quite strict and, therefore, "was not liked at first." Jones, he continued, "made the officers and men stand around and mind their Ps and Qs". See Bates, *Pennsylvania Volunteers*, vol. 2, p. 791; Burns diary, June 16, 1862.

71. "B.F.H.", "Journal of the California Regiment," November 18, 1862.

72. Banes, *Philadelphia Brigade*, p. 73; "B.F.H.", "Journal of the California Regiment," November 18, 1862.

73. *OR* 11, pt. 2, p. 226; Welcher, *Union Army*, vol. 1, p. 821.

74. Ibid.; *OR* 11, pt. 2, p. 463.

75. Banes, *Philadelphia Brigade*, p. 74; Ward, *One Hundred and Sixth*, pp. 61-62; "B.F.H.", "Journal of the California Regiment," November 18, 1862.

76. Ibid.; Ward, *One Hundred and Sixth*, p. 62; Burns diary, June 28, 1862.

77. Welcher, *Union Army*, vol. 1, p. 822; Ward, *One Hundred and Sixth*, pp. 62-63; "B.F.H.", "Journal of the California Regiment," November 18, 1862.

78. *OR* 11, pt. 2, pp. 50 80,90; Burns diary, June 29, 1862.

79. Ward, *One Hundred and Sixth*, p. 63.

80. Child, *Fifth New Hampshire*, p. 92.

81. *OR* 11, pt. 2, pp. 50, 90; Bates, *Philadelphia Brigade*, p. 79; Burns diary, June 29, 1862.

82. *OR* 11, pt. 2, p. 80; Welcher, *Union Army*, vol. 1, p. 822; "B.F.H.", "Journal of the California Regiment," November 18, 1862.

83. "B.F.H.", "Journal of the California Regiment," November 18, 1862; Bates, *Pennsylvania Volunteers*, vol. 2, p. 791; *OR* 11, pt. 2, pp. 90, 91.

84. Bates, *Pennsylvania Volunteers*, vol. 2, pp. 791-792; *OR* 11, pt. 2, p. 91; Banes, *Philadelphia Brigade*, p. 78.

85. Welcher, *Union Army*, vol. 1, p. 822.

86. *OR* 11, pt. 2, pp. 50,91; "B.F.H.", "Journal of the California Regiment," November 18, 1862.

87. *OR* 11, pt. 2, pp. 54,91; Ward, *One Hundred and Sixth*, p. 63; "B.F.H.", "Journal of the California Regiment," November 18, 1862.

88. Ibid.; Ward, *One Hundred and Sixth*, p. 63; Banes, *Philadelphia Brigade*, p. 78; Welcher, *Union Army*, vol. 1, p. 822; *OR* 11, pt. 2, p. 50.

89. Banes, *Philadelphia Brigade*, p. 79; *OR* 11, pt. 2, p. 25; Six men were killed and mortally wounded in this action. See Fox, *Regimental Losses*, p. 278.

90. *OR* 11, pt. 2, p. 50.

91. Banes, *Philadelphia Brigade*, p. 79; Ward, *One Hundred and Sixth*, p. 65; Burns diary, June 29, 1862.

92. *OR* 11, pt. 2, pp. 50, 91; Banes, *Philadelphia Brigade*, p. 79.

93. "B.F.H.", "Journal of the California Regiment," November 18, 1862; Ward, *One Hundred and Sixth*, p. 66.

94. Welcher, *Union Army*, vol. 1, p. 823.

95. Ibid.; William B. Franklin, "Rear-Guard Fighting During the Change of Base," in Johnson and Buel, eds., *Battles and Leaders of the Civil War*, 2, p. 374.

96. "B.F.H.", "Journal of the California Regiment," November 18, 1862; Franklin, "Rear-Guard Fighting," p. 373.

97. *OR* 11, pt. 2, p. 91; Welcher, *Union Army*, vol. 1, p. 823; Franklin, "Rear-Guard Fighting," p. 373.

98. Welcher, *Union Army*, vol. 1, p. 824; Franklin, "Rear-Guard Fighting," p. 374; O.R 11, pt. 2, p. 91; Bates, *Pennsylvania Volunteers*, vol. 2, p. 792: Jones would finally relinquish brigade command after the army reached Harrison's Landing.

99. *OR* 11, pt. 2, p. 50; Welcher, *Union Army*, vol. 1, p. 823.

100. Ibid.; Burns diary, June 29, 1862; Franklin, "Rear-Guard Fighting," p. 374.

101. Burns diary, June 29, 1862; *OR* 11, pt. 2, p. 91; "B.F.H.", "Journal of the California Regiment," November 18, 1862.

102. Ibid.; Welcher, *Union Army*, vol. 1, p. 824; Burns diary, June 29, 1862; William Fox claimed that two men of the 71st were killed and mortally wounded in the fighting at Savage's Station. See Fox, *Regimental Losses*, p. 278.

103. Welcher, *Union Army*, vol. 1, p. 824; "B.F.H.", "Journal of the California Regiment," November 18, 1862.

104. Ibid.; Banes, *Philadelphia Brigade*, p. 82; Burns diary, June 29, 1862.

105. Child, *Fifth New Hampshire*, p. 94.

106. Welcher, *Union Army*, vol. 1, p. 824.

107. Banes, *Philadelphia Brigade*, 82; Burns diary, June 29, 1862; "B.F.H.", "Journal of the California Regiment," November 18, 1862; Bates, *Pennsylvania Volunteers*, vol. 2, p. 792.

108. "B.F.H.", "Journal of the California Regiment," November 18, 1862.

109. Welcher, *Union Army*, vol. 1, p. 824; "B.F.H.", "Journal of the California Regiment," November 18, 1862; The time of arrival was probably closer to 3 a.m. The 71st and the brigade reportedly began crossing the bridge over the swamp near daylight. See Banes, *Philadelphia Brigade*, p. 83; Ward, *One Hundred and Sixth*, p. 69.

110. "B.F.H.", "Journal of the California Regiment," November 18, 1862; Burns diary, June 29, 1862.

111. *OR* 11, pt. 2, p. 55.

112. Welcher, *Union Army*, vol. 1, p. 825.

113. "B.F.H.", "Journal of the California Regiment," *Bucks County Intelligencer*, November 25, 1862; Banes, *Philadelphia Brigade*, p. 83; Ward, *One Hundred and Sixth*, p. 69; Burns diary, June 30, 1862.

114. Welcher, *Union Army*, vol. 1, p. 826; *OR* 11, pt. 2, p. 92.

115. Welcher, *Union Army*, vol. 1, pp. 825, 826; Banes, *Philadelphia Brigade*, 83; Ward, *One Hundred and Sixth*, p. 69.

116. Welcher, *Union Army*, vol. 1, p. 826; *OR* 11, pt. 2, p. 92.

117. Ibid., pp. 51, 92; Banes, *Philadelphia Brigade*, p. 92; Welcher, *Union Army*, vol. 1, pp. 825, 826, 827; Ward, *One Hundred and Fifth*, p. 70.

118. "B.F.H.", "Journal of the California Regiment," November 25, 1962; Welcher, *Union Army*, vol. 1, pp. 826, 827; *OR* 11, pt. 2, p. 92.

119. "B.F.H.", "Journal of the California Regiment," November 25, 1862; *OR* 11, pt. 2, p. 92; Burns diary, June 30, 1862.

120. "B.F.H.", "Journal of the California Regiment," November 25, 1862; Burns diary, June 30, 1862; *OR* 11, pt. 2, p. 92.

121. G.D. Carrow, *The Model Soldier; A Memoir of Lieut. George W. Kenney, of the (First California) 71st Regiment Pennsylvania Volunteers* (New York, c. 1870), pp. 8-9; "Lieutenant Kenney," The Philadelphia Inquirer, July 11, 1862.

122. "B.F.H.", "Journal of the California Regiment," November 25, 1862; Burns diary, June 30, 1862.

123. Welcher, *Union Army*, vol. 1, p. 827; *OR* 11, pt. 2, p. 51: The move south had not specifically been ordered by General McClellan, who was not on the field.

124. "B.F.H.", "Journal of the California Regiment," November 25, 1862; Welcher, *Union Army*, vol. 1, p. 828; Carrow, *Model Soldier*, p. 9; Lieutenant Kenney died in Confederate hands.

125. Welcher, *Union Army*, vol. 1, pp. 828, 829; *OR* 11, pt. 2, pp. 202-203, 229.

126. Ibid., p. 52; Welcher, *Union Army*, vol 1, p. 829; Burns diary, July 1, 1862; "B.F.H.", "Journal of the California Regiment," November 25, 1862.

127. Ibid.

128. Welcher, *Union Army*, vol. 1, p. 830; *OR* 11, pt. 2, p. 80.

129. "B.F.H.", "Journal of the California Regiment," November 25, 1862: Burns diary, July 1, 1862; *OR* 11, pt. 2, p. 81.

130. Welcher, *Union Army*, vol. 1, p. 830; "B.F.H.", "Journal of the California Regiment," November 25, 1862.

131. Banes, *Philadelphia Brigade*, p. 88.

132. "B.F.H.", "Journal of the California Regiment," November 25, 1862; Burns diary, July 1, 1862.

133. *OR* 11, pt. 2, p. 81; Banes, *Philadelphia Brigade*, p. 89; Though General Sedgwick did not mention the move toward Richmond, Banes was very specific about it in his account. Banes seemed to imply, however, that the movement toward the Confederate capital may have been dictated by the poor condition of the main road south to Harrison's Landing. Thus while it appeared to the rank-and-file that they were about to make the long awaited move on Richmond, they were, in fact, only taking a different route to the James River. See Banes, *Philadelphia Brigade*, p. 89.

134. *OR* 11, pt. 2, p. 81; Banes, *Philadelphia Brigade*, p. 89; Burns diary, July 2, 1862; Ward, *One Hundred and Sixth*, p. 71; Elliott diary, July 2, 1862.

135. Ward, *One Hundred and Sixth*, p. 72; Burns diary, July 2, 1862.

136. Ward, *One Hundred and Sixth*, p. 72; Burns diary, July 4, 1962.

137. Ibid., July 15,17,18 and 22, 1862; RG-19, Records of Military Affairs, Office of the Adjutant General, Pennsylvania State Archives, Harrisburg, Pennsylvania; Bates, *Pennsylvania Volunteers*, 2:793; It was also on this day that the V and VI Corps, heretofore officially known as the V Provisional and VI Provisional Corps, were officially confirmed and their designations changed to the V and VI Corps. See Welcher, *Union Army*, vol. 1, p. 253.

138. Child, *Fifth New Hampshire*, p. 96; The 4th Ohio of General Kimball's II Corps brigade was evidently put out of commission through the Antietam campaign because of illness contracted at Harrison's Landing. The Buckeyes, who had left the Shenandoah Valley for the Virginia Peninsula late in June, arrived at Harrison's Landing on July 1. On August 24, regimental surgeon H.M. McAbee wrote that of the 909 enlisted men in the regiment, only 300 were healthy enough to be present for duty. McAbee attributed the poor health of the 4th Ohio to sickness acquired while at Harrison's Landing. See William Kepler, *History of the Three Months and Three Years' Service of the Fourth Regiment Ohio Volunteer Infantry in the War for the Union* (Cleveland, 1886), pp. 81-83.

139. Catherine H. Vanderslice, ed., *The Civil War Letters of George Washington Beidelman* (New York, 1978), p. 75; "B.F.H.," "Journal of the California Regiment," November 25, 1862.

140. Bates, *Pennsylvania Volunteers*, vol. 2, pp. 810, 811, 813, 814, 818, 822; RG-19, Records of Military Affairs, Office of the Adjutant General, National Archives, Washington, D.C.

141. Vanderslice, George Washington Beidelman, p. 77; Burns diary, August 10, 12, 13 and 16, 1862; "B.F.H.", "Journal of the California Regiment," November 25, 1862.

142. Vanderslice, *George Washington Beidelman*, p. 81.

143. Burns diary, August 20, and 21, 1862; Child, *Fifth New Hampshire*, p. 104; Vanderslice, *George Washington Beidelman*, pp. 82-84.

144. Ibid., p. 85.

145. Ibid., p. 86; "B.F.H.", "Journal of the California Regiment," November 25, 1862; Banes, *Philadelphia Brigade*, p. 100; Burns diary, August 27, 1862.

146. *OR*, 11, pt. 1, p. 758, pt. 2, p. 25.

147. McClellan, "Peninsular Campaign," p. 187.

148. William M. Runkel, "The *Philadelphia Brigade*: Its Part, Under Sedgwick and Howard, at the Battle of Antietam," *Philadelphia Weekly Times*, April 8, 1882; "B.F.H.", "Journal of the California Regiment," *Bucks County Intelligencer*, December 9, 1862; Dyer, *Compendium of the War*, vol. 3, p. 1597; Bates, *Pennsylvania Volunteers*, vol. 2, pp. 794-795, 801.

"He is a good soldier"

Johnston, Davis and Seven Pines:

The Uncertainty Principle in Action

Steven H. Newton

1. 36th Congress, 2d Session, Senate Document No. 3, *Report of the Commission appointed under the eighth section of the act of Congress of June 21, 1860, to examine into the organization, system of discipline, and course of instruction of the United States Military Academy at West Point* (Washington, D.C., 1860), p. 186.

2. Quoted in Grady McWhiney and Perry D. Jamieson, *Attack and Die, Civil War Military Tactics and the Southern Heritage* (University, AL, 1982), p. 153.

3. For a discussion of the tendency toward mechanistic interpretations of battle, see John Keegan, *The Face of Battle* (New York, 1976), pp. 15-46. For two quite different uses of statistical quantification with respect to the Civil War, See McWhiney and Jamieson, *Attack and Die*, pp. 18-24, and Hermann Hattaway and Archer Jones, *How the North Won, A Military History of the Civil War* (Chicago, 1983), pp. 721-732. A wide gamut of available "conflict simulations" are consistently marketed which explore the "what if" possibilities of the war. Of recent titles, Eric Lee Smith, *Across Five Aprils* (Baltimore, 1993), is of particular interest, as it presents the Battle of Bentonville, Johnston's last attack.

4. For an extremely readable consideration of quantum physics, including the uncertainty principle, and its implications for human experience, see David Z. Albert, *Quantum Mechanics and Experience* (New York, 1993).

5. Richard M. McMurry, "The Enemy at Richmond: Joseph E. Johnston and the Confederate Government," *Civil War History*, vol. 27 (1981), p. 31.

6. Jefferson Davis to Varina H. Davis, June 23, 1862, in the Jefferson Davis Papers, Museum of the Confederacy, Richmond, Virginia.

7. Steven E. Woodworth, *Jefferson Davis and his Generals, The Failure of Confederate Command in the West* (Lawrence, KS, 1990), p. 178; William C. Davis, *Jefferson Davis, The Man and His Hour* (New York, 1991), p. 423.

8. Davis, *Jefferson Davis*, p. 424.

9. Steven H. Newton, *The Battle of Seven Pines* (Lynchburg, 1993), p. 84.

10. Woodworth, *Davis and his Generals*, p. 178.

11. Craig L. Symonds, *Joseph E. Johnston, A Civil War Biography* (New York, 1992), pp. 174, 183.

12. Joseph T. Glathaar, *Partners in Command, the Relationships Between Leaders in the Civil War* (New York, 1993), p. 118.

13. U.S. War Department, *The War of the Rebellion: The Official Records of the Union and Confederate Armies*, 128 volumes, (Washington D.C., 1890-1901), series I, vol 11, pt. 3, p. 536. Hereinafter cited as *OR*. All references are to series I unless otherwise noted.

14. *OR* 11, pt. 1, p. 933-941.

15. Janet B. Hewett, Noah Andre Trudeau, and Bryce A. Suderow, eds., *Supplement to the Official Records of the Union and Confederate Armies*, 3 volumes to date (Wilmington, N.C., 1994), Part 1, vol. 2, pp. 381-383. Hereinafter cited as *SOR*.

16. *SOR*, part 1, vol. 2, pp. 935, 937-941; Gustavus W. Smith, *The Battle of Seven Pines* (New York, 1891), pp. 20-22; Newton, *Seven Pines*, p. 84.

17. Newton, *Seven Pines*, pp. 98-99; Steven H. Newton, "Joseph E. Johnston and the Defense of Richmond" (Dissertation, The College of William and Mary, 1989), pp. 387-388.

18. *OR* 11, pt. 1, pp. 943-946, 986-987.

19. Symonds, *Johnston*, p. 193.

20. Richmond *Examiner*, November 10, 1862, p. 2; P.W. Alexander, "Confederate Chieftains," *Southern Literary Messenger*, vol. 35 (1863), p. 35.

21. *OR* series IV, 1: p. 999; Newton, "Defense," pp. 18-22; Symonds, *Johnston*, pp. 128-129.

22. Symonds, *Johnston*, p. 193.

23. These were the brigades of J.R. Anderson, Branch, Daniel, Gregg, Ransom, Ripley, and Walker. See Newton, *Seven Pines*, pp. 104, 109-110.

24. Newton, "Defense," pp. 313n, 372-373n.

25. Ibid., pp. 383-384, 404-405, 414, 416-418, 425-426, 454-455.

26. *OR* 11, pt. 3, p. 524.

27. Ibid., pp. 523-524.

28. Joseph E. Johnston to William Browne, May 27, 1862, in Jefferson Davis papers, Chicago Historical Society; A.L. Long, *Memoirs of Robert E. Lee* (New York, 1886), pp. 158-159; Newton, "Defense," pp. 425-426, 454-455.

"What Men We Have Got Are Good Soldiers & Brave Ones Too"

FEDERAL CAVALRY OPERATIONS IN THE PENINSULA CAMPAIGN

Robert O'Neill

1. W. W. Blackford, *War Years With Jeb Stuart* (Baton Rouge, 1993 ed.), pp. 26-27; John Hennessy, *The First Battle of Manassas: An End To Innocence July 18-21,*

1861 (Lynchburg, 1989), p. 80; William C. Davis, *Battle at Bull Run: A History of the First Major Campaign of the Civil War* (Baton Rouge, 1977), p. 80.

2. Hennessy, *The First Battle of Manassas*, pp. 113, 117-119; Albert G.Brackett, *History of the United States Cavalry*, (Freeport, 1865), p. 212. A battalion of seven companies of cavalry (two companies of the 1st regiment, four of the 2nd and one company of the 2nd Dragoons) was attached to Col. David Hunter's Second Division. Some of these men dashed out of the woods near the 3rd and 5th Maine Infantry, scattering many of the men. An account in the *National Tribune* (Washington, D.C.), August 20, 1881, gives a soldier's view of the impact of the Black Horse Cavalry on the men as they retreated.

3. Thomas F. Thiele, "The Evolution of Cavalry in the American Civil War; 1861-1863," (Ph.D. dissertation, University of Michigan, 1951), pp. 1, 5.

4. Ibid., pp. 11-14.

5. Ibid., p. 22.

6. Ibid., pp. 19-20; Stephen W. Sears, *George B. McClellan: The Young Napoleon*, (New York, 1988), p. 25.

7. Thiele, "The Evolution of Cavalry," pp. 30-32. Early calls for troops specified "No Cavalry". The debate would develop early, and Lincoln began calling for cavalry as early as June. By the end of July, the flood gates had opened as recruiters enlisted regiment after regiment of cavalry.

8. Brackett, *History of the United States Cavalry*, p. 144.

9. George B. McClellan, *The Armies of Europe,* (Philadelphia, 1862), pp. 386, 389.

10. New York *Times*, June 1, 1861.

11. Ibid., July 24, 1861.

12. Thomas M. Eddy, *The Patriotism of Illinois*, 2 vols. (Chicago, 1865), vol. 1, p. 566. Barker's Battalion was mustered out in September of 1861 and the men re-enlisted as McClellan's Dragoons in October of 1861. The unit was assigned to the 12th Illinois as Companies H and I in February 1862 but served detached until November 1863. On the Peninsula they were referred to as Barker's Battalion and McClellan's Dragoons but not the 12th Illinois.

13. Stephen W. Sears, ed., *The Civil War Papers of George B. McClellan: Selected Correspondence, 1860-1865* (New York, 1992), pp. 71-75; U.S War Department, *The War of the Rebellion: The Official Records of the Union and Confederate Armies*, 128 vols. (Washington, D.C., 1890-1901), series III, vol.1, pp. 324, 337, 346, 357, 392. Hereinafter cited as *OR*. All references are to series I unless otherwise noted.

14. *OR* 5, pp. 12-14, 567, 575.

15. Ibid., 2, p. 288, The other men listed were Maj. R.B. Marcy, Lt. Col. Delos B. Sacket and Brig. Gen. Frederick Lander. Marcy, who was McClellan's father-in-law, would serve as his inspector general and later chief of staff, Sacket would also serve as McClellan's inspector general. Lander, who held a field command under McClellan, died of disease in March 1862. Sears, *The Civil War Papers of George B. McClellan*, p. 94; *OR* 11, pt. 3, p. 40.

16. Sears, *The Civil War Papers of George B. McClellan*, p. 89.

17. *OR* series III, 1, p. 622.

18. Ibid., p. 873.

19. Rochester *Daily Union & Advertiser*, March 6, 1862; Sears, *The Civil War Papers of George B. McClellan*, pp. 134-135. This proposal appears in draft copies of a letter to Simon Cameron of November 15, 1861. His final draft did address the possibility of modifying the course at West Point but not in this detail. See also *OR* 5, p. 13 where he speaks to the weeding out process through courts-martial and examining board.

20. Detroit *Free Press*, January 9, 1862.

21. Rochester *Daily Union & Advertiser*, January 30,1862. By August 1862 an examination in horsemanship was required of recruits, see *OR* series III, 2, p. 380.

22. *OR* series III, 1, pp. 722, 724.

23. Ibid., pp. 728-729; Thiele, "The Evolution of Cavalry," pp. 84-85. Numerous other states were effected in addition to New York. This issue was also taken up by the Committee on the Conduct of the War in December 1861. See U.S. Congress, *Report of the Joint Committee on the Conduct of the War, Part 1: Army of the Potomac* (Washington D.C., 1863), pp. 174-186.

24. Daniel Peck letter, February 2, 1862, in Jamestown *Post Journal*, February 6, 1961; Nelson Taylor, *Saddle and Saber: The Letters of Civil War Cavalryman Corporal Nelson Taylor*, edited by Dr. Gray Nelson Taylor (Clifton Park, 1993), pp. 17-18. See also the Jamestown *Journal*, March 14, 1862.

25. James B. Burrows to Dear Mother, March 9, 1862, from Camp Fenton, Washington, D.C., James Baldwin Burrows Papers, Civil War Miscellaneous Collection, United States Military History Institute, Carlisle, Pennsylvania. Hereinafter cited as USAMHI; Fredonia *Censor*, March 26, 1862; Taylor, *Saddle and Saber*, pp. 19-21. The 9th New York Cavalry had adopted the nickname "The Stoneman Cavalry" by December of 1861.

26. Fredonia *Censor*, March 19, 1862; Jamestown *Journal*, March 28, 1862.

27. James B. Burrows to Dear Mother, March 11, 1862, In the Field, USAMHI.

28. Taylor, *Saddle and Saber*, p. 23; James Burrows to Dear Mother, March 22, 1862, Alexandria, Va., USAMHI.

29. Detroit *Free Press*, December 12, 1861; *OR* series III, vol. I, pp. 788-789, 922.

30. Hillman Hall, *History of the Sixth New York Cavalry*, (Worcester, 1908), p. 37.

31. James Burrows to Dear Mother, April 1-3, 1862, on board Schooner "Eliza Williams" off Ft. Monroe, Va., USAMHI. See also Newel Cheney, *History of the Ninth Regiment, New York Volunteer Cavalry* (Poland Center, NY, 1901), pp. 34-35. The dates between these two accounts vary by a day or so, and I have used the dates in the Burrows letter as it was written at the time. See also the Jamestown *Journal*, April 4,1862; Taylor, *Saddle and Saber*, pp. 25-27. I have used Taylor's dates for the 2nd and 3rd Battalions.

32. Jamestown *Journal*, April 4, 1862 (letter dated March 28, 1862).

33. Ibid., April 11, 1862.

34. Ibid., April 25, 1862.

35. *OR* 11, pt. 3 , 105. Nelson Taylor claimed that Col. Henry Hunt had the order countermanded in an effort to retain the men now under his command. See Taylor, *Saddle and Saber*, pp. 30-32, 37-38.

36. Charles S. Wainwright, *A Diary of Battle The Personal Journals of Colonel Charles S. Wainwright, 1861-1865*, edited by Allan Nevins (Gettysburg edition) p. 43.

37. Thomas Benton Kelley to Dear Mary, April 20, 1862, Alexandria, Va.; Ibid., May 1, 1862, from Ship Point, Virginia, in the Private Collection of Dr. James Milgram, Chicago, Illinois.

38. James B. Burrows to Dear Mother, May 4, 1862, from Camp Winfield Scott, Va., USAMHI; *OR* 11, pt. 3, p. 165.

39. Daniel Peck letter, May 6, 1862, in Jamestown *Post Journal*, February 9, 1961; Taylor, *Saddle and Saber*, pp. 36-37; *OR* 11, pt. 3, pp. 182-183.

40. Cheney, *History of the Ninth New York Cavalry*, pp. 43-47; Taylor, *Saddle and Saber*, p. 37-40.

41. Jamestown *Journal*, September 13, 1861, December 13, 1861 and May 30, 1862.

42. George B. McClellan, *McClellan's Own Story* (New York, 1887), pp. 237-238. In his report for the campaign chief quartermaster Brig. Gen. Stewart Van Vliet lists the total number of ships used as 405, see *OR* 11, pt. 1, p. 158.

43. Sears, *The Civil War Papers of George B. McClellan*, pp. 209-210; *OR* 11, pt. 3, pp. 16, 26, 36. Not every regiment listed in the March 24 special orders served on the Peninsula. Also used was the order of battle as listed in Stephen W. Sears, *To the Gates of Richmond: The Peninsula Campaign* (New York, 1992), pp. 359-385.

44. Jamestown *Journal*, April 4, 1862.

45. Aurora *Beacon*, May 1, 1862; Sidney Morris Davis, *Common Soldier UNcommon War*, edited by Charles F. Cooney (Bethesda, 1994) p. 103.

46. James H. Stevenson, *Boots and Saddles: A History of the First Volunteer Cavalry of the War*, (Harrisburg, 1879), p. 93; William H Beach, *The First New York (Lincoln) Cavalry* (New York, 1902), pp. 98-100; Thomas Kelley to Dearest Mary, May 1, 1862, from Ship Point, Va.

47. *OR* 11, pt. 1, pp. 285-299; William Brooke Rawle, *History of the Third Pennsylvania Cavalry* (Philadelphia,1905), pp 43-52.

48. C.C.W. letter, March 12, 1862, from Alexandria, Virginia, in *True Republican & Sentinel*, March 19, 1862.

49. *OR* 11, pt. 3, pp. 133-134. The 8th Illinois was also attached to Stonman but got underway late and was never involved in the fighting that afternoon. They went into bivouac at Lebanon Church, see George Cook letter, May 11, 1862, in Aurora *Beacon*, May 22, 1862. Men of the 9th New York Cavalry were assigned to Gibson's, Benson's and Tidball's Batteries, see Cheney, *History of the Ninth New York Cavalry*, pp. 29, 39-41.

50. *OR* 11, pt. 1, pp. 400, 423-424. See also Davis, *Common Soldier UNcommon War*, p. 115. See also J.W. Minnich, "Incidents of the Peninsula Campaign," *Confederate Veteran*, vol. 30 (1922), p. 53, for a Southern view of these torpedoes.

51. *OR* 11, pt. 1, p. 444. Confederate accounts of this fight are few and it is difficult to put their side of it together. Many Northern accounts mention the 1st North Carolina Cavalry as being involved at Fort Magruder but it was not on the Peninsula yet.

52. *OR* 11, pt. 1, pp. 423-24, 525-526, 434, 440-441; *Report of the Joint Committee,* p. 568.

53. *OR* 11, pt. 1, pp. 440-441.

54. Ibid., pp. 440-441, 534; pt. 3, p. 140.

55. Ibid., pp. 426, 526.

56. Ibid., pp. 433-435, 445; Rawle, *History of the Third Pennsylvania Cavalry*, p. 53; Thomas P. Nanzig, *3rd Virginia Cavalry* (Lynchburg, 1989), p. 16. The standard, which is not mentioned in Union accounts, must have been taken from the McClellan Dragoon's.

57. *OR* 11, pt. 1, pp. 441-446; *Source Book of the Peninsula Campaign in Virginia*, (Fort Leavenworth), p. 100.

58. *OR* 11, pt. 3, pp. 431-432, 427-428; Rawle, *History of the Third Pennsylvania Cavalry*, p. 56.

59. *OR* 11, pt. 1, pp. 436-439; Davis, *Common Soldier Uncommon War*, pp. 118-119. Major Williams got involved in a debate with General Cooke over his orders which plays out in the reports.

60. *OR* 11, pt. 1, p. 436; Davis, *Common Soldier Uncommon War*, pp. 118-119. General McLaws was also confused as to their identity, apparently thrown off by their casual approach, see *OR* 11, pt. 1, p. 442.

61. *OR* 11, pt. 1, p. 439, 442-443; Davis, *Common Soldier Uncommon War*, pp. 119-120.

62. *OR* 11, pt. 1, pp. 431-432.

63. Ibid., pp. 428-430, 432, 439, 445; Kenneth L. Stiles, *4th Virginia Cavalry* (Lynchburg, 1985), p. 10; *The Returned Battle Flags*, edited by Richard Rollins (Redondo Beach, 1995), p. 46; For the two day period May 4 and 5 the cavalry losses were listed as 15 killed, 33 wounded and 1 missing. Stuart reported that Captain Newton was captured on the 4th, other sources indicate that he was captured on the 5th.

64. *OR* 11, pt. 1, pp. 526-527.

65. Minnich, "Incidents of the Peninsula Campaign," p. 53; Archibald Gracie, "Gracie's Battalion at Williamsburg in 1862," *Confederate Veteran*, vol. 19, 1911, p. 31; O. O. Howard, "Personal Reminiscences of the War of the Rebellion," *National Tribune* (Washington, D.C.), December 27, 1883; Alexander S. Webb, *The Peninsula: McClellan's Campaign of 1862* (New York, 1881), p. 70; *Report of the Joint Committee*, p. 570. Sprague was governor of Rhode Island. His reasons for being with Stoneman are unknown.

66. McClellan, *McClellan's Own Story*, p. 324.

67. *Report of the Joint Committee*, pp. 429, 568.

68. Stevenson, *A History of the First Volunteer Cavalry of the War*, pp. 97-99.

69. *OR* 11, pt. 1, p. 633; pt. 3, pp. 145-146, 148-149, 151, 153.

70. Elisha Hunt Rhodes, *All For The Union: The Civil War Diary and Letters of Elisha Hunt Rhodes* (New York, 1985), p. 65; Davis, *Common Soldier UNcommon War*, pp. 129-136; Janet B. Hewett, Noah Andre Trudeau, and Bryce A. Suderow, eds., *Supplement to the Official Records of the Union and Confederate Armies*, 3 volumes to date (Wilmington, N.C., 1994), part 1, vol. 2, p. 117. Hereinafter cited as OR Supplement; *Source Book of the Peninsula Campaign*, p. 117. Other sources put the Federal loss at four killed and three wounded.

71. *OR* 11, pt. 2, p. 247; Augustus Woodbury, *The Second Rhode Island Regiment: A Narrative of Military Operations* (Providence, 1875), p. 79; Abner Hard, *History of the Eighth Cavalry Regiment Illinois Volunteers, During the Great Rebellion* (Dayton, 1984), pp. 117-118; Robert J. Driver, Jr., *1st Virginia Cavalry* (Lynchburg,

1991), p. 34; Davis, *Common Soldier UNcommon War*, pp. 132-133. Davis incorrectly gives the date of this skirmish as the 11th.

72. Woodbury, *The Second Rhode Island Regiment*, pp. 80-81; Hard, *History of the Eighth Cavalry Regiment*, pp. 118-119; *OR* 11, pt. 3, p. 166; *Report of the Joint Committee*, p. 431. This period is difficult to put together with certainty. The regiments were so broken up that they could arrive at a given point more than once as each detachment came in. Furthermore there are no reports from the cavalry covering this period leaving one to rely on histories written well after the war.

73. *OR* Supplement part 1, vol.2, pp. 51-52; *OR* 11, pt. 3, pp. 157-158, 160-161; Silas Wesson Diary, Civil War Times Illustrated Collection, USAMHI.

74. Samuel P. Bates, *History of Pennsylvania Volunteers, 1861-1865* (Harrisburg, 1869-1871, Broadfoot edition, Wilmington, NC),. vol 3, p. 569; Muncy *Luminary*, May 27, 1862.

75. Ibid., letter from Williamsburg (date in May uncertain), July 8, 1862.

76. McClellan, *McClellan's Own Story*, pp. 340-346.

77. Hard, *History of the Eighth Cavalry Regiment*, pp. 120-123.

78. Ibid., p. 123; Chicago *Tribune*, May 21, 22, 1862, Davis, *Common Soldier UNcommon War*, p. 140; Thomas Kelley to Dearest Mary, May 23, 1862, from camp eight miles from Richmond.

79. Ibid.; Chicago *Tribune*, May 23, 1862; *OR* Supplement part 1, vol. 2, p. 120; Davis, *Common Soldier UNcommon War*, p. 142.

80. *OR* 11, pt. 1, p. 650.

81. Ibid., pp. 655-656; Hard, *History of the Eighth Cavalry Regiment*, p. 124; Chicago *Tribune*, May 26, 1862.

82. *OR* 11, pt. 1, pp. 652-654; pt. 3, pp. 198-199; McClellan, *McClellan's Own Story*, pp. 362-364.

83. *OR* 11, pt. 1, pp. 675-676; Rawle, *History of the Third Pennsylvania Cavalry*, pp. 73-75; Chicago *Tribune*, June 3, 1862.

84. *OR* 11, pt. 1, p. 27; pt. 3, p. 186.

85. Ibid., pt. 1, pp. 666-668; pt. 3, p. 191.

86. Ibid., pp. 677-678, 738; National *Tribune*, September 6, 1883.

87. *OR* , pp. 686, 689, 692-693.

88. Ibid., pp. 682, 685-686, 692.; National *Tribune*, January 10, 1884.

89. *OR* , p. 736; Davis, *Common Soldier UNcommon War*, p. 148.

90. *OR* 11, pt. 3, p. 197; Hard, *History of the Eighth Cavalry Regiment*, p. 126; Chicago *Tribune*, June 6, 1862. These accounts are at odds. Hard, writing three years after the war, stated that darkness kept the regiment from reaching the Richmond and Fredericksburg bridge, but the second account carries a date of May 27, 1862. It

may be that because Gamble took only one battalion with him Hard was not aware of it. The Stoneman dispatch while not mentioning the second incident does not preclude it. He does mention that a detachment was sent out and ran into an enemy force but seems to go no further. The early hour at which it was written may indicate that Stoneman was not yet aware of the success of Gamble's mission.

91. *OR* 11, pt. 1, pp. 688-690, 726, 736; pt. 3, p. 200.

92. Ibid., pp. 690-691.

93. Ibid., p. 37. He saw the expedition only in terms of clearing the way for McDowell.

94. Hard, *History of the Eighth Cavalry Regiment*, pp. 128-129.

95. Theo. Rodenbough, *From Everglade to Canon with the Second Dragoons*, (New York, 1875), p. 260; *OR* Supplement part 1, vol. 2, p. 122. For a comprehensive analysis of the logistical problems of supplying the army see William J. Miller, "Logistics, Friction and McClellan's Strategy for the Peninsula Campaign," in William J. Miller, ed., *The Peninsula Campaign of 1862: Yorktown to the Seven Days*, vol. 2 (Campbell, CA, 1995), pp. 129-188.

96. *OR* 11, pt. 3, p. 212; Rawle, *History of the Third Pennsylvania Cavalry*, p. 75.

97. Rodenbough, p. 263. See *OR* 11, pt. 1, pp. 1052-1060 for more on this truce party.

98. Thomas Kelley to Dearest Mary, June 7, 1862 from Mechanicsville.

99. Aurora *Beacon*, June 26, 1862 (letter of Abner Hard dated June 15, 1862). Evidence of this warning is found in *OR* 11, pt. 1, p. 1007, but it was not the issue since Stuart did not move through this area.

100. *OR* 11, pt. 3, pp. 202-203.

101. Emlen N. Carpenter to Dear Mr. Herszey, June 20, 1862, Alexander R. Chamberlin Collection, USAMHI. The events generally known as Stuart's Ride Around McClellan have been covered in detail in the first volume of this series and will not be examined in detail in this article.

102. Aurora *Beacon*, July 3, 1862, (letter of Abner Hard, June 21, 1862); Hard, *History of the Eighth Cavalry Regiment*, p. 137; *OR* Supplement part 1, vol. 2, p. 125. Hard in his regimental gives the date of this affair as the June 25.

103. Rawle, *History of the Third Pennsylvania Cavalry*, pp. 77-81; William Woods Averell, "With the Cavalry on the Peninsula," in Robert U. Johnson and Clarence C. Buel, eds., *Battles and Leaders of the Civil War*, 4 vols. (New York, 1884-89), vol. 2, p. 430. Most of these accounts refer to the village as Aylettsville however the correct name was Ayletts and it is now Aylett. See Dorothy F. Atkinson, *King William County in the Civil War*, (Lynchburg, 1990), p. 1.

104. *OR* 11, pt. 3, p. 253; William Hyndham, *History of a Cavalry Company*, (Philadelphia, 1870), p. 48; Bates, *History of Pennsylvania Volunteers*, vol. 3, p. 523.

105. David Ashley to Dear Parents, Brothers & Sisters, June 25, 1862, from Camp between Dispatch and Tunstall's Station, The Ashley Family Papers, Civil War Miscellaneous Collection, USAMHI.

106. *OR* 11, pt. 3, pp. 242,256-257.

107. Sears, *To the Gates of Richmond*, pp. 183-187; Beach, *The First New York Lincoln Cavalry*, pp

108. Thomas Kelley to Dearest Mary, July 4, 1862 from City Point Landing; Hard, *History of the Eighth Cavalry Regiment*, p. 137; *OR* 11, pt. 2, p. 528; A. Wilson Greene, *Whatever You Resolve: To Be:Essays on Stonewall Jackson*, (Baltimore, 1992), pp. 43-44. One Federal account claimed that Jackson's men were observed disembarking from trains at the station but this is unlikely as Jackson rode the rails only as far as Beaver Dam Station, five miles from Ashland.

109. Greene, *Whatever You Resolve To Be*, p. 45.

110. *OR* 11, pt. 2, pp. 232, 399, 406; Richard A. Sauers, "The Pennsylvania Reserves: General George A. McCall's Division on the Peninsula," in William J. Miller, ed., *The Peninsula Campaign of 1862: Yorktown to the Seven Days*, vol. 1 (Campbell, CA, 1993), p. 26; Philadelphia *Inquirer*, July 10, 1862.

111. *OR* 11, pt. 2, p. 232; Hard, *History of the Eighth Cavalry Regiment*, pp. 138-139; Chicago *Tribune*, July 21, 1862; *True Republican & Sentinel*, July 23, 1862.

112. *OR* 11, pt. 2, pp. 233, 289; Hard, *History of the Eighth Cavalry Regiment*, p. 140; Chicago *Tribune*, July 21, 1862.

113. *OR* Supplement part 1, 2, p. 127.

114. *OR* 11, pt. 2, pp. 41, 43; Lt. Col. Abraham K. Arnold, "The Cavalry at Gaines' Mill," *Journal of the United States Cavalry Association*, vol. 2 (1889), p. 356. The author of this article was in the attack and seriously wounded. Hard, *History of the Eighth Cavalry Regiment*, p. 145; Philadelphia *Inquirer*, July 10, 1862. Of the other units known to be with the army, the 1st New York was entirely on escort duty, the 3rd Pennsylvania was on picket duty and the 2nd United States was on the field but their location is uncertain.

115. *OR* 11, pt. 2, p. 224; Arnold, "The Cavalry at Gaines' Mill," p. 357; Wesley Merritt, "Life and Services of General Philip St. George Cooke, U.S. Army," *Journal of the United States Cavalry Association*, vol. 8 (1895), p. 89.

116. Philip St. George Cooke, "The Charge of Cooke's Cavalry at Gaines's Mill," *B & L*, 2, p. 345; Arnold, "The Cavalry at Gaines' Mill," pp. 358-359.

117. Charles F. James to Dear Sir, January 3, 1899, Richmond National Battlefield Park Library.

118. Arnold, "The Cavalry at Gaines' Mill," pp. 359-362; Merritt, "Life and Services of General Phillip St. George Cooke," pp. 90-91.

119. William Biddle to Fitz John Porter, August 10, 1895, Porter Papers, Library of Congress Manuscript Division, Washington, D.C.; Merritt, "Life and Services of General Phillip St. George Cooke," p. 84; Phillip St. George Cooke to George B. McClellan, May 2, 1885, Porter Papers.

120. *OR* 11, pt. 2, pp. 232-233, 406-407; Philadelphia *Inquirer*, July 10, 1862.

121. Thomas Kelley to Dearest Mary, July 4, 1862, from City Point.

122. *OR* 11, pt. 2, pp. 223, 330-334; Chicago *Tribune*, July 7, 1862.

123. *OR* 11, pt. 2, pp. 482-483; pt. 3, p. 273, 275; *History of the Eleventh Pennsylvania Volunteer Cavalry* (Philadelphia, 1903), pp. 43, 45; Chicago *Tribune*, July 7, 1862. General Silas Casey's report regarding the withdrawal from White House is the most complete account found. He insinuates that Stoneman's cavalry was responsible for burning the White House.

124. Silas Wesson Diary, Civil War Times Illustrated Collection, USAMHI.

125. *OR* 11, pt. 2, p. 525; Averell, "With the Cavalry on the Peninsula," pp. 672-673; Philadelphia *Inquirer*, July 4, 1862; Walter Clark, *Histories of the Several Regiments and Battalions From North Carolina in the Great War 1861-1865*, 5 vols. (Raleigh, 1901), vol.1, p. 420; Greg Mast, "A Few Good Tarheels," *Military Images*, vol.16 (September 1994), p. 30; Nanzig, *3rd Virginia Cavalry*, pp. 17-18.

126. *OR* 11, pt. 2, pp. 47-49.

127. Ibid., p. 235; *Walter S. Newhall: A Memoir* (Philadelphia, 1864), pp. 68-73. Treichel's ride to Heintzelman is not as well documented but Heintzelman's diary seems to refer to it. See *OR* Supplement part 1, vol. 2, p. 88.

128. Silas Wesson Diary, Civil War Times Illustrated Collection, USAMHI.

129. *OR* Supplement part 1, vol. 2, p. 128.

130. Chicago *Tribune*, July 10, 1862.

131. *OR* 11, pt. 3, pp. 307-308, 312.

132. *OR* Supplement part 1, vol. 2, p. 130. No orders have been found confirming this however the evidence indicates that the 6th cavalry was assigned to Gregg, who would be replaced by Pleasonton in early August. Averell, in his article in Battles and Leaders states that the 5th Cavalry was assigned to his brigade.

133. *OR* 11, pt. 3, p. 316; Rawle, *History of the Third Pennsylvania Cavalry*, p. 98; Rodenbough, *From Everglade to Canon*, p. 265.

134. Hyndman, *History of a Cavalry Company*, p. 60; *OR* Supplement part 1, vol. 2, p. 131.

135. Sears, *The Civil War Papers of George B. McClellan*, pp. 375-376; *OR* 11, pt. 3, p. 326.

136. *OR* 11, pt. 3, p. 328. McClellan's dispatches during mid-July are peculiar. He mentions that returned prisoners reported the movement of Jackson while his cavalry "amused" themselves at Malvern Hill. He knew that no large enemy force was within 10 miles of him but chose inaction and speculated that Jackson was going to aid Confederate forces in the west against Buell.

137. *OR* 11, pt. 2, pp. 934-946; Rawle, *History of the Third Pennsylvania Cavalry*, p. 100; Bates, *History of Pennsylvania Volunteers*, vol.3, p. 524; Gracey, *Annals of the Sixth Pennsylvania Cavalry*, p. 82; *OR* Supplement part 1, vol. 2, p. 132.

138. *OR* 11, pt. 2, pp. 946-948; Averell, "With the Cavalry on the Peninsula," p. 679. In this account he identifies his foe as the 13th Virginia Cavalry. That unit did not yet exist as such but companies that later formed the 13th Virginia were in the area and may have been involved.

139. Sears, *To the Gates of Richmond*, p. 354; *OR* 11, pt. 2, pp. 951-952; *OR* Supplement part 1, vol. 2, p. 481.

140. Ibid., pp. 481-483, 496-497; Chicago *Tribune*, August 10, 1862.

141. Ibid.

142. Ibid., *OR* 11, pt. 2, pp. 962-963.

143. Ibid., *OR* Supplement part 1, vol. 2, pp. 133-134; Davis, *Common Soldier UNcommon War*, pp. 198-199.

144. *OR* 11, pt. 2, pp. 954-955, 960-962; Robert J. Driver, Jr., *10th Virginia Cavalry* (Lynchburg, 1992), pp. 22-23.

145. *OR* 11, pt. 2, pp. 964-967.

146. Thomas Kelley to Dearest Mary, August 24, 1862, from Yorktown, Va.

147. Beach, *The First New York (Lincoln) Cavalry*, p. 161; Hyndham, *History of a Cavalry Company*, p. 64; *OR* 11, pt. 1, p. 88, 92; pt. 3, pp. 367-370.

148. Sears, *The Civil War Papers of George B. McClellan*, p. 418.

149. Thomas Kelley to Dearest Mary, August 24, 1862.

150. Averell, "With the Cavalry on the Peninsula," p. 678.

151. New York *Times*, September 3, 1862.

152. *OR* 11, pt. 3, pp. 484, 645. There are at least seven dispatches calling for more cavalry in the Southern correspondence.

153. Ibid., p. 565; Emory M. Thomas, *Bold Dragoon: The Life of J.E.B. Stuart* (New York, 1986), pp. 103-105; Robert J. Trout, *With Pen & Saber: The Letters and Diaries of J.E.B. Stuart's Staff Officers* (Mechancisburg, 1995), p. 61.

154. Trout, *With Pen & Saber*, p. 68.

155. "The Union Cavalry," *Journal of the United States Cavalry Association*, vol. 5 (March 1882), p. 11; Charles Rhodes, *History of the Cavalry of The Army of the Potomac* (Kansas City, 1900), p. 7.

"To Alleviate Their Sufferings"

A REPORT OF MEDICAL PERSONNEL AND ACTIVITY AT SAVAGE'S STATION
DURING AND AFTER THE SEVEN DAYS BATTLES
edited by William J. Miller

1. The Citizens' Association, *A Typical American; or Incidents in the Life of Dr. John Swinburne of Albany* (Albany, 1885), pp. 24-25.

2. Major John Jefferson Milhau, medical director of the Third Corps, Army of the Potomac. Dr. Milhau was born in France and entered the U.S. Army in 1851. *U.S. War Department, The War of the Rebellion: The Official Records of the Union and Confederate Armies*, 128 vols. (Washington, D.C., 1890-1901), series I, vol. 11, pt. 1, p. 196. Hereinafter cited as *OR*. All references are to series I unless otherwise noted.

3. Hundreds of physicians served with the Army of the Potomac on the Peninsula and not all of them were enrolled as members of the U.S. Regular Army or U.S. Volunteers from the various states. Many of the physicians were civilian volunteers—like Swinburne—or "contract surgeons" hired by the army to assist during the campaign. Not all of these surgeons appear on army rolls or on those kept by the adjutant generals of the various states, nor do their full names always appear in the *Official Records*, so not all of the doctors mentioned by Swinburne could be identified. Furthermore, Swinburne was careless about spelling names correctly or even consistently (this failing might be the typesetter's). For example, Dr. John Jefferson Milhau is referred to as "Milhem." One of Swinburne's associates at Savages's Station is referred to as "Millner" in one place, "Milner" in another and "Millnor" in a third. Swinburne refers to Capt. Chauncey McKeever, chief of staff for the Third Corps, as "McKelver" and "McKelvey." This inconsistency makes it unusually difficult to determine precisely to whom Swinburne refers. Physicians and officers who could be identified with a reasonable level of accuracy are named in the notes. Men who could not be identified appear only in Swinburne's text with no further annotation. Furthermore, since titles—acting assistant surgeon, assistant surgeon and surgeon—were subject to change during the five-month-long campaign, and the dates of appointments and promotions are elusive, I have refrained from listing the titles.

4. Lieutenant Colonel Edward Perry Vollum, U.S.A., of New York, entered the service in 1853 and served as medical inspector with the Army of the Potomac in June 1862.

5. O. Munson was surgeon of the 5th New York (Duryea's Zouaves). *OR*. 11, pt. 2, p. 383.

6. Joseph Underwood. *OR* 11, pt. 1, p. 205.

7. A. P. Clark, 37th New York.

8. Joseph Sim Smith of Virginia entered U.S. service May 1861.

9. Probably G. F. Perkins, 22nd Massachusetts.

10. William Faulkner, surgeon of the 83rd Pennsylvania.

11. William P. Russell, surgeon of the 5th Vermont, was reported wounded and taken prisoner June 26, 1862. See William W. Potter, *One Surgeon's Private War*, edited by John Michael Priest, et. al. (Shippensburg, 1996), pp. 36, 132,

12. William W. Potter, assistant surgeon of the 57th New York. Readers interested in gaining greater insight into the extent of the carnage wrought by the Seven Days Battles and the efforts of Federal surgeons to care for the wounded will benefit from Potter's memoir, *One Surgeon's Private War*.

13. Probably the surgeon referred to as "former state assistant" of Vermont, W. T. H. Brooks's brigade *OR* 11, pt. 2, p. 374.

14. Probably N. Millner, 22nd Massachusetts. Ibid., p. 304.

15. Henry Sayler Schell, U.S.A., of Pennsylvania, entered U.S. service in August 1861.

16. Charles Ravenscroft Greenleaf, U.S.A., aide to Dr. Charles S. Tripler, formerly assistant surgeon in 5th Ohio. *OR* 11, pt. 1, p. 196.

17. A. K. Smith, U.S.A., aide to Dr. Charles S. Tripler. Ibid.

18. Ely McClellan of Pennsylvania, aide to Dr. Charles S. Tripler, entered U.S. service in August 1861. Ibid.

19. Captain Chauncey McKeever, assistant adjutant general of Gen. Heintzelman's Third Corps.

20. Swinburne again refers to Capt. McKeever.

21. Colonel Lucius Mirabeau Lamar, 8th Georgia Infantry, had been severely wounded and taken prisoner June 28, 1862.

22. Dr. Hunter Holmes McGuire.

23. Swinburne refers to Maj. Gen. D.H. Hill's Division.

24. Swinburne left this space blank.

25. Confederate division commander John Bankhead Magruder

26. Swinburne left this space blank.

27. Lafayette Guild, former assistant surgeon, U.S.A.

28. Brigadier General John H. Winder.

29. Swinburne left this space blank.

30. Swinburne left this space blank.

31. Swinburne refers to the battle fought on June 30, 1862, most commonly known as Glendale or Frayser's Farm.

32. Here Swinburne, or his typesetter, begins enclosing the document numbers in parentheses.

33. Swinburne addresses Dr. Guild, not "Gould."

34. *Who Was Who in America Historical Volume 1607-1896* (Chicago, 1967), p. 589.

"Weather Still Execrable":

CLIMATOLOGICAL NOTES ON THE PENINSULA CAMPAIGN,

MARCH THROUGH AUGUST 1862

William J. Miller

1. Martin Blumenson, *Patton: The Man Behind the Legend, 1885-1945* (New York, 1985), p. 251.

2. Peter G. Tsouras, *Warriors' Words* (London, 1992), p. 475.

3. Ibid.

4. U.S. War Department, *The War of the Rebellion: The Official Records of the Union and Confederate Armies*, 128 vols. (Washington D.C., 1890-1901), series I, vol. 11, pt. 1, p. 137. Hereinafter cited as *OR*. All references are to series I unless otherwise noted.

5. George B. McClellan, *McClellan's Own Story* (New York, 1887), p. 276.

6. Ibid.

7. Ibid., p. 356.

8. Ibid.

9. *OR* 11, Pt. 3, p. 174.

10. *McClellan's Own Story*, p. 358.

11. John B. Kitching, *Memorials of Col. J. Howard Kitching* (New York, 1873), p. 66.

12. *New York Times*, June 1, 1862.

13. *McClellan's Own Story*, p. 396.

14. In his memoirs, General McClellan stated: "With the exception of the 25th, it rained heavily every day from the 22nd to the battle of Fair Oaks." The observations in this journal do not bear out that claim. Ibid., p. 365.

15. Ibid., p. 400.

16. Ibid., p. 402.

17. Ibid., p. 403.

18. *Anti-Rebel: The Civil War letters of Wilbur Fisk*, Emil Rosenblatt, ed. (New York, 1983), p. 36.

19. *McClellan's Own Story*, p. 406.

20. Ibid.

21. Kitching, *Memorials*, p. 70.

22. *McClellan's Own Story*, p. 407.

23. *Lebanon* (Pennsylvania) *Advertiser*, July 30, 1862.

24. Ibid., August 6, 1862.

25. Heros Von Borcke, *Colonel Heros Von Borcke's Journal*, translated with an introduction by Stuart Wright (Palaemon, 1981), p. 89.

26. Joseph P. Elliott Diary, Civil War Miscellaneous Collection, USAMHI.

27. Ibid.

28. Henry Fogle diary, Western Pennsylvania Historical Society, Pittsburgh, Pa.

29. U.S. Weather Bureau Climatological Records, Microfilm T-907, National Archives, Washington, D.C.

30. Figures for Norfolk and Richmond represent the mean number of days with precipitation of 0.01 inch or more over the span of years indicated (30 years and 41 years respectively). See National Climatic Center, Comparative Climatic Data for the United States (Asheville, NC, 1979), p. 24. Figures for the Tidewater Region were drawn from the data presented in this article. It is important to note that the historical figures for Norfolk and Richmond reflect measureable precipitation while the figures for 1862 reflect any rainfall.

31. This figure reflects only the number of days with precipitation between March 10 and March 31.

32. This figure reflects only the number of days with precipitation between August 1 and August 26.

33. For details of how rain and mud hindered Federal logistics, see William J. Miller "'Scarcely Any Parallel in History': Logistics, Friction and McClellan's Strategy in the Peninsula Campaign," *The Peninsula Campaign of 1862: Yorktown to the Seven Days*, William J. Miller, ed., 3 vols. (Savas Woodbury Publishers, Campbell, CA, 1995), vol. 2, pp. 128-188.

INDEX